The Keswick Week 1971

In the official photograph of the Convention Council and speakers are, from the left, *back row*: Mr. Martin Burch, Revs. D. N. Carr, Peter Coombs, R. C. Lucas. *Middle row*: Canon Alan Neech, Mr. E. R. Appleton, Canon T. F. C. Bewes, Archdeacon H. W. Cragg, Major W. F. Batt, Revs. K. A. A. Weston, Michael Baughen; Mr. H. G. Wheeler (Secretary). *Front row*: Revs. James Dunlop, G. B. Duncan, Alan Redpath; Canon A. T. Houghton, Rev. J. A. Caiger (Chairman), Maj.-Gen. D. J. Wilson-Haffenden, Dr. William

The
Keswick Week
1971

Marshall, Morgan & Scott
London

MARSHALL, MORGAN & SCOTT
BLUNDELL HOUSE,
GOODWOOD ROAD,
LONDON S.E.14 6BL

The Official Record of the Keswick Convention 1971
produced by the courtesy of the Keswick Convention Council
Copyright © 1971
Marshall, Morgan & Scott

The official group photograph of Convention Council members
and speakers by W. P. Haworth, of Keswick. All other photographs and snapshots by the Editor of *The Keswick Week*, the
Rev. H. F. Stevenson, Editor of LIFE OF FAITH, except as otherwise acknowledged.

The colour photograph on front cover is of Lake Windermere.

THE KESWICK CONVENTION FOR NEXT YEAR
July 8th–15th

ISBN 0 551 05077 2

*Printed in Great Britain by The Anchor Press Ltd, and
bound by William Brendon & Son Ltd, both of Tiptree, Essex.*

Contents

Saturday July 10th

8 pm OPENING MEETING

Spiritual Health
Rev. G. B. Duncan

TAPE NO. 290

Keswick's Trumpet Call

"Called . . . unto holiness" was the keynote for Keswick 1971 given to the speakers by the chairman, the Rev. John A. Caiger, at the prayer meeting for members of the Convention Council and speakers, on Saturday afternoon, July 10, before the Convention officially began. As usual, those responsible for the ministry and smooth running of the Convention waited unhurriedly upon God, before facing the gathered congregation.

The call to holiness, Mr. Caiger indicated, comes not from the Council or speakers, but from God, by the Spirit, and through the Word. It should be sounded forth in trumpet tones, as when Gideon "blew a trumpet" when the Spirit of the Lord came upon Him—and the people rallied to the call.

Never was the call to sanctification—to practical and Scriptural holiness, as the Keswick "fathers" defined it—more needed than it is today, the chairman affirmed. That call should re-echo through all the gatherings at Keswick.

It was a beautiful summer evening as the great crowd of roughly five thousand people, who had come to Keswick from all parts of the land—and a considerable number from overseas—assembled for the opening meeting at 8 p.m. The vast tent was filled except for a few seats on the very fringes. Hearts and voices were lifted up with fervour in the singing of the traditional opening hymn, "Full Salvation!" Then Canon A. T. Houghton led in prayer, voicing the expectation of a week of happy fellowship, and the desire to meet with God.

The chairman welcomed several distinguished visitors, including the Bishop of Carlisle, clergy and ministers of Keswick, and the chairman of the Keswick Town Council. On behalf of all these "locals", as he put it, the Bishop expressed a warm welcome to Convention visitors to "this lovely part of the world". The majesty and wonder and beauty of the hills should lead us, as they did the Psalmist, to the Creator of the hills, for refreshment of body, mind and spirit.

The Bishop then referred to those Greek tourists to Jerusalem who found their way to a Convention—or festival, as they called it—and made the request to Philip, "Sir, we would see Jesus." That should be the unspoken desire of every listener to every Convention speaker. To see Jesus is to face the challenge of commitment. If we do that, the mind will be convicted and convinced; the heart moved; and the will dedicated.

In a brief address as chairman, the Rev. John Caiger stressed that the purpose of Keswick through the years has been to wait upon God, and meet with Him.

After the hymn, "Speak, Lord, in the stillness", the Rev. George Duncan spoke searchingly from the story of the woman who was healed from an issue of blood. Spiritual *health* is the purpose of God for His people; and Mr. Duncan asked his hearers directly, "How *are* you?"

The meeting closed with the paraphrase, "Come, let us to the Lord our God with contrite hearts return . . ." And it was a glorious finale that, as the congregation dispersed, the hills encompassing Keswick were invested with an almost ethereal beauty, bathed in the golden light of the setting sun.

Spiritual Health

By the Rev. George B. Duncan, M.A.

As I have been praying about this opening meeting, Mark 5:24–34 has been laid on my mind and heart. It has often been said that the opening message of a Keswick Convention sets the tone. I should hate to think that the Holy Spirit should be thus bound and limited: but surely in some sense the purpose of the opening message is that it should at least help to set our faces toward the right objective; that right at the beginning there should be some definition of the way in which our thought and mind will move during the days that lie ahead.

I want to say that the purpose of this Convention is surely no different from the total purpose of God for His people. And I believe that that purpose is that we should not only have spiritual *life*, but that we should have spiritual *health*. Jesus said, "I am come that they might have life, and that they might have it more abundantly." In my early days I often used to hear from this platform the Convention described as a kind of spiritual clinic. And who would deny today the statement that the church is sick, and therefore that Christians are very far from living lives that are spiritually well?

No doubt during these days we shall be meeting friends: Keswick is a great place for meeting friends. And the usual question-cum-greeting will be spoken, "How are you?", to which the usual untruth will be spoken, "Very well, thank you!" I wonder if it is not more important that we should meet the Lord, and should hear Him say in greeting to us, "How are you?"

I believe that in the early days of the revival movement in Ruanda, a frequent greeting from one Christian to another was, "How is your heart in the Lord today?" "How *are* you?" "Very well, thank you"? Physically it is seldom true; spiritually, I would submit, it is almost never true. There is a hymn that is sung with great fervour—but I sometimes shrink from singing it—where the chorus affirms, "It is well with my soul." Is it? It is possible to have spiritual life without having spiritual health. And surely health is God's purpose, and our purpose this week. The prophet Isaiah brought this same charge against the people of God in his day: "The whole head," he said, "is sick, and the heart faint; from the sole of the foot to the crown of the head there is no soundness."

Well, let us look at the incident in which health came to one who was sick. There are just three points, and I trust and pray that these may, as it were, clarify the direction of our thinking and of our intention during these days together. First, we see here—

A LIFE FROM WHICH HEALTH HAD GONE. "A certain woman, which had an issue of blood twelve years, and had suffered many things of many physicians, and had spent all that she had, and was nothing bettered, but rather grew worse." Note, *the presence of a crippling disease*. Twelve years she had been sick—and that is a longish time. But I wonder how long some of us have been living in spiritual ill-health.

What about your spiritual *appetite*? Is your appetite for the Word of God healthy? Those of you who have small children will know that a loss of appetite is an indication of ill-health. When your child turns away from the plate in front, you say, "Hallo! What's the matter with you?" What is your spiritual appetite like?

What about your *heart*—your love for the Lord? For the house of God? Your love for the world that God loves? How much caring is there in your life; and with the caring, giving?

What about your *breathing*? I hope you are not sitting next to somebody whose breathing is not quite right! It is possible that there may be somebody; but if their breathing is not right, you know that there is something wrong. What about your *praying*—your breathing? That O.K.?

What about your *tongue*? One of the first things the doctor says is, "Can I have a look at your tongue?" What about your tongue? Is there a testimony there? Can you bring a real, humble, sincere testimony as to what Jesus Christ means to you? I do not ask, Do you know the Gospel? You know that. But if this was turned into a testimony meeting right now, have you a testimony on your tongue? Or is your tongue more often filled with frivolous or unkind things?

What about your *temperature*? Is that normal? Or is your temperature a bit high? Are you inclined to lose your temper? Or maybe it is a bit below normal: folk find you unfriendly and cold.

What about your *skin*, your appearance? Sometimes you can tell by the very look of a person that they are not well. Are you so obviously spiritually well that you do not need to tell anyone you are a Christian? They can tell it.

Here was a woman who had been sick for twelve years with a crippling disease. How long some Christian lives are lived tragically below the standard set out in the Word of God!

I note also *the pressure of a crushing despair*. At least this woman wanted to do something about it. She was ready to go anywhere, to listen to any voice, to pay any price to anybody else, if only they would help. All we are told is that she suffered many things of many physicians, and had spent all that she had and was nothing better: although Dr. Luke omits, "but rather grew worse"! If ever a life was utterly bankrupt and crushed into despair, this woman's life was like that.

I wonder if there is somebody here—bless your heart—and that is just where you are. You are not only spiritually sick, and living below the level of God's intention and God's provision, but you are absolutely at the end of your tether. You have tried everything, read every book you can, you have listened to preachers . . .

Well, a great Christian like Paul knew what it meant to be brought to the end of his tether, so you are in good company. He wrote in 2 Corinthians 1:8, "At that time we were completely overwhelmed, the burden was more than we could bear; in fact, we told ourselves that this was the end." I wonder if this visit to Keswick is for you the last gasp: you are at the end. Every possible remedy exhausted; every bit of money gone. She was utterly bankrupt. Paul adds: "We believe that we had this experience—of coming to the end of our tether—that we might learn to trust . . . in God."

10

I had a book sent to me the other day, and the very title is suggestive—
Crowded to Christ. For if this was a life from which health had gone, it
was also—

A LIFE IN WHICH HOPE WAS BORN. "She heard of Jesus" (Mark 5:27). She
"came in the press behind, and touched His garment. For she said, If I may
touch but His clothes, I shall be whole." A life in which hope was born. Oh,
I pray that this is going to be a week in which hope is going to be kindled in
every heart: for my! don't we need hope today!

What did all this mean? First, it meant that there had to be *a learning of
Christ*. Reports reached her of this Jesus, of what He said and of what He did,
of what He asked and of what He gave; and what she heard of Him brought
a ray of hope into a dark sky.

I believe that at the root of much of our problem today in the church at
large, there lies a basic ignorance about Jesus Christ. Recently one of the
leading personalities in the Roman church in Holland visited Edinburgh.
The Roman church in Holland is in a state of ferment and change, in which
this churchman is playing a leading part. And he was asked by a Presbyterian
minister interviewing him, what he reckoned would be needed to produce the
same kind of upsurge and ferment of spiritual vitality in Scotland. His reply
was significant: "It will happen when you begin to take Jesus Christ
seriously."

And, let us face it, most Evangelical Christians don't take Jesus Christ
seriously. "My people are destroyed for lack of knowledge" was God's
charge in the days of Hosea. And the church today desperately needs to learn
what Christ has said; what He claims to be able to do; what He wants us to
do; and how He wants us to live. "Faith cometh by hearing, and hearing by
the Word of God." God has no time for ignorance. Faith is not a feeling;
it is a response to truth learned. And faith and hope will begin to kindle in
your hearts and mine, as they kindled in this woman's heart when she heard
of Jesus. A learning of Christ.

That means getting down to your Bible in your own home, and in your
own room. It means being in your place in church twice on Sunday, not once
in the morning, and then in the evening lounging in front of your television
set watching the play! It means getting to a Bible study if there is one; if
there isn't, starting one in your own home. Learning of Christ. There is no
substitute for this kind of basic knowledge of Him.

How tragic it is that there is so much ignorance: and we have to be fair
here, as ministers and clergy, and accept our share of responsibility for this.
On holiday recently I went to a service on the Sunday morning, and I went
with a hungry heart. And when it came to the time when the Word of life was
to be broken, the minister lounged back on one elbow in the pulpit, blethered
away for five minutes, and then finished: and we went away empty and hungry.

Then there are those pathetic folk who say that a sermon must not be
longer than ten minutes. Poor creatures! They send their little five-year-olds
to school: and the lessons that these little five-year-olds have to go through
are longer than ten minutes, you know; and they have more than one lesson
a week. When we begin to take Jesus Christ seriously, that means learning;
just sheer, disciplined learning.

Are you not frightened sometimes when you see on your television screen
a documentary from China, and you see tens of thousands of Chinese young

people holding in their hands a book that they know off by heart? A book that doesn't come within a mile of the Book that you and I have, that we neither have in our hands, nor in our handbags, nor in our pockets—and most of which we know nothing about.

When you begin to take Jesus Christ seriously, this means learning. What this woman heard of Him was not much: but it was a starting-point. And not only was there a learning of Christ here, but *a longing for Him*. "If I may touch but His clothes," she said, "I shall be whole." What she had learnt she believed, and what she had believed she wanted to see in her own life. With a passion and a purpose she was determined to reach Him and touch Him. While the multitudes thronged, she touched.

Years ago in Portstewart—Keswick's daughter Convention in the North of Ireland—one of the great figures who ministered the Word of God there for many years was Alexander Fraser, a Scotsman who was very difficult to understand to begin with: but once you could understand him, what treasures he would unfold! I remember him speaking on this incident on one occasion: and one little phrase that he said then has stuck: "The flesh throngs, but faith touches." There are plenty of folk who throng around Jesus Christ. You will find them in every church every Sunday. But out of the many who throng, there are the few who touch Him.

There are many here at Keswick who will be thronging around Him. But I wonder how many hands—the hands of faith—will be reached out with intention and purpose, to touch Him; to tap the resources that are in Him, and relate those resources to our need. Interested, curious, enjoying it all, with no desire, no intention, no resolve, no determination . . . Not so with this woman. A learning of Christ was followed by a longing for Him. She said, "If only I get within range of Him, and reach out! And even if I touch just His clothes, I shall be whole." I trust that we shall learn enough about Christ during these days to make us long for Him.

A life from which health had gone; a life in which hope was born; and finally—

A LIFE FOR WHICH HELP WAS FOUND. "Straightway the fountain of her blood was dried up; and she felt in her body that she was healed of that plague. And Jesus, immediately knowing that virtue had gone out of Him, turned Him about in the press, and said, Who touched my clothes? And his disciples said unto Him, Thou seest the multitude thronging Thee, and sayest Thou, Who touched me? And he looked round about to see her that had done this thing. But the woman fearing and trembling, knowing what was done in her, came and fell down before Him, and told Him all the truth. And He said unto her, Daughter, thy faith hath made thee whole; go in peace and be whole of thy plague." A life for which help was found.

What can we learn from these final touches in this miracle of a message? I think we learn two things: first, that *what Christ gives must be received personally*. And so He isolates this woman, who has the touch of faith, from the thronging crowd, to make this principle absolutely clear. What Christ can do, what Christ will do, He will do for us personally. "My soul, wait thou only upon God." I hope that we shall have some wonderful meetings here. But a wonderful meeting, to be meaningful, must be a personal encounter. One of the great American preachers said that a sermon, to be a true sermon, must be *an event*; something that is not just heard, but something in which there is a happening. And what is that happening? It is a personal encounter, and an involvement, between the individual and the Master.

"Somebody hath touched me!" That is what Jesus said, in Luke's account. A personal confrontation with Christ—and those who criticise the Billy Graham type of crusade, or others who criticise this type of Convention, where there is a great throng, overlook this one tremendous spiritual factor: that is that the Holy Spirit can isolate the individual in a multitude, just as Jesus did it with this woman. And if I know anything about Keswick from the experience of a quarter of a century, it means exactly this, that you will find yourself some time or other during these days in a situation where, as far as you are concerned, there is nobody else in the tent but you and your Lord. What Jesus gives must be received personally—maybe not here; maybe in the quiet of your room, or in one of the local churches, or by the lakeside: but it must be received personally.

And what Jesus gives *must be revealed publicly*. In other words, what Christ does in us and for us is not something to be kept to ourselves. It is something that others are bound to know about. And in that knowing, all the glory must be given to Jesus Christ. Luke's account reads that she "declared unto Him before all the people for what cause she had touched Him, and how she was healed immediately." The people then went away, not thinking, What a wonderful experience this woman had; but, What a wonderful person Jesus was.

A life from which health had gone; a life in which hope was born; a life for which help was found. And if to somebody there comes a new experience of Jesus Christ this week, when we go back shall we be honest, and bear our witness to the Christ who has met our need?

We are living in a world which is absolutely filled with clamouring voices. It seems as if the only voices that are not heard are the voices of those who have been saved by Jesus Christ. We never bother to write to the BBC to tell them that we don't want that kind of muck and filth shoved into our homes under the guise of "art". We don't write to the papers; we don't lift up our voices in the office. Everybody else is talking except the converted Christians. We stay dumb. Jesus said, "No, my dear woman. What's happened to you is something that you must let others know about; because otherwise you will get the glory. And the glory is mine."

I wonder how many times during this week those surrounding the throne, and close to the presence of the risen, ascended, and enthroned Lord, will hear Him whisper to Himself, as this Convention goes on day after day, "Someone hath touched me," and the hand of faith go out to Him, and you and I lay hold of Him in all His fulness in a new and fuller way, and go out to live to His glory? It is possible to have life; you've got that; you are born again. Have you got health?

Years ago at a Convention in Leicester I remember the Rev. W. H. Aldis saying that a telegram had been received from a Convention in China—this was in the days of long ago—and in this they said they were praying for their Convention, not that they should be better Christians, but that they might be *well* Christians. There is all the difference in the world between being better, and being well.

View of Derwentwater

Photo: Rev. K. W. Coates

Sunday July 11th

11 am Convention Service

The Need of the Times (OVERSEAS BROADCAST)
Rev. R. C. Lucas

TAPE NO. 297a

The Heart Finds Rest
Archdeacon H. W. Cragg

TAPE NO. 296

3 pm Afternoon Service

The Word and the Day
Rev. James Dunlop

TAPE NO. 296a

7 pm Evening Service

Christian Revolution
Rev. Alan Redpath

TAPE NO. 297

Call to Worship

A glorious morning, with the sun shining brightly from a clear sky, greeted those rising early on Sunday for the first of the prayer meetings, at 7 a.m. A goodly number made their way through the quiet streets of the slumbering town, to the Eskin Street tent; and there was liberty in prayer, not only for the Convention, but for the "home" churches from which visitors had come.

A change in BBC requirements for the Overseas Broadcast Service necessitated adjustments to the day's programme. Instead of being sent out "live" at 6.15 p.m., the broadcast was pre-recorded during the first half of the morning service in the tent. A hurriedly constituted "choir" was rehearsed beforehand by Mr. Tim Buckley, and led the singing of familiar "Keswick" hymns.

The scene was set by the chairman; then "Ye servants of God" prepared the way for prayer by Canon A. T. Houghton. Mr. Martin Burch read Ephesians 3:14–21, and the Rev. R. C. Lucas took 2 Peter 3:11 as the text of his challenging address. Response to this trumpet call was made in the hymn, "Jesus, Master, whose I am", and the Rev. John Caiger brought the broadcast to a conclusion in prayer.

Immediately following the recording of this half-hour service, "Oh, worship the Lord" was sung; and then the Ven. H. W. Cragg preached a sermon which clearly spoke to many hearts. He linked together Psalm 55:6, "Oh, that I had wings . . . I would fly away and be at rest" and Matthew 11:28, "Come unto me . . . and I will give you rest".

On a gloriously sunny afternoon it showed a singleness of purpose on the part of a thousand or more people to attend the meeting at 3 p.m., and they were rewarded with a stimulating address by the Very Rev. Dr. James Dunlop, chairman of the Portstewart Convention and a former Moderator of the Presbyterian Church in Ireland. Meanwhile, in the small tent, a large number of children enjoyed the meeting conducted by SU staff workers.

The churches were—as in the morning—well filled for their evening services, when Convention speakers again occupied their pulpits. As the broadcast service had already been recorded, no meeting was held in the tent until 7 p.m., when the customary evangelistic service was led by the Rev. John Caiger. The hymn, "Crown Him with many crowns", was followed by prayer by Archdeacon Cragg. Then the chairman read John 4:14–24 and Revelation 2:1–7, and "Oh, worship the King" preceded Dr. Alan Redpath's stirring message on "Christian Revolution".

As the superb summer day drew toward its close, clouds gathered and hung low upon the hills. It was a calm, cool eventide, however, as the under-thirties filled the small tent at 9 p.m. for the first of the young people's meetings—yes, the "upper limit" was raised this year from twenty-eight to thirty. At the same time a very large crowd practically filled the Market Place for the open-air meeting.

The Need of the Times

By the Rev. R. C. Lucas, M.A.

For very many years now Christian people have assembled here annually, coming literally from the four corners of the earth to meet with God and with one another in this most beautiful spot, Keswick in Lakeland. We meet to consider, and to face, the strong logical demands that our Christian faith makes upon us for a life of true holiness and godliness.

I want to begin with a verse from the Epistle we shall be studying this week: "Since all these things are disintegrating, what sort of people ought you to show yourselves in the holiness and godliness of your lives?" (2 Peter 3:11).

This powerful sentence comes from the writings of the apostle Peter. He is telling us to look ahead (something we don't do very much, but which the Bible frequently asks of us); and he sees the approaching end of the present world order, when his Lord and Master will return to sit in judgment on everything and everyone, and to create a new world in which righteousness dwells.

"Since all things are disintegrating"—it's possible that he does not speak of this disintegration as being entirely a matter of the last day. The sentence can imply that all things are already beginning to disintegrate. In other words, Peter may be telling us that there were already signs in his own day of decay in the world around him. The same can be said of the world and society in which we live today. Just because of this, here and now, in the light of the situation we face, Peter's exclamation comes to us with the greater force— what kind of people ought *we* to be in the quality of our Christian lives?

Well, what kind of people *ought* we to be if, in our modern day, we name the name of Jesus Christ?

The first thing I would say is that certainly we should be *rich* men.

At a Keswick Convention a year or so back, I went one evening to the youth meeting to find myself down to be interviewed by Mr. Tim Buckley. One question, suddenly shot at me, demanded quick thinking. What, I was asked, is the point of the Convention? What are we here for? On the spur of the moment the answer I gave may have been incomplete, but it certainly clarified my own mind, if no one else's! It was, quite simply, that we Christians were here at Keswick to learn that we might be *rich men* (indeed, that we were already rich men if we only knew it!). The point of our meeting together was to discover the wealth that we had through our knowledge of Jesus Christ, and then to discover how to enjoy it and to make use of it in daily life.

Unfortunately, as everyone knows, our Christian lives too often appear poverty-stricken. And if they do not appear so to others, we know well that they are! The light of our joy flickers feebly. Our spiritual batteries are low. We achieve little through our prayers; and our witness to men makes comparatively little impression.

17

It is the apostle Paul who especially loves, in his letters, to speak to Christians who feel like this. He delights to tell them of the unsearchable riches of Christ, and he urges them to recognise what their Lord can be to them. It is particularly marvellous to see this in his letters from prison, when circumstances must have been anything but pleasant; although it is true to experience that it is often just when we are in hard or lonely places that we rediscover the worthwhileness of being a Christian.

After this broadcast, I suggest you might open a New Testament and read straight through the Ephesian letter, with whoever is with you, noting all the references to the riches and wealth that belong to the Christian believer. Then carefully work out its meaning for yourself, and claim for your own lives the enjoyment and experience of all that God gives in Christ.

This concept of the riches to be found in following Jesus was a great stimulus to me some ten years ago, when I was appointed in charge of a church strangely, but strategically, situated in the heart of the business quarter of the city of London. All around were, and are, big office blocks, where much of the wealth of the nation is administered, and in which a young man may still seek and make his fortune. The ancient church building to which I came, standing as it does among modern skyscrapers and similar buildings, seemed to symbolise an antiquated faith with little to offer modern men. Certainly I would not have had the nerve to join others in an evangelistic ministry there unless I had been fully persuaded that we were able to offer, in Christ, something of far deeper value than any business house could offer. Tonight this broadcast will, I hope, be picked up by people in different parts of the world who first found the riches in Christ in that church in the city, or came there to value them more.

Christian men and women, then, should be people with great resources, In meeting them, others who feel the bankruptcy of purpose and meaning in their lives will be drawn to ask, and to find, the source of this real human experience at its best in Jesus Christ.

Then, today we Christians are called to be *strong* men.

I can recall, as a boy, once sending off 6d in stamps (you got a great deal in those days for six old pennies!) for a course of body building. I had been attracted, as boys are, by a photograph of a completely muscle-bound man with glistening skin and vast torso, and I wished to be similarly developed. Now, I am glad to report, I admire a rather different kind of strength, though it is not less rare.

I mean that strength in the inner man which the Spirit of God supplies to the people of God. In everyday terms, it is the strength which makes it possible to continue as a Christian in loneliness and when the winds are contrary. It is the strength which makes it possible in godless times and places to adhere to standards and outlooks which others easily dismiss or decry. This strength gives a man quickness of eye to see what is compromise, and the strength of nerve to refuse it. It enables a man to persevere in times of failure, and, often far more difficult, remain true to his convictions in times of success.

In short, it is the very quality that is indispensable for Christian living today. Such strength enables us to give comfort, rather than demand it. It gives backbone to young Christians in days when a false and flabby tolerance of evil is fashionable. It equips Christian parents to take the responsibility for the guiding of their children, even in bewildering times. And it energises the Christian man or woman to take a proper share in the toil of real Christian work and witness.

Listen to Paul, writing about such strength: "I have been very fully initiated into the human lot with all its ups and downs—and I have strength for anything through Him who gives me power."

Finally, in the light of both present and future, it is essential that we Christian people should be *good* men.

This short second letter of Peter's contains an impressive call for an ethical revival among Christian people. Just as he shows clearly how false teaching must lead to lax living, so he demands that true Christian beliefs must lead to true Christian goodness. And by that, I mean attractive goodness.

There is something here very characteristic of New Testament teaching, I think. Christian doctrine and duty are so closely interwoven. In Paul's letters there is frequently a very careful arrangement of his material; the first part of the letter dealing with the facts of Christian faith, and the second part with the manner of Christian living. In this way he shows that it is hopeless, even absurd, to expect Christian behaviour without Christian belief.

For some years, as you will know, this has been seriously and widely challenged. Indeed, people become very indignant at such an idea. "How can you say that a man must be a Christian," they protest, "if he is to lead a decent life? Why, we can show you plenty of people who make no particular claim to be Christians whose lives are far better than those of certain Christians we know!"

The misunderstanding here comes from a failure to see that the widespread preaching of the Christian Gospel in this country and in the West, say, for example, in the 18th and 19th centuries, led inevitably to the widespread adoption of Christian standards. The resulting patterns of Christian behaviour have proved to have immense staying power (thank God), and have remained long after the *raison d'être* for them, the Christian faith, has lost its hold on the nation.

This Christian structure, however, can be destroyed. Near my home in London, some large office blocks have recently been demolished. It was all done in a matter of weeks. But just suppose that instead of such a frontal attack plans could have been made fifty years ago to remove one brick a week from the massive foundations of the same office. After some twenty years only 1250 bricks would have been removed! It would be many years before a collapse would come; but one day the cracks would appear, and one day, still further in the future, the crash must come.

We live in days when the cracks in the Christian structure of our land have been widening in a frightening way. There are also signs of imminent collapse.

If the older Christian standards do disappear, in the home, and in the market place, what can we expect to be rebuilt in their place? What will the younger generation construct? (and since the majority of the world population is now under 25, and in fifteen years' time 35 per cent will be less than 15 years of age, the younger generation have obviously got to do a lot of the building). Well, one of the attractive things about our young peoplell toda is their determination to be themselves. To do this they say they wi takey nothing on trust, and think everything out for themselves. They feel that we, their elders, have been conformists, fitting into a pattern, often unthinkingly.

19

Well now, what will be the result of this building of theirs? A new pattern of behaviour and living will inevitably begin to emerge, based upon new convictions. But these convictions are unlikely to be distinctively Christian ones.

It is in this context that the determination "to be oneself" can be very frightening. We shall see in this country for the first time for over two hundred years, non-Christian standards espoused and justified as being the only consistent behaviour since God is dead and gone. Did I say, we shall? Already we are beginning to see this. The process of disintegration is visible around us.

In the light of this, what sort of people should we Christians be? We must, by the grace of Christ, and the love of God, and the power of the Spirit, be *distinctly* Christian in the way we live. This will increasingly mean being distinctly *different*.

It will not be enough that this goodness be a negative thing; that we do not steal, or lie, or live covetously—though these negatives will never cease to be important. We shall need positive Christian energy in our lives, so that the hands that do not steal, work hard to provide the needs of others; the lips that do not lie, speak rather grace and truth to their neighbours; and the lives which renounce cupidity, embrace instead the way of sacrifice for the sake of Christ and the Gospel.

Yes, this is what the times demand. More important, it is what the truth demands. And to find afresh the incentive and the grace for such a life, we meet here at this great Convention. But though we wish that you might be here with us, that isn't necessary. The throne of God is open to you in the Name of Jesus Christ; the book of God is yours as well as ours; and the power and presence of Christ the Lord can be yours wherever you are. May God bless you and us, through them.

The Heart Finds Rest

By the Ven. H. W. Cragg, M.A.

I wonder how deep the disintegration has gone in your life? If I may be allowed to pick on that word from the first address, in beginning to bring you the second address—thereby establishing a record, I believe, for never before has a Sunday morning congregation at Keswick listened to two addresses at the eleven o'clock service. I guess you are a pretty good lot; but how deep has the disintegration gone, so far as your heart is concerned? This is my theme;

and I want, if I may, in opening it up to link together two texts of Scripture, which I shall later tear apart.

The first is Psalm 55:6, and the second is Matthew 11:28; and there is a common factor in these two verses, though there is a diverse approach to the realisation of that factor. Psalm 55:6, "Oh that I had wings like a dove! for then would I fly away, and be at rest." Matthew 11:28, "Come unto me . . . I will give you rest." Most people know the first of my two Scriptures, because of the song that is built around the words so beautifully. And most people know the second, because of the very familiarity of these words from the lips of Christ. But how few people know the *rest* about which both verses speak. Do you? Do I? I know you did once: I did once; but how deep has the disintegration gone in your heart?

Psalm 55:6 is an attempt to gain rest by running away; and it doesn't work, because when you run away you take yourself. Matthew 11:28 is the way to receive rest by coming to Christ. The verses are alike in their expression of need, but poles apart in their approach to the remedy.

I want to consider with you some of the situations in which it is essential that we abandon the idea of Psalm 55:6, as the psalmist himself did before he came to the end of this same psalm; and we welcome the invitation of Matthew 11:28. May I speak simply with you, first, about what I should like to call—

REST IN SUFFERING. Romans 8:18 reminds us that all our sufferings are sufferings of "this present time". They are the backcloth of the disintegration of which we have heard; and they are "not worthy to be compared with the glory which shall be revealed in us"—that glory which is the ultimate when disintegration has run its course, and Christ takes over; that glory which is available now for all who will turn to Christ to receive it. Rest in suffering.

Do I speak with a sufferer this morning? Suffering in body, distressed and distraught in mind? I have been literally amazed to discover in the course of my Christian ministry—and never more so than in recent years—how many there are who bear about in their body day by day more than their nearest neighbour knows anything about. Am I speaking with somebody who has just about escaped to get to Keswick from the long-drawn-out nursing of a dear one? How hard it has been, and yet how rewarding; and how wonderful the atmosphere as you have gone about your task. I want to speak about rest in suffering. Do we know this?

Do you remember Hagar, turned out of Abraham's household with her boy Ishmael? Abraham provided her with the wherewithal for the first part of the journey, but very soon the water was spent in the water-skin. And you remember how she found some brushwood in the desert, and there she laid down her boy; and she said, "Let me not see the death of the child. This is more than I can face." And so she took herself a little way further off, and herself lay down to rest. But the boy began to pray, and God answered the child's prayer for the mother's salvation. "And the Lord opened Hagar's eyes," and she saw a well of water; and she went to find the salvation from her distress and sorrow, which she scarcely hoped to find. Her first prayer was, "Oh, that I might fly away." But God said, "No, you don't! You come to me."

As I mingle among my suffering friends—and they are quite numerous—I find that this is the lesson they have to learn; and they learn it so well, so many of them. They have stopped trying to fly away, and they keep on coming to Christ, day after day, hour after hour; unable to escape, and not even trying to, they come as they are to Jesus, and they find in Him all they need.

The apostle Paul, stung deeply and permanently with that thorn in the flesh, "the messenger of Satan to buffet" him. Three times he besought the Lord that it might be taken away: "Oh, that I might fly away, and be at rest." But back from the throne of God comes the best and most blessed answer to prayer: "My grace is sufficient for you. Don't run away; come to me."

Bishop Handley Moule, who spoke from this platform in years past so graciously, had lying at home in Bishop Auckland an invalid daughter, Mary. Mary never regained strength; she lived the life of an invalid. I have a little book, long since out of print, which tells the story of Mary Moule, her suffering, her faith, her confidence in God, her quiet rest, her total witness to Christ. Some poets of an earlier day had written verses that fitted her story; and some of these were taken from their setting and set down on the flyleaf of the book called *Mary E. E. Moule.* Years ago I discovered one I have never been able to forget. This is how it reads:

> *Is the cross heavy? Does thy sorrow tire?*
> *Never fear;*
> *When the refiner's gold is in the fire*
> *He is near:*
> *Whom the Lord chasteneth most He loveth best,*
> *Harming never;*
> *By Golgotha the way to heavenly rest*
> *Passeth ever.*

Don't run away. Come to Christ, just where you are, just how you are, just how you are going to remain. A miracle of peace and rest can be infinitely more blessed than a miracle of healing, if that is God's way. Rest in suffering. And what about—

REST IN CIRCUMSTANCES. How we should love to change these, so often. Perhaps it is the person next door who makes all the trouble; perhaps it is the situation in your work, in your church, whatever it is. And yet the Christian believer surely understands, without anybody to explain to him, that his circumstances are overruled by God; and that if they ought to change, God will change them in His good way and time. But the circumstances—or, as the word means, the things that stand around me, or in the centre of which I stand—are all divinely controlled. Why, therefore, always try to run away?

It was like that with Elijah, wasn't it? In 1 Kings 19, you can see him fleeing at the threat of Jezebel—this mighty man of God, who had been so triumphant on Carmel. Eight hundred and fifty prophets had not been able to withstand his faith and courage, or to resist the power of his God; yet the threat of one woman, Jezebel, sent him skedaddling away. "Oh, that I had wings like a dove! for then would I fly away, and be at rest."

But was he at rest? Could he ever be at rest in the wrong place? Could "flying away" from the plan of God ever give anybody any rest? God called him back, and in effect He said, "No, you don't, Elijah! You come to me. I can give you what a journey of a thousand miles will never lead you to discover. And I can give it right here, and right now, without any change of scene."

You recall the woman at the well in John 4, coming in the burden and the heat of the day to be alone from the critical eyes of those who gazed upon her. She would come when it was hottest and hardest, to get away from the unrest that her own sin and shame had brought upon the locality in which she moves. How graciously and how tenderly the Lord Jesus came and sat opposite to her on the other side of the well, and said in effect, 'Woman, you won't get what you need by running away. You'll get it by coming to me."

What are you trying to escape, in the vain hope that somewhere else, in some other setting, with circumstances entirely changed by your own ingenuity, and somebody else's scheming, that somehow or other deep down in your heart you will find rest by running away? That will, in fact, be the supreme mark of your disintegration. "Come unto me, all ye who labour and are heavy laden, and I will give you rest."

I visited the blacksmith one day, and while chatting with him I leaned my arm on the old-fashioned bellows that were still in his smithy; and the fire was alight and the stonemason's tools were in the furnace fire, ready for sharpening. As I leaned on the handle of the bellows I moved it slightly up and down in sheer simplicity and joy. And at once: "Stop it!" he said. I thought I had committed the biggest crime ever possible to be set down to my name! Then he added—and I have never forgotten it: "I know just how hot to make the fire; you don't."

Are you not happy to stay in the fire when God's hand is on the bellows, and not ours? Rest in suffering. Rest in circumstances.

REST FROM SIN—not rest *in* sin; there is no resting-place there. But rest *from* sin. For, after all, sin is the root cause of all unrest; and we need rest from this more than anything else. Possibly in a happy congregation of this sort there are more people who need rest from sin than rest in suffering or in circumstances; and it is only to be found as we welcome the invitation of Matthew 11:28.

Unrest is often caused by *conviction of sin*. Do you remember that Bunyan's pilgrim had a burden on his back, so often described by preachers as the burden of his sin? It wasn't anything of the kind. It was not the burden of his sin, but the burden of conviction of sin. An unconvicted man does not find his sin a burden; he finds it a wonderful opportunity to express himself in the way he wants at that moment. But when God comes to convict of sin, then it is the very convicting of sin which is the burden.

"If I ascend up into heaven, thou art there ... If I take the wings of the morning, and dwell in the uttermost parts of the sea . . ." thou art there also. "The darkness hideth not from thee; but the night shineth as the day . . ." Wings of a dove can never give me a rest in a place far from conviction, for conviction is where God and I meet. And that is wherever I try to fly.

Some have lost their rest through *a consciousness of failure*. I read somewhere a lovely little sentence about the awareness of weakness and failure and disintegration. The writer put it like this, so simply: "There's a sob in every Christian's heart." So when I find there is a sob in my heart, perhaps it is that it is a Christian heart, and it knows the sense of breakdown and failure that has come.

What must I do? Run away? That will only increase the failure. "Come unto me. Let my cleansing blood deal with every spot and stain that remains. Let me wash you white. Let me pardon your iniquity, for it is great. Let me take hold of that life with its breakdown, and mould it afresh. Come closer; don't run further."

Some need rest from sin, because they do not yet understand what is the supreme inner heart of this Convention's life and ministry, the sense of conflict with inbred sin. The old nature within, and the world without, combine to throw me down—and you, too! "The flesh lusteth against the Spirit, and the Spirit against the flesh: and these are contrary the one to the other: so that ye cannot do the things that ye would," wrote the apostle Paul. A modern translation that does not appear in any printed Bible was one made to read, "The flesh lusts against the Spirit, and the Spirit against the flesh, so that you need not do the things you otherwise would . . ." How is the thought and the sentence changed, by coming afresh to Christ! Sin is the cause of your unrest, isn't it?—the conviction you won't allow, to get it put straight; the failure you cannot forget, in spite of Christ's promise to put it behind His back; and the inner conflict you cannot resolve, because you are trying the wrong way. Rest is where you and Jesus get right close, and stay close. "Come unto me—in your suffering, in your circumstances, and away from your sin—and I will give you rest."

"Come unto me." Will you do it?

The Word and the Day

By the Very Rev. James Dunlop, M.A., D.D.

In Isaiah 30:21 we have the words: "Thine ears shall hear a word behind thee, saying, This is the way, walk ye in it, when ye turn to the right hand, and when ye turn to the left." It would, I suppose, be somewhat trite to say that we meet in a day of great need, of unrest in the world, when questions are arising in men's minds as to the things that are coming or may come on the earth. And we meet in a day of great need in the church, when the necessity for a spiritual revival, and the restoration of moral and scriptural standards, is being borne home to many.

And we meet, as a company of God's people set in this world, in this age, members of Christ's church, conscious to a greater or lesser degree of our failure and shortcomings and inadequacies, longing for a word from the Lord that might vitalise and quicken, and maybe revolutionise, our living and our ministry. Let us have no doubt in our minds: God is here to meet with His people, to speak the word, if we are earnest and ready and willing to receive

24

and obey it. "Thine ears shall hear a word behind thee, saying, This is the way, walk ye in it . . ."

That is the word of Isaiah to Israel in his day, and it is still the message for the spiritual Israel today. There is a way that God has for us to walk; a way clearly indicated for His people amid the perplexities of such times as these; a way full of glory to Himself, and instinct with blessing for us; and a way of spiritual power and effectiveness in relation to the world of men around us—a way which in all these things fulfils His will.

Now, what is that way? I want to suggest to you three things, First, I suggest to you, it is—

THE WAY OF SPIRITUAL VISION. Spiritual vision was the thing that Israel of Isaiah's day lacked; and the lack was evident in the tendency of the nation to rely upon other things, rather than God alone. The people of Israel always felt the difficulty of sustaining themselves on the height of simple dependence on the unseen spiritual power of God; and in Isaiah's time they were constantly oscillating between alliances with the northern and southern powers, leaguing themselves with Assyria against Egypt, or with Egypt against Assyria—the effect of which was, that whichever was victorious, Israel suffered. She was a battle-ground for both. She became the prize of each in turn. And so for Israel to depend only upon God was political reason, as well as religious.

But it was on the latter ground that the prophet warned Israel. At this particular time an alliance with Egypt was being sought, and it seemed to many a prudent thing that they should make that alliance. But Egypt was a nation of idolaters, and God had expressly warned against such alliance: it would be supremely a godless policy, making friends with the enemies of God, turning a deaf ear to all God's counsels. And so Isaiah put before the people the grand alternative of trusting wholly and simply in God. He told them that they had lost God-reality; but let them come back now to Him in faith, and trust only in Him. God was real, eager and willing to manifest Himself and put forth His power for His people. Let them lay hold of His strength. Let them rest in Him, and in this quietness and confidence should be their strength. Their God was all-sufficient. "Thine ears shall hear a word behind thee, saying, This is the way, walk ye in it, when ye turn to the right hand, and when ye turn to the left." The way of spiritual vision.

And that principle given to Israel is the one wise and holy rule for God's people in all ages. We in our day are called to trust only in God, and thereby prove His power. But, as for Israel, to hear and respond to that message we need a new spiritual vision. For our eyes have turned to other things, and other considerations, and other authorities than the living God. A strange blindness can easily and persistently assail the church of Jesus Christ: and a blind church, as someone has truly said, is the chief hindrance to God and truth in this world. And let us remember, as we say that, that "the church" means ourselves, the people of God in this age. And with God's people, when there is "no vision, the people perish".

What is the vision that we need? Why, very much the vision that Israel needed—a vision, an understanding of *the reality and the sufficiency of God.* We have been busy, we have been fretted about many things; and we have lost the spiritual balance. We need to get things back into their right perspective. And God is calling us to turn our eyes upon Him, to look unto Him and be saved. That is to say, we need to see Him as the active and living God who is interested and concerned for His cause and for His people, whom He so wants to trust Him that He can prosecute His cause through them, even in such a day as this.

Remember, the work of God in this world is not our work for God: it is God's work for, and in, and through us. He is the Captain and the Lord in this fight, and He has power, wisdom, and guidance for His church; and in and by Him alone can the church hope to overcome. We need to recover this vision. That is the vision that was given to Joshua when he was commissioned to lead the people of Israel forward into the land of promise. Joshua was anxious in that day: he was haunted with weakness he may have been fearful of the future; he may even have been tempted to compromise with the enemy. But to Joshua the Lord Himself came and said, "As Captain of the Lord's host am I come now unto you!" and Joshua knew that he and Israel could go forward and prove invincible with that divine Captain.

In a richer and fuller way God comes and says exactly the same thing to us, the people of God today. "As Captain of the Lord's host am I now come to *you*." He says it expressly in the Lord Jesus Christ, His blessed Son, who came forth from the side of God for this very purpose. What we need, above all things, is a new vision of Jesus Christ, our Lord and Redeemer, with all power and all authority given unto Him, both in heaven and on earth.

We need the vision that John was given on Patmos, the vision of Christ in all that He is for and over His people; the complete conqueror of all the powers of darkness, in this age as in every age; the Christ who now lives and intercedes for His people, and the Christ who has now come to them also, that He might indwell them and fill them with His Holy Spirit.

Let me remind you that the life and death and resurrection and ascension of our Lord, and the coming of the Holy Spirit, have turned the tide for ever for those who believe in Him, and are seeking to serve Him. For He rose and ascended "far above all rule and authority and power and dominion, and above every name that is named". It was established beyond doubt that whereas man in himself is no match for the forces of evil, yet man in Christ, in union with the Son of God through the living Spirit, is more than conqueror, destined to overcome.

The church must see the supreme power of her Lord, and she must trust herself and her conflict only to Him. Have we lost that vision? Is it a dull vision, or is it burning clearly for us? Such a vision that God waits to give us— if we have been losing it—a vision of Jesus Christ His Son in the place of pre-eminence; Jesus Christ set on high; and on the midst of His people in all His greatness and power and fulness and sufficiency.

And with that we need a vision of what the church of Christ is, and is meant to be; of her high calling in Christ. The people of God in this world— mocked and despised, and written off, it would seem, by the great majority— are actually the body of Christ in the world, the habitation of God through the living Spirit, the "fulness of Him that filleth all in all". This is what we, God's people, are in the purpose of God. The possession and the delight of Jesus Christ, purchased by His blood, to be holy unto Him without stain or shame of sin or compromise, and mighty through God to the spreading of His Gospel to mankind, throwing down the strongholds of evil. We need that vision restored: and then, with shame, in this vision of reality, we can see ourselves very different from that, and perhaps see ourselves defeated and sinful and traitorous, living in such a way that with this "name to live" we are denying the very power thereof.

And we must be challenged to do something about it. Can we get the spiritual vision? The way of spiritual vision exalts God and humbles us, and drives us to bow in humility and contrition; and be assured that that is part of God's great purpose of blessing in this Convention. The way of vision.

Secondly, there is—

A WAY OF DECISION. Decision—which simply means that the vision will have to be translated into reality. The voice that speaks to us, pointing the way, will be obeyed. Jesus Christ waits for His people to repent. He waits for our honest confession of sin and failure; for our confession of looking to worldly expedients, for self-chosen ways, instead of trusting the divine power. He waits for our obedience to His Word, as it tells us to repudiate self, and to believe in Him, and to choose Him as Lord wholeheartedly.

God expects a decision from us in this Convention: we must make our choice: we must come to decision as God speaks. This means, essentially, I think, that there will have to be separation unto God, and unto God alone. Separation. That word "separation", I find, is not very popular in present-day thinking. But God's people are clearly called to separate from all that is not of God or in His will. That was a large part of Isaiah's call to the people of Israel. There must be no alliance, no compromise with the enemy, or with those who know not the Lord and His ways—be they Egypt, or Assyria, or anyone else, on the right hand or on the left.

I wonder, does the principle of separation seem to us today to be something harsh and bigoted and narrow, or—what seems almost worse to many people today—out-of-date. Maybe. But not, I submit, to a warfaring man. For him it is a matter of common sense. The fifth column is too great a menace to admit of compromise or of acceptance of doubtful help.

A Brigadier in the army, a great Christian man, an Irishman—there have been many great Irishmen in the British army!—was talking to me and to a group of boys many years ago about his experiences in the first world war. He talked about the armistice day coming. The message came through that at 11 a.m. on the eleventh of November, 1918, hostilities would cease, the firing would stop; but they would stand to. And, said the message, there would be no fraternisation with the enemy. My dear people, when we rise to God's vision and conception of our Christian calling in this world as a warfare, and as a continuous warfare against a very cunning foe, we realise that this is still a matter of sheer common sense: no fraternisation with the enemy.

When I say this, I do not mean separation from other Christians; selective, divisive, shutting-off of part of the body of Christ by those who seem to think they must have some special monopoly of truth, or purity, and won't have fellowship with other people who are Christians. This is one of the gravest curses in Christian work, one of the most wounding things for the body of Christ.

I am speaking of the enemy, who must be recognised as such. And that enemy can be found within the camp, within the true body of Christ, within the heart of the Christian, within you and me. Its chief marks are the acceptance of unspiritual standards, rebellion against God's ways of truth and

27

purity and single-heartedness, an unwillingness to be wholly the Lord's and to follow Him only and fully. Wherever that enemy gains foothold, and is recognised as such, he must be cast out: there must be separation. This is the way: and as God's way of full blessing is open to us, He expects us to walk in it.

Well, let us look at it quite clearly. This way of separation may well mean for us a way of unpopularity; a way of persecution maybe; certainly a way of self-abnegation. To make choice of the way of Christ our Lord is a decision to put away the energy of the flesh on which we have been relying, and to turn from the way of worldly wisdom and worldly manoeuvring and expedients, to the way that Jesus Christ walked; a way that follows Him who "when He was reviled, reviled not again; when He suffered, He threatened not; but committed Himself to Him that judgeth righteously". It means ceasing to judge by worldly values, and to walk according to worldly standards; and instead becoming nothing, becoming even fools for Christ's sake. To stop vindicating ourselves, and justifying our position and attacking other people's, and striving in carnal energy and with carnal weapons—but turning from that, that the power of Christ may really rest upon us. Our warfare is spiritual.

The way of decision to which we are called is a decision to believe in the supreme spiritual resources that we have in Christ, and in Christ alone, and in all simplicity to put them to the test. He wants us to cease from ourselves, and to find our all in Him. Are you ready for that?

Then, in the third place, it will be—

THE WAY OF FULL BLESSING. If we, God's people, are willing in the day of His power, there will be no doubt of this. God by His Spirit wants to bless and lead His people forward in a victorious experience. He wants our witness to be vital and our message to be clear. He wants us to possess our possessions in Him—and this is the way. Let us not have the idea that God is sterile and harsh, and waiting to judge us in severity for our failure. His heart is full of love and yearning toward us. His arm, though "strong to smite" is also "strong to save"; and He is far more willing to bless us than we are to seek the blessing. And He is glad beyond our human comprehension when we do seek Him, and allow Him to have His way. He is determined to bless and to use us—even us—for the outworking of His great purpose.

A text that I am very fond of quoting is Psalm 65:9, "The river of God is full of water." There is all-sufficiency in our God, and if we die of thirst the responsibility is our own. We have our sufficiency in God—our all-sufficiency. "By strength shall no man prevail." His strength alone must fill us. And it will, if we obey His words and yield to Him.

As His people are holy—that is, separated unto Him, and given to Him—the overflowing life of God will be there. The Holy Spirit, remember, has come forth from the side of the Father and of the Son, to yoke His strength to His people's weakness in a victorious experience. And that is what God expects and awaits. We are to be filled with the Holy Spirit. And as we fulfil the conditions in all reality and honesty, His Spirit will fill us. This is the way, walk ye in it.

My dear people, God is already speaking to us, setting before us the way of vision, the way of decision, and the way of full blessing. And hearing His voice, let us turn no more to the right hand or to the left, but walk in the way. Let us begin to do so here and now. God is longing to manifest Himself in such a day as this, and there is no hope unless He does. He is waiting to manifest Himself for the glory of His Name, for the honour of His Son, for the good of His people, for the blessing of mankind.

The only thing up to now that has hindered Him has been our human blindness, or our human pride, or—can it be?—our disobedience to His will. Well, deal with that now, as He reveals it. Cast it out. Turn from it. Tell the Lord that you are willing to follow Him, to trust in Him only, as He enables. Or perhaps as Christian workers we have been feeling baffled and discouraged before the problems that we have been tackling, in the church, in our service for Him. We have put forth our best efforts; we have copied the methods of others; we have followed the teaching from platforms like this as far as we have known how. And yet we seem to have been like sea birds that have fallen after dashing themselves against the lighthouse tower, with broken wings; and disappointment claims us for its own. And now God has spoken to us, reminding us that the race is not to the swift, nor the battle to the strong, and that the best of human skill or wisdom or the energy of the flesh cannot avail in this warfare; and He has shown us that He is the captain of the fight. And He will, as we give ourselves to Him, undertake for us. He is ready to exert omnipotence on our behalf, if we will believe Him, and open a channel for His power by our yielding in faith.

Well, if we make the surrender, and fulfil our humble little costly part as we believe in Him and put our full trust in Him, do you think that He will fail on His part? That He will dishonour and deny His word to us, having brought us to this position? Of course not. But we've got to trust God, and believe in Him. "He is faithful that promised, who also will do it." Let Him, then, have this opportunity for which He seeks, for which He longs. He delights to be gracious; He waits to bless us with His full blessing. He will fulfil His word, and He will be true to Himself. This is the way of full blessing, which *God* is waiting to give. Listen again. "Thine ears shall hear a word behind thee", speaking clearly, "This is the way, walk ye in it . . ." Spiritual vision, decision, fulness of blessing. So may it be, and all the praise and glory shall be His.

Rev. Dick Lucas and Dr. James Dunlop

29

Christian Revolution

By the Rev. *Alan Redpath*, D.D.

*I am the Lord thy God, which have brought thee out of the land of Egypt,
out of the house of bondage. Thou shalt have no other gods before me—Exodus
20:2–3.*

It is a trite saying, but nevertheless true, that we live in a world in revolt.
In the past four years I have been going round it, almost non-stop. And
everywhere the order of the day is rioting, street-marches, protest, revolution,
in every country in the world. This is what we face just now, and for a Christian
I think it is a most exciting day in which to be alive. I am so glad I know the
Lord Jesus tonight. I am so sorry for people who don't.

But my great concern is that somehow we all might be stabbed awake in
our conscience, to understand that the message of the living Christ is the only
answer to the problems of men today. Thank God our message never needs
altering, never needs watering down. The same old truth, the same old wonderful story, presented, perhaps, with a different emphasis and in different
ways, is the message—not *a* message, but *the* message—for the salvation of
men in these tremendous days.

I don't think there has ever in history been a generation which has had
so much, but hasgrumbled so constantly, and has sought so persistently to
have more and more of what they already have. It is an amazing world,
really. A society which is clever enough, brilliant enough to relay live by
satellite on television, the British Lions rugger match in New Zealand the
day before yesterday. To land men on the moon—wonderful! But at the same
time to meet racial animosity with revolution, assassination and tyranny;
to try to settle our problems by strikes and lock-outs.

I believe there is a sinister force at work in this country determined to
pull us down: and unless the Christian church wakes up to this, there is no
answer; it is so sinister, and so subtle. I heard on television a man say during
the electricity strike: "All that we want to do is to cause the most amount of
suffering we can to the greatest number of people in the shortest possible
time!"

There is a spirit abroad in our country, and in the world, which threatens
our very existence. And we Christians must wake up to this, for we live in a
country and a civilisation which has gone crazy. The only hope for peace,
in the mind of many people, the United Nations, has been reduced to total
impotence in the Holy Land and in Vietnam. In universities, which assert
their role to be the critical centre of society, the moral vacuum that exists has
completely eliminated the Word of God and the law of God, the Ten Commandments.

Dope, drugs, addiction! Of course, we Christians love to get together and
lament it all; we enjoy speaking about it, indeed, and link it with our hope

30

that the Lord will soon come again. But we don't do anything more about it. I mean, we don't want to get involved; we don't want to get our feet wet; we don't want to face this situation. We want to live in our cosy little huddle.

The sin of our day, I feel, might well be the blindness and heartlessness of Christian people, who leave others way out there, just because we don't know what to do about it. We go to meetings, do a bit of evangelism; but we don't do anything more. We don't get involved where people are, where the action is. My dear friends, I am sure of this, that we are finished, absolutely finished, if this generation does not seek the will of God afresh in society today, and get to know God's restoring purpose in Jesus Christ our Lord—which is expressed for us in the words of the first commandment: "I am the Lord thy God. Thou shalt have no other gods before me."

There is a madness in the world which God wants to deal with. And because you and I are in the world, He wants to begin with us. I believe the hour is come for a Christian revolution—not revival only, but revolution: a sheer down-to-earth revolt against the popular, happy-go-lucky, easy-going Christianity which costs us literally nothing, which can be as like the world as anything else, and which gets nowhere, cuts no ice, and leaves people totally unmoved. Oh, for a Christian revolution to take place this week in our hearts!

That's what Paul said the Christian is: "If any man be in Christ, he is a new creature", a totally different kind of person inside. He hasn't put on a Sunday suit; he hasn't just got a few new habits, and lost a few old ones. He is totally different inside; something happened to him. He has revolted from his old master, the devil, and is under the sovereignty of Jesus Christ the Lord. He has taken part in the Christian revolution.

Now, this is our theme tonight, this first commandment, which demands a revolt from all other gods. "I am the Lord thy God. Thou shalt have no other gods before me."

Before I go any further it might be well to say a word to dispose of one line of thinking that may be yours when you turn to a passage and a text like this. Some people might say, "Oh, this is only for the Jews. This is purely national. This is dispensational. It hasn't anything to do with today." Now, I believe that is not only highly dangerous, but totally unscriptural. Let me put three passages from the Word together, and read them to you.

Deuteronomy 8:2, "Thou shalt remember all the way which the Lord thy God led thee these forty years in the wilderness, to humble thee, and to prove thee, to know what was in thine heart, whether thou wouldest keep His commandments, or no. And He humbled thee, and suffered thee to hunger, and fed thee with manna, which thou knewest not, neither did thy fathers know; that He might make thee know that man doth not live by bread only, but by every word that proceedeth out of the mouth of the Lord doth man live."

Matthew 4:4, "Jesus answered and said, It is written, Man shall not live by bread alone, but by every word that proceedeth out of the mouth of God."

Matthew 5:17, "Jesus said, think not that I am come to destroy the law, or the prophets: I am not come to destroy, but to fulfil. For verily I say unto you, Till heaven and earth pass, one jot or one tittle shall in no wise pass from the law, till all be fulfilled. Whosoever therefore shall break one of these least commandments, and shall teach men so, he shall be called the least in the kingdom of heaven: but whosoever shall do and teach them, the same shall be called great in the kingdom of heaven. For I say unto you, That except your righteousness shall exceed the righteousness of the scribes and Pharisees, ye shall in no case enter into the kingdom of heaven."

Now what do these verses teach? Just this, that my life and yours are only perfectly conditioned, can only see their maximum potential, when they are governed by every word that proceeds out of the mouth of God. The law that God gave to the Hebrew people was directed to the end of expressing His intention for their happiness and their holiness—and for ours, too. And to show to us that a man can only be holy if he is living by every word that proceeds out of the mouth of God, and with unquestioning obedience to it all. The Lord Jesus lived constantly, without exception, by the words which proceeded out of the mouth of God.

One tremendous day He died on a cross outside the city wall. He bore the penalty of our disobedience. He took the rebels' place. He died for rebels like you and me.

> *In my place—and yours—condemned He stood;*
> *Sealed my pardon with His blood:*
> *Hallelujah! what a Saviour!*

In His resurrection He took His life again. Because of His obedience it was absolutely impossible for Him to stay dead. He couldn't stay dead. He was dead, but He couldn't stay dead because He had obeyed God perfectly. "I lay down my life, that I may take it again. No man taketh it from me . . . I have power to lay it down, and I have power to take it again." This was a terrific, tremendous, omnipotent word of our Lord Jesus Christ. He took it again, in order that He might communicate to each one of us that life he lived of obedience, so that when I am saved and born again of His Spirit, I am immediately indwelt of the Holy Ghost, whose natural thing is to obey God all the time. God in me obeys God in heaven. God in me shows out the Lord Jesus. This is the wonderful transformation that takes place when a man is born again.

Paul describes it in the words of Romans 8: "What the law could not do, in that it was weak through the flesh, God sending His Son in the likeness of sinful flesh, and for sin, condemned sin in the flesh, that the righteousness of the law might be fulfilled in us, who walk not after the flesh, but after the Spirit."

Listen, my friend, if you think the Gospel is an easy way out, if you think it is old hat, if you think it irrelevant, if you think it is a nice, smooth, easy, tricky psychological way of escape from reality, it's not. We have not come to Keswick to escape from reality: we have come to face it. We have come to be apart for a while that we may face reality, and go back empowered, to changed lives in the power of Jesus Himself. The Gospel is not an easy way of escape from the law. It is God's plan to fulfil God's law in my life—a redeemed man, redeemed by the blood of Christ.

The new life of the Holy Spirit in me, when I am born again, must be regulated by the Ten Commandments. It is not a further knowledge of truth that I need: it is sheer, down-to-earth obedience to what I already know. That is what God is after. And it is the consistent teaching of the Bible that man can only fulfil the possibilities of life if he is living by the words which proceed from the mouth of God. We are not only born for time, but for

32

eternity. The trouble is that so many of us live down here as though we were going to live for ever. Today we sow, and tomorrow we reap. And the reaping depends on the sowing.

If the ultimate end of our lives is to be absolute harmony with the will of God, then we must live by every word that proceeds out of His mouth. If you live without any reference to God's law, and hope one day you will make it somehow or other to heaven, then, if I may say so respectfully, you are foolish in the extreme.

Here, then, in these Ten Commandments, are the words of God uttered for the government of a people whose glory lay in the fact of their absolute obedience to law, and whose shame would lie in their constant revolt against His authority. And they speak to us today with renewed force in this permissive age of the society in which we live. There is no permissiveness about God. His law does not water itself down to suit the 20th century. The glory of His people consists in their obedience to the Lord Himself, and our shame consists in our revolt against His authority.

Of course the commandments presuppose failure and sin—they won't have any place in heaven, because when I get to heaven I shall have a nature which cannot disobey God. As long as I live here, though, Christian or otherwise, I am living in touch with a nature which is altogether and always sinful. I've been a Christian now for forty-two years. I was converted in a public house, forty-two years ago. I like to go there when I come up to Keswick, just to see it again—that dirty old pub where Jesus met me for the first time, through the ministry of a business colleague. And I'm no better a man now than I was then: I am potentially just as sinful, just as evil, but for the grace of God. The only good thing about a Christian is Jesus in his life. So I say that as long as I live here I have a nature which is altogether sinful: and but for the grace of God it would always be sinful. And these words and law are of constant importance, for although the Christian needs to be reminded that "the law of the Spirit of life in Christ sets him free from the law of sin", it does not set him free from the law of God.

Liberty is not being away out on our own somewhere, independent. That is lawlessness. And those people who want to tear up society, revolt against the regime, the tradition, the establishment—well, hold it a minute. Before you do that just consider what you are going to put in its place. Are you sure you've got something instead? Liberty is not being independent. Many countries like to have independent churches. Well, bless your hearts, if you are a member of one, thank the Lord! But independence is not a Bible word: dependence is the Bible word.

Liberty is not being independent, living in a separated field all on your own. That's lawlessness. Liberty—praise God!—is fulfilling our destiny to do the will of God. That's liberty. Liberty leads to law. Indeed, the epistle of James talks about "the law of liberty"—that's a wonderful phrase: "The law of liberty." And what is law? It is a rule of life, which one intelligent being lays down to another intelligent being, having the absolute right to total authority over his life.

If there is somebody here who says, "Oh, what awful legalism that must be!" I want to say to you, "Blessed legalism!" For the thing that I need in my heart twenty-four hours a day, seven days a week, is the sovereignty of God expressed in my heart by the indwelling of Christ. The law of liberty.

I saw a programme on TV a while ago, in "Twenty-four Hours", interviewing some folk on drugs. The interviewer asked a girl aged seventeen, "Who's your father?" "Don't know," she said. "Who's your mother?" "She left me when I was two." "Where have you been for seventeen years?" "Oh, just any old where." That's what she said: "Any old where." "Taking drugs?" "Yes," she said. "What are you taking?" "Heroin." "Going high on it?" "Yes, going high. Been going high for two years." "Aren't you afraid that drug will kill you?" I can hardly describe the sense of horror as I saw the look on her face as she replied, "I hope to God it will!"

That's freedom! That's what this generation has come to! Where on earth does that lead anyone? Freedom is not licence, not doing what you like. It is fulfilling the Word of God and the will of God in your life day by day.

Augustine said, "Love God, and do as you like!" That may sound dangerous, but it is wonderfully true. Because when I love Him I accept His laws as a sheer delight; and while this law makes demands on me that are absolutely impossible, He gives me grace to meet them all.

Well, the law of God leaves me helpless, because it tells me I'm a sinner. The law, as someone has said, opens my eyes and shuts my mouth. It makes me see that I am without excuse; that I am a rebel against Almighty God. And the Ten Commandments are interpreted in the New Testament with added force and authority. What does the Lord Jesus say about it? "You have heard it said, Thou shalt not kill: I say unto you, He that hates is guilty. You have heard it said you shall not commit adultery. I say unto you, He that looks to lust is guilty." You say the Gospel is easy: you say grace is a way of escape. It isn't: it is a way of fulfilment by the power which He can give us all.

Why is God's law so severe? Believe it or not, it is the most perfect expression of His love. His goal for every one of us is perfection. It is to make us like the Lord Jesus, to blot out the image of the devil and blot in the image of Christ. That He wants to do: wipe out Satan's image and put in the image of Jesus. He is perfect love.

The cross frees us from every bit of condemnation, but it does not free us from obligation. And He that is alive today, the Lord Jesus, is the one who has the right to rule your heart and your life.

I hope what I have said has come through by the power of God's Spirit to your heart, that we are free from the law's condemnation by the blood of Jesus, and that you have put your faith in Him, and you are free. "There is therefore now no condemnation to them which are in Christ Jesus."

That is the verse that my office friend gave me when I was converted. I underlined that word now so heavily that I went right through to the epistle to the Philippians, and ruined my Bible the first day! But it was worth it. "There is therefore now no condemnation . . ." But listen. There is no condemnation, but there is total obligation. Absolute obligation. We are not free from that. Therefore as we listen to this obligation to revolt, this divine requirement and call to revolt against every false god—listen to the words of the Lord Himself: "I am the Lord thy God." He confronts us with Himself, by the name *Jehovah*. And that is a combination of three words: "He that will be; He that is; He that was." At once I find myself in the presence of eternal God: and if I really believed this, I would feel that I should have to stop preaching, and we should all be on our faces crying to Him for a new sense of His power and authority in our lives. He that is; He that was; and He that will be.

If I reach out to the future, all unknown to me, limitless, without end, He is the God that will be. If I face life today, with all its problems and all its bewilderment and all its confusion, "I am He that is." If I look back, way back to the beginning, "I am He that was." And whether I think of my origin, or my present state, or my eternal condition, He is saying to me tonight, "*I am!*" None can escape the immense revelation of the character of God.

"I am the Lord thy *God*." And the word here is *Jehovah-Elohim*, and it means the supreme object of worship. He faces us and says, "I am the Lord thy *God*." Upon that fact rests the command, "Thou shalt have no other gods before me." And if He is what He claims to be, it would be a most unreasonable thing to have another god before Him. There cannot be two who fulfil this description of an endless life: every other god must be limited. "Oh," but you say, "I haven't any gods." Haven't you? How interesting! You're an atheist? Wonderful! You don't believe in a god? Fine! But you do, you know. If you say you don't, then you are no better than your dog, your cat, your sheep, if you have no god. You don't want to be put down there! The Bible says, "All we like sheep have gone astray—"; but there is something about human nature, that there is a shrine in every heart in which there is a god whom we worship every day.

The very composition of a man, a woman, demands a centre of worship as a necessity of existence. The question is, who is your god? Can I help you to discover that? I'll tell you who it is. It is the person you think most precious. It is the thing or the person for whom or for which we should make the biggest sacrifice. It is the thing or the person which, if it left us, we should be desolate; if we possessed it, we should be happy.

Here in this commandment there is a declaration from heaven that at the very centre of our beings, enshrined in our hearts, there is to be enthroned— not a rabble of little tin gods, not a hypothetical unknowable being, not sex or drugs or addiction or anything, but a living Person who can arrange my plans, and utter His commandments and expect my obedience. At just the moment a man loses this vision of Him as Jehovah, at that moment he puts something else in the place of God.

The gods of Old Testament days are quite interesting. If a man worshipped Molech—the god of the Ammonites—we find out about him in Leviticus 20—he became cruel, ruthless. To worship Baal was to descend to bestiality, immorality. Mammon—to worship possessions and things. These gods go by other names, but they are here today.

How many of us worship Molech, the god of cruelty? People tell us that Christianity and Communism are much alike. They are as unlike as can be: totally different. Christianity says, "What's mine is thine, and you can have it out of the love of my heart." Communism says, "What's thine is mine. And I'll have it with the barrel of a gun!" They are as different as that; so don't let anybody kid you they're alike: they are not. How cruel Communism is. Oh, but you do not need to go to Communism. How cruel I am! How cruel you are! How often we just want to get on, at anybody else's expense. You first—after me! We are out for number one, and all the time. The cruelty of human nature.

And the god of Baal. How many prostitutes are on the streets of London

35

today? Who keeps them going? Those who worship Baal, the god of bestiality, the god of immorality. Man has lost his God and worships sex.

The god of Mammon? The abundance of things that we possess. My, how this first commandment needs to be preached in Britain today! The greatest country in the world is now the greatest gambling nation in the world. Six hundred million pounds spent in Scotland alone between Christmas and New Year on alcoholic drinks. This Britain of ours! The god of Mammon that we worship. And in the New Testament I find Paul speaking like this: "For many walk, of whom I have told you often, and now tell you even weeping, that they are the enemies of the cross of Christ, whose end is destruction, whose god is their belly" (Phil. 3:18–19). Just one god—of animal appetite. "What shall we eat, and what shall we wear?"

Let me say it to you gently, that I know so much of this god in my life—the god of myself. You've got a god, and I have—the god of myself: self-respect, self-esteem, self-preservation. If you had not got that god in your heart, some of you, you would be on the mission field tonight. The god of self-preservation. "How much am I going to get? Will the missionary society insure me for life? Will they give me an old age pension? Will I be secure? I don't think I will, so I'll buy my house at home, and I'll build up my practice, and I shall have possessions and things." Self-preservation!

My beloved brother and sister, you have never touched the heart of Christianity when you live like that. For the heart of Christianity is not self-preservation, but self-sacrifice. "I lay down my life that I may take it again" could be said of every child of God who is really living in the will of God.

God is saying tonight, "Thou shalt have no other gods before me." Who is your god? The god of cruelty, the god of self, the god of impurity? Who is at the centre of your life—a little puppet king who has never been dethroned? Or has there been a moment when you have stepped off the throne and you have knelt and said, "Jesus, take the place of pre-eminence, of lordship, of authority!" Listen to the words of Jesus: "Thou shalt love the Lord thy God with all thy heart, with all thy soul, and with all thy mind. If any man will come after me, let him deny himself, and take up his cross, and follow me."

I ask you, What is your life devoted to? Is it some of these gods that I have been talking about? I am saying that heaven is calling upon us all to revolt from their authority, and come under the authority of Jesus Christ. And thank God I do not have to revolt in my own strength. "The weapons of our warfare are not carnal, but mighty through God to the pulling down of strongholds."

How I should love to know that strongholds of sin in your heart and mine have crashed, because of my determination to turn to Him and the power of His Holy Spirit let loose in my heart. But this costs: it does not permit of any substitute. The woman of Samaria soon found that out. It was not a question of place; it was not a question of denomination. No, no! It was reality. Reality. How people long for that today in Christians. Reality.

I know a man who had his silver wedding; and for ten years he had been getting very concerned about his wife, because she had got so indifferent to him. And at their twenty-fifth anniversary he thought he would pluck up courage and ask her why. He took her out for a good meal first: that was a good idea. Then he said, "Dear, there's something I want to ask you. For the last ten years, I've given you new cars every year; and you've had new homes and new clothes. You've had everything that a woman can possibly want. But why is it that you are so cold to me; why are you so lacking in any affection?" "Oh," she said, "I'm so glad you've asked me that. I've been trying for years to pluck up my courage to tell you. I'm grateful for all the new cars I've had, and all the new clothes, and the new homes, and for all that you have done for me. But I want you to know that you've never given me the love of your heart!"

"Simon, do you love me?" said Jesus. "If any man love me he will keep my commandments, and my Father will come to him." What a promise! No substitutes. The church in Ephesus got a mighty shock. It was one of the fundamentalist churches of the day; sound, orthodox, wouldn't have any-thing to do with anything that wasn't dotting its i's rightly, and crossing its t's correctly. All those sort of people were outside; liberals were not heard of in Ephesus: they were terribly sound, thorough-going fundamentalist believers; nothing wrong with their doctrine. "I have somewhat against thee," was the word that Christ spoke to them from heaven, "for you have left your first love."

Is Jesus saying that to you tonight? He does not permit any substitute. I tell you, He demands all you've got. For the woman of Samaria, it meant repentance. "Go, call thy husband! Come out into the light. Tell me the whole story. I know all about it; but I want you to tell me. Tell me the truth. Go, call thy husband." Repentance. Ephesus was such a respectable church: "Except ye *repent* . . . Repent, or else . . . Change your mind, or else . . ." Worship demands all you've got.

A little boy was putting on his shirt one morning: nice shirt, it was, beautiful colour. But he was having such a battle putting the buttons in the right holes. He was getting so frustrated; and his mother, looking at him, said, "Take it easy! Look, here's the top hole, and here's the top button. Put those two in first, and all the rest will fit in."

Friends, have you got your priorities right? Where is Jesus in your life? First, second, third, or one of the also-rans? "Thou shalt love the Lord thy God with *all* thy heart, with *all* thy soul, with *all* thy mind." He demands all I've got. But I want to say this: Worship creates tremendous power. Oh, how I long for this in my heart and yours tonight. I am talking to my own heart, the most needy of all. How I long for the power that came to that woman of Samaria; for she went into the city of Sychar, and told them that she had met a Man who told her all things that she ever did. And Jesus saw them coming, and said to His disciples, "Look! the fields are ripe to harvest." And then we read, "Many believed in Him because of the word of the woman." What did they see? A great theologian, a PhD? No, an ordinary woman, a sinful woman, transformed with the water of life—who had met and confronted Jesus Christ, and honestly repented. And through that life immediately there were signs of the reality of the love of Jesus.

This is my message to you, given with a tremendous sense of concern for a Christian revolution. Will you join me in a thorough-going, down-to-earth revolt against every god that takes the place of Jesus?

Young people in our churches today—programmes of all sorts and kinds; anything's all right as long as you have devotions at the end. You can play the fool, do anything you like—social drinking at parties—anything is per-mitted these days: there are no barriers. Put the barriers up, my friends. Seek to live in the will of God, and then you will be happy. Remember that the more a Christian becomes like the world, the less like he is to Jesus. And the whole purpose of God the Father is to make us like God the Son—a new humanity, redeemed by the blood of Christ, indwelt by the Holy Ghost, and submitted to the authority of the risen Lord!

Are you one? Who is your god? Are you willing to rebel, to repent? Are you willing to take part in a Christian revolt against false gods, and to enthrone Jesus as King and Lord? He will give you the power: you cannot do it. But are you willing?

St. Kentigern, Crosthwaite, Keswick
Photo: Rev. K. W. Coates

Monday July 12th

11 am Bible Reading

The Way to Christian Stability
(1) The Possession of the Knowledge of Christ (2 Peter 1:1–11)
Rev. R. C. Lucas

TAPE NO. 291

11.50 am Forenoon meeting

The Tragedy of Permissiveness
Rev. Alan Redpath

TAPE NO. 298

3 pm Afternoon meeting

Righteous Lot
Rev. William Culbertson

TAPE NO. 298a

7.45 pm Evening meeting

Drifting is Dangerous
Rev. Michael Baughen

TAPE NO. 299

Thou Art the Man!
Rev. James Dunlop

TAPE NO. 299a

Call to Repentance

Keswick 1971 will live long in the memory of great numbers of Christian people. Not for any dramatic events or moments: for there were none. But everyone present was saying, "This is a *good* Convention"—sometimes varying the adjective to *excellent*. Perhaps the most apposite word would be *purposeful*. The keynote sounded at the start, "called unto holiness", set the tone to the whole week. There was a quiet spirit of reverent waiting upon God, an intent listening to His Word.

The weather was most kind. Gloriously sunny days gave place on Wednesday to overcast skies and a cool breeze; but the sun returned on Friday. Attendances at the meetings were splendid, with a comfortably filled tent for the Bible Readings and evening meetings. The forenoon and afternoon gatherings were naturally thin in such enticing weather, with the hills and lake alluring holiday visitors; but day visitors swelled the congregations mid-week.

An outline of the Bible Readings on 2 Peter, provided in the official programme, had whetted appetites and evoked eager expectation as the tent filled up at 10 a.m. on Monday for the first of these studies in "The Way to Christian Stability". They proved to be most satisfying and deeply appreciated, blending as they did lucid exposition with practical application. The impact of the Word was apparent throughout the Convention; and although no open response was invited, counsellors were kept busy on several evenings. It was a week, pre-eminently, of quiet instruction in the Word; and that Word effected its gracious work of illumination, challenge and invitation in countless hearts and lives.

A powerful address was given by Dr. Alan Redpath at the noon meeting on "The Tragedy of Permissiveness" as illustrated in the life of Solomon. And in the afternoon Dr. William Culbertson gave a characteristically penetrating Bible study on "Righteous Lot"—imparting to the adjective a rather astringent flavour!

Both addresses at the evening meeting continued the theme of sin in the believer, and called for repentance. The Rev. Michael Baughen—colleague of the Rev. John Stott as vicar of All Saints, Langham Place, and a new speaker at Keswick—stressed the dangers of *neglect* in the spiritual life. It leads to carelessness of heart; hardening of heart; and eventually to an unbelieving heart.

These thoughts were taken up by Dr. James Dunlop, who went on to show, from the story of David, how grievously a man of God may fall into sin. But through repentance he was restored. Very compassionately, Dr. Dunlop urged anyone conscious of sin and failure to make their way back to the One who is ever ready to say, "Go in peace, and sin no more."

The Way to Christian Stability

1. THE POSSESSION OF THE KNOWLEDGE OF CHRIST (2 Peter 1: 1–11).

By the Rev. R. C. Lucas, M.A.

It is a great privilege to look with you at this remarkable little letter, the second letter of Peter. I want to put on one side, straight away, a debate which has raged in ancient and modern times, concerning the question, Does this letter have apostolic authority? Should it be part of the sacred Scriptures? Canon Michael Green, in his Tyndale Press Commentary on *2 Peter and Jude*, and his monograph, *Two Peter Reconsidered*, deals with these matters.

One of the hallmarks of Scripture is that *it speaks with force and power to one's own heart*. The second hallmark of Scripture is that *it speaks with power to one's own day*. Holy Scripture is always contemporary. You feel that Peter might have been reading our own daily papers of the last two or three years. He seems to know so well the world in which we live. He might also have been reading some of the church papers—some of our church debates. He seems to know the weakness and frailty of our church scene.

The relevance of this short letter came to me almost as an awe-inspiring thing. It is really quite startling, and it reminded me where the church should look in its search for relevance today. The church sometimes looks in an almost frantic manner to all sorts of modern ways and means to impress people with what we have got to say. We are conscious that our problems are so difficult that we despair, and often we forget the secret, which is simply to get up, unashamed and with courage, to expound the Word of God. People will be amazed when we do that. They have never heard it, and they have no idea how these books that they dismissed when they were at school could speak with such power to the situation in which they live, to their own hearts and for their own day. We shall find this letter speaking to the problems we Christians face, both in the church and in the world.

In vv. 1 and 2, we are introduced to the author and his readers. This is the customary greeting, of course, of the day. Paul's greetings are very like it. But it is not so very different from the way that we greet each other when we write a letter which is addressed to a number of people. Just as though Mr. Caiger might send me a letter a few months before Keswick, and on the top of the letter it would say "From the Chairman of the Keswick Convention Council." And then it might say, "To the Council Members and Speakers at the Convention." And then underneath, "With the purpose of preparing you for 1971." So that there was nothing strange in this: it is exactly how we should write a semi-formal letter today.

41

Peter tells us who he is; he tells us to whom he writes; and he gives us some clue as to the themes he is going to write about, and the desires that were in his heart.

The particular points worth noting are these: First, *the way in which he refers to himself*. The old spelling of Simon, Simeon, that is in some translations, is probably better: it is the Hebrew version of his name, which comes again in Acts 15:14. It is one of the little touches which make the careful reader so sure that the real Simon is writing here, just as in 2:1—where you get that little phrase that the false teachers "deny the Master who bought them", the very thing that Peter himself had done. These small touches are wonderfully convincing and assuring.

He is "a servant and an apostle"—a servant, a title of absolute humility, of course: a slave. An "apostle", a title of absolute authority. He is our brother, and he stands among us as our brother to lead us into the powers of Christ. But he is more than our brother: he is our authoritative teacher. We do not stand on the same level as he does. What he has to say is uniquely Scripture to us, and uniquely authoritative; therefore, although he is our brother, he is also our teacher, and what he says is indeed the Word of God to us.

Then notice the way in which he refers to *his Christian readers*. They are not his servants, nor are they his inferiors. They are "those who have obtained a faith of equal standing with ours in the righteousness of our God and Saviour Jesus Christ." This is a remarkable phrase for an apostle to write. He is writing to people who are second-generation Christians, but that does not mean that they are second-class citizens of the Kingdom of heaven. But of course they would be tempted to think that. They would say, "We never walked with Jesus in the flesh as you did, and so of course we realise that your Christian life is beyond our reach." He contradicts that right at the beginning, and writing to Christians down the ages throughout the world, Peter says that we have a faith which through the grace of God is of equal standing with that of the apostles. Isn't that a wonderful thought?

I am not going to look at many cross-references, because of our old enemy, time. But 1 Peter 1:8—these references to 1 Peter are particularly helpful— has that same theme, "without having seen Him you love Him; though you do not now see Him you believe in Him and rejoice with unutterable and exalted joy". Yes, Hallelujah! That is so, isn't it? You have not seen the Lord, but you love Him; you rejoice in Him with great joy. And so do I. And so although we are far removed in years and time from Simon Peter, we have the same love and the same faith for Jesus.

How does this come about? Well, this faith has been allotted, or granted, to us: that is a better translation, really, of v. 1. This emphasises that great truth which George Whitefield as a young man rejoiced to preach: free, sovereign grace. The Bible is full of it from cover to cover. The one great thing the Bible is talking about from end to end is not our faith, but the grace of God, without which we should not have begun the Christian life; without which none of us would reach the portals of the eternal Kingdom of our Lord and Saviour. And it is because of God's free grace that we have a faith of equal standing with all other believers, and with Peter and his brethren, too.

This is because of the justice, or fairness, of our God and Saviour. I do not think he uses "righteousness" here in the same way as Paul does; he is simply saying that election, or free grace, is not a mark of God's injustice, but on the contrary, it is a proof of his justice, and fairness, and righteousness.

So the way he refers to his readers is, I think, very heartening to us. Then there is the way that he refers to *his Lord and Master*. At the end of v. 1 he talks about "our God and Saviour Jesus Christ". This is the *RSV* translation, and almost certainly preferable to any other translation here. "Our God and Saviour"—so right at the beginning of his letter he shows us the very high position that his Master, Jesus Christ, has in his thinking. He is God; God come to earth. The idea still lurks in men's minds today that this great assertion that Jesus is God, God incarnate, is not somehow original; that it grew up over the years, rather like legends in the unreformed churches. And that if you go right back to the beginning of the story you will find a Jesus, meek and mild, with no claims of dogma—as people say today. Now that cannot be substantiated. From the first day of the Christian church, from the first day on which Peter, bold as a lion, stood up in Jerusalem and preached the Gospel, in his first sermon the climax is this: "Let all the house of Israel therefore know assuredly that God has made Him both Lord and Christ, this Jesus whom you crucified" (Acts 2:36). Can there be any doubt of what he believed, right from the beginning?

There was never a church without that foundation stone. There was never a sermon without that theme. There was never a believer without that Lord and Master, right from the beginning. So let all Christians today know assuredly that Jesus is God, conqueror, and now risen again, and ascended, and reigning. We shall see through this letter the wonderful that place Peter has for our Lord Jesus Christ.

Then, fourthly, notice the way in which he refers to *the Christian life*. It is essentially a knowledge of God and of Jesus. "May grace and peace be multiplied to you in the *knowledge* of God and of Jesus our Lord." In a lovely phrase which was used very much to me when first I was converted, to become a Christian is "to come to know Jesus Christ". To know a person, of course, is the deepest knowledge that we can have: the knowledge of husband and wife, the knowledge of two friends, of a David and a Jonathan. This is the deepest knowledge of which we are capable. It is a deeper knowledge than that we get by going to college, of course. That is why it is open to everybody, whether we go to college or not. To know a person, and to come to appreciate a person, and to love a person, that is right at the heart of life. If we did not know one another, life would not be worth living; if we did not have friends and family then, well, we should commit suicide!

And right at the heart of Christianity is to know God; the deepest knowledge which alone makes life really worth living. But, be careful! Though it is true to say that we Christians know Christ, rather than knowing truths about Him, it is also true to say that we cannot go on to know Christ better without knowing more about Him. There is no false distinction in the Bible between knowing Christ and knowing truths. I have to know truths, to know Christ better. This is going to come out in this letter all the time.

That is why this week we shall study this book. Please do not feel that this kind of study is something which is unnecessary: that we can love Christ without it. No, we have to study; we have to know what the Bible says if we

43

are to know the true Person, and to know Him truly. That is why when a man comes to Christ, immediately his mind is awakened.

Some young people in the church where I work have recently been to an approved school. A remarkable work, as some of you know, is going on among some of these approved school boys and girls. In this school, twenty or so young men professed conversion. One of these men could not read at all. Only two weekends ago they paid a return visit, when another number of men came to faith in Christ. But perhaps even greater joy than that was the growth they discovered in many of the boys who had professed conversion before. And this boy who could not read had learnt to read, and was reading the Bible. Christianity has always brought education in its train, because it awakens men's minds to explore the world that God has made around them, and to explore the Word of God that He has written for our learning.

So that one of the results of Christ entering our lives should be a quickening of our mental capacities. And that is not just for young people and students. Every mother and father, yes, every grandfather and grandmother, and every child, can be quickened to cope with these Bible Readings that we have on these mornings. It is not beyond any of us to explore the depths of God; and it is His desire that in the knowledge of God, grace and peace may be multiplied to us. And let us get it quite clear, that grace and peace will not be multiplied to us in any other way. You do not wander into an increasing experience of God.

Now this is what He wants from us in this letter. Verse 2 in a delightful way hints at the real theme of 2 Peter. It is the theme of both 2 Peter and 1 Peter: the theme of spiritual growth, progress, multiplication in the Christian life. Peter's desire is that a young Christian may grow, and that an older Christian may grow still more. His desire is that the grace and peace of God may be multiplied in your life and in mine, through our knowledge of God and of Jesus.

Now let us get straight down to this magnificent passage, vv. 3–11, which is the most classic statement in the New Testament concerning growth in grace. In a sense, every theme that we shall meet this week is in this preliminary passage. This will make it impossible for me to sound all the depth of this passage: we shall come back to it again and again.

Verses 3–4 tell us that two things have been granted to us: the power of God, and the promises of God.

First, *the power of God*. God has called us, as v. 3 says, through the knowledge of Himself, "to His own glory and excellence"—I prefer the "to" there, to "by" as in the *RSV*. He has called us, in other words, to glory and excellence; to holiness. He has called us to an entirely new kind of life. But He has therefore called us to something which is quite impossible in our own strength. I haven't got the power to live a life like Jesus Christ. So, as in the same breath He tells me that He has called me to His glory and excellence, He tells me also that He has provided the means by which such a life can be lived. He has given me His divine power. And—to put it more exactly—that divine power has given to me "all things that pertain to life and godliness". Now isn't that a striking phrase! It is a comprehensive phrase. Everything that I need for a life of godliness is provided by the power of God when He calls me to a knowledge of Himself, and calls me to His excellence and glory.

44

What God asks of us, He makes possible for us. This is absolutely fundamental to the Bible picture. Jesus comes up to a man who is standing before Him with a withered arm which he is quite incapable of lifting. "Lift up your arm!" "I can't do that, Lord. It's no good asking me to do the impossible." But he does lift it up—because with the command is the power. There is much misunderstanding concerning this. If in the New Testament God commands me to do anything, I don't have to ask Him for power: the power is there. He wouldn't ask me to do it, if He had not given me the enabling. And I can obey—it is the obedience of faith, isn't it; I can't obey in my own natural wisdom, because I haven't the strength to lift up my arm—but I can obey through faith. I can lift up my arm because if He tells me to do something, I know that He will make it possible.

God is always asking us to do the impossible. He is going to ask many of us before this week is finished to do some impossible thing for Him—it may be small, or it may be big; it may refer to your own family life; it may refer to the whole nature of your career in the future. And when God calls you to do this thing, it is going to take your breath away. You are going to say, "I can't do that!" But God's power always comes with God's call. So "His divine power has granted to us all things that pertain to life and godliness, through the knowledge of Him who called us to his own glory and excellence."

With the power of God come *the promises of God*: "By which He has granted to us His precious and very great promises" (v. 4). Now your promises summarise what you are going to do. "I promise to do this," you say, referring to something in the future that you purpose and will to do. The promises of God, which have such a prominent place in the Bible—the promises of God in the Old Testament, for example, tell the people of God in the Old Testament what their Lord and Master is going to do.

Now we cannot understand too clearly that all the promises—and I mean all the promises: every promise of the Old Testament finds its fulfilment in, not an event so much as in a person, in Jesus Christ. This is a rather difficult thing to take in at first: it is such a tremendous thing to say. But it is very important to see it. As I study the promises of the Old Testament, if I try to find their fulfilment out of relationship to Jesus Christ, I shall be led astray, "All the promises of God are Yea and Amen in Christ"—that is to say, they are fulfilled in Him, and in what He came to do. And as God poJints to esus Christ through the Spirit, He can say to us, "Now I have done what I promised to do."

Let me immediately qualify this by saying that the promises refer not simply, or not mainly, to the first coming of Christ. In fact, so prominent is the Second Coming of our Lord and Saviour in this letter, that it is simply referred to as "the Coming". This entirely different perspective has been one of the major lessons for me. We tend to think of the first coming of Jesus as being the crucial coming, and the second as completing His first coming. The Bible thinks of his Second Coming as being *the* coming of Christ; and the first as anticipating that. It puts the whole centre of history, not in the past, but in the future. So the promises of God are already fulfilled in part in Jesus Christ, but their complete fulfilment will, of course, only be seen in the coming of Jesus in glory.

But in those two phrases brought together under the phrase "the coming of Christ", every promise that God ever made will be fulfilled. Isn't that a

45

tremendous thought? That there is not a single promise that God has made that is not going to be fulfilled. If you look around at the world today, you are bound to say that there are many things that have not begun to be fulfilled by God. No, exactly: because, you see, we so often think around the first coming, without that picture of *the* coming of Christ in glory. And if our minds are focused there, all our thinking will be illuminated. It is there that everything that God has promised is going to be seen to be done. At the moment it can only be seen to be done by faith.

So we shall find that the promises in 2 Peter refer primarily to the coming of Christ in glory. But of course they also refer to the coming of Christ in meekness as the world's Saviour. So v. 4 has a double reference: it refers to what God will do now, and what He is going to do.

What will He do now? Well, I think v. 4 is a better description of conversion than any other in the New Testament, in some ways. Look at this description of conversion. First look at the *negative* side. The negative side is that we "may escape from the corruption—or pollution (we shall come on to that word later)—that is in the world because of desire, or passion"—the world's desires. The new-born Christian is a man who has escaped.

Now that does not mean, of course, that Christianity is escapism, as the world claims. Sometimes in history Christians have acted as though that were the case. They have fled from what was obviously a wicked world into the desert. They have enclosed themselves in communities to get away from the wickedness all around them. And it is easy to understand why. But that is not God's purpose. His purpose is for us to be the salt of the earth; therefore we have got to be right in among people, we have got to live in the world, we have got to live on Monday morning, and not only Sunday morning.

But in order that we may do this safely, and not be swamped by the world, as is so possible for us, we first have to escape from the desires of the world. The desires of the world have to be rooted out of us. Love for the world has to be taken out of us. The fear of the world has to be taken out of us— isn't that almost as bad as love for the world? And God by His Spirit has to do a mighty, liberating work in our hearts, to loosen the grip that the world has on every one of us.

The more I grow as a Christian the more sure I am that the world has a grip on all of us. It wants to make us all the same: children of the world— if you like, children of the devil. And God comes to free us from that grip; to help us to escape from this stifling, suffocating atmosphere; to free us from fear of what others think about us; to make us bold and strong and very courageous; to help us to stand outside the world, and to see where the world is going. And then, when we have lost our love for the world, and have been liberated from it, then to plunge us back into it.

In this sense the Bible is full of coming and going, as I once heard a Christian say. We have to come out of the world, before God can send us back into the world. God cannot trust you to live in the world until He has taken you out of the world. And this separation from the world and its desires is at the moment taboo in Christian circles, isn't it? We have reacted against a no drink, no cinema, no this, no that, no what-not doctrine; and we are too frightened to say "separation" at all. Well, we have to bring it right back into our teaching, haven't we? We have to tell young Christians that they will

46

never be able to do anything in the world for God at all until they have been separated from the world; until they cease to love the world; until they have got out of the grip of the world.

There is no possibility of influencing the world until it stops influencing me. I therefore have to escape from the corruption that is in the world because of passion; and only God the Holy Spirit can do this for me. It is, of course, a progressive work: it is a work that God goes on doing all our lives. The world is always calling us back. "You didn't really mean to go; let's keep in close touch, anyhow, by long-distance telephone. I know you didn't mean to go as far as that. Come back just for a day or two!" Oh, no. Let us get this clear into our minds, that we have escaped once for all from the pollution that is in the world.

And *positively*, what? "We have partaken of the divine nature". This is what it means to be a Christian. A cross-reference to 1 Peter 1:23 says, "You have been born anew, not of perishable seed but of imperishable, through the living and abiding word of God." The seed of God has been implanted into us, and new birth has taken place. Therefore, by His marvellous grace and plan, we partake of Him. He dwells in us: we dwell in Him.

Don't you think that is a wonderful description of what it means to be a Christian: to "escape from the corruptions that are in the world" and to become "a partaker of the divine nature"? And how hungry people around us in the world today are for this! Many young people, for example, far outside the church, are hungry for this. They see the decay and corruption that is written into the world. They often see it more clearly than their elders, who seem satisfied with it. They long to get out of the pollution and corruption and decay in the world. That is why they say they want to drop out. And they hunger after an experience that will fulfil themselves. They live, of course, in the far country, and the only food you can find in the far country is the food of the pigsty: but don't blame them for that. That is the only food to be found in the far country. But if they will only come back from the far country, if they could only be brought back to the Father, then there will be food in His house, enough and to spare. We must spread the dish before them of what is in the Father's household, and plead with them to come from the far country. They don't know what they are missing.

A positive note is needed from the Christian church today, so that when a young person comes into our churches he sees that there is a feast spread before him: that people there are obviously satisfied with the food of God; that they have escaped from those things that he knows to be wrong; and that they are partakers of the divine nature; and that alone is their satisfaction and joy. What has been granted to us? The power and promises of God.

What is *demanded of us* (vv. 5–7)? A very feeble translation here, "beside this." Better the *Revised Standard Version* or other modern translations: "For this very cause"—for this very reason, because of what has been given to us, this is what I demand of you. What does he demand? That we should make every effort, strain every nerve, do our best, to grow in grace. "Make every effort to supplement your faith with virtue, and virtue with knowledge, and knowledge with self-control, and self-control with steadfastness, and steadfastness with godliness, and godliness with brotherly affection, and brotherly affection with love."

May we just go off the main road for a moment, into a lay-by? And may

47

I be permitted to give you a small lesson in Bible logic? Because this particular chapter is very rich in two remarkable cases of Bible logic. The question, How can I be holy? cannot, of course, be answered by your own efforts. Some of us, when we first went to church, that was all we heard. To live the Christian life you have to pull up your socks, and do your best, and be sincere, and try your hardest. And that was no good news to us. No wonder people soon give up that! What good news it was, then, to hear the Gospel, that the power of God is available; and that the life of Christ can be in me. And many books and testimonies have been written on the realisation that has come to men, that Christ lives in them by His Spirit, and can energise them to live a holy life.

But then we may slip into the opposite danger, and say among ourselves, as Christians, that all that is needed is the power of God, and faith to appropriate it. But the Bible does not talk like that. Having told us that our holiness depends upon the power of God, and without that power we could not live a holy life, it then goes on to say, Through your faith, work to add to your faith virtue, knowledge, self-control, and steadfastness. Now this is not a synthesis: it is not saying that the truth is a mixture of faith and works. The truth lies in both extremes, as old Charles Simeon said. Holiness is entirely by faith in Jesus, and entirely by making every effort. It is entirely divine, and entirely human. It is of God, and it is of us as renewed Christians. Remember that—*as renewed Christians*: that is the point. And the renewed Christian is asked to do things that the unsaved person is not asked to do. The unsaved person is never asked to do anything, but to repent, and come as he is. Is not that right? The only thing he can do is to bring the sins that he has committed to the Redeemer.

But the renewed man is asked to do a lot, because the power of God is at work in him. He is asked to supplement his faith with virtue, to supplement his virtue with knowledge . . . and this is a matter of human effort: knowledge does not fall out of the sky!

The same Biblical logic can be seen in an even more striking case in v. 10, "Therefore, brethren, be the more zealous to confirm your call and election." Now every well-instructed Christian knows that the rock on which his assurance is built is his call and election. That is the unshakable rock. Peter is very certain of this truth, as he shows at the beginning of his first letter, where he talks of the Christians as being chosen, and destined by God, for obedience. How strange now, that in v. 10 Peter should say something that we do not often say: "Make every effort"—for that is what the phrase "more zealous" means; it is exactly the same phrase, virtually; it is the verb instead of the noun—"make every effort to confirm your election".

Let me put this as startlingly as it is in the original: "to make secure your security." Now in a sense that is nonsense! If God has made my security sure in His election in Christ, and on the basis of the cross of Christ, how can I make that more sure? Well, yes, I can make it more sure by the life that I live. I must secure my security. I am not to sit back and say, "I am elected through the sovereign grace of God, through the grace of Christ, through the Holy Spirit." No, I am to say, "I must live this life out. I must confirm my call. I must secure my security." As Paul would put it, I am to "work out my salvation with fear and trembling".

Yes, the emphasis is on me; but of course—as you know—"it is God

48

who worketh in us both to will and to do of His good pleasure." God has to work to will as well as to do. And yet I must work. That is Bible logic. The Bible puts these two extremes: and much harm has come by Christians teaching one extreme, without the other—without the paradox, without the balance. They are both needed in a full Christian representation of New Testament truth; and I think that this passage is particularly helpful because it shows us that in holiness there is needed first faith in the power of God that is ours, and then effort to translate that power into a holy character.

Now then, back to v. 5. What is demanded of us? We are to exert ourselves to be holy, to richly supply, with our faith and through our faith, all these things. Now I prefer to take this—not as a ladder, although it is a lovely ladder, with rungs from faith to love. Notice where Christian life starts, with faith; and where it finishes and is completed, with love (at the end of v. 7). But I prefer to take this, as I believe it is meant to be taken, as seven couplets.

Now let me, if I may, give you these seven couplets. It will not be possible to look at every one in detail, but I think you will agree with me that it gives a wonderful portrait of a balanced Christian character and life. And that these couplets are not just put higgledy-piggledy: he is not just putting them in a pot, and taking out one that he thinks will fit. He has very carefully balanced one against another: you will see this as we go on.

"To your faith add—generously—virtue." Now this is the first balance of the Bible; it is the balance of Paul's letters—first doctrine, then duty; first belief, then behaviour. Turn your Christian faith into Christian goodness. Incidentally, that word was used in Peter's day by the heathen of a *good*, upright life. And Peter is not ashamed to say that if I am a man of faith, I should show to the heathen a life that they see and recognise to be good. So that is the first and basic balance: to my faith I must add virtue. It takes quite a long time to learn it, all the same. It is grand to rejoice in faith, but not if there is not a life of virtue to back it up!

To virtue I must generously add knowledge. Why does he say that? Well, because mere goodness without an understanding of why we live like this, and what this means in the world today, is not enough. I want to stress that. Knowledge is a keynote in this letter. The false teachers won their way so quickly and easily because people did not have any knowledge to put over against them. People were naive: the Christians knew so little. And every new wind of doctrine that came along swayed them, and knocked them off their balance: so like so many young Christians today, and sometimes older Christians!

To our virtue, there must be knowledge. We must know why we stand where we stand; why we think what we think; why we do what we do. We must be able to give a reason not only for the faith, but for the life that we live. We must grow in grace *and* knowledge.

To knowledge must be added self-control. Now this is a lesson that every growing Christian finds. He begins to be expert in Bible study; he begins to talk to the Youth Fellowship; he is asked by the pastor to "give a word"; he begins to be a person who knows his Bible—the young people in the church are sure he is, or the assembly begin to come to him over knotty problems. And a strange thing then begins to happen. We say, "Well, I know it, you know. I know the truth. I know the Christian doctrine." And we begin to be careless in our own Christian lives. Don't ask me to explain

49

that: it is just a fact. The strange thing is that the Christian who has become knowledgeable often becomes careless about the practical details of a consistent Christian life.

This was true of the false prophets, who were notorious for their lack of self-control. They indulged the flesh (2:10); they felt that they could "get away with it". Now, is not that a temptation as we grow in knowledge? We know the way back to God; we know that the blood of Christ cleanses us; we feel, "I do not have to be so careful as I was when I was a young Christian. I know how to deal with these problems. I could have given that talk that the speaker gave this morning at Keswick." Ah, there is great danger when we get to that stage, isn't there?

And so, to your knowledge, he says, add self-control. If you aspire to be a teacher of the Word of God—and I hope many of you young men and women do aspire to be teachers of the Word of God: not only in this country, but to the far corners of the earth—aspire also to have, through the grace of God, an iron self-control. I *must* be a master of myself. It is one of the first lessons a teacher has *got* to learn. Of course, only the Holy Spirit can give that fruit. But I have got to make every effort to see that that fruit becomes mine.

Now look at the next balance. Self-control and steadfastness. You see, I may learn to control myself, but I cannot control my circumstances. They often get out of control; and so I have to have patience with circumstances that don't fit—that call to another church that did not come; that change in my direction that I wanted. I have got to learn patience. God is sometimes not in the hurry that we are.

"To steadfastness, godliness." When the false teachers lost this steadfastness, and gave up hoping that God would intervene, they became godless. And when we learn patience, we also learn godliness. Godliness is always the fruit of patience. It is patience that really makes a godly man. And that, in a sentence, is why I don't believe holiness can ever come suddenly, because it is only through patience that I can ever be made godly.

The next balance, godliness with brotherly affection—something that Peter loves very much. You will find a reference to brotherly affection in every chapter of 1 Peter—though the time does not permit us to look at it. Peter valued affection among the brethren; that warmth in the church circle which is so attractive.

To love God, I must love my brother also. And if I do love my brother, then God must so invade my heart that I love the whole world. And there is something within us, when the Holy Spirit fills us, that wants to embrace the whole world; that wants to love the whole world, and to bring that love into a very cold world, and begin to melt down all that frigid opposition to the truth and grace of God.

What kind of Christian are you? (vv. 8–9). Now Peter very skilfully pictures two kinds of Christian. First, those who are *increasing and growing* (v. 8); and then those who are *static*, and do not grow (v. 9). This is a natural thing for a teacher to do: having said what it means to grow, he pictures the man who does grow, and the man who does not.

The man who does grow: "If these things are yours and abound . . . " if you possess them as your own possession, and they increase, ". . . they keep you from being ineffective . . ." that is, literally, idle, or unproductive. Two different things: first, God will put you to work if you grow; but if you don't grow, He won't. You will be idle—no work to do. And if you did do any work, you would be unproductive and unfruitful. But "if these things are yours, and abound", then if you do work, you will be fruitful. So if I am an idle Christian because I am not growing, I shall be unfruitful. But if I am a working Christian, whom God has put into His vineyard, I shall be effective and fruitful. That is the picture.

So if these things are yours, and abound and multiply, they will keep you from being an idle and unproductive Christian; they will make you an effective and fruitful one. Incidentally, I would ask you to see what are the real qualities and essentials that are needed for a fruitful Christian life. This is a life of progress in holiness and Christian character; in wholesome integrity. "Oh, God, use me, use me!" prays the young Christian. I used to pray that so much. And after some years I began to realise why God gave me blessing in such small dollops—that if He gave me blessing in any larger dollops I got conceited and swollen-headed, and lost my Christian character. The trouble is that God cannot use us very much when we are young Christians, for that very reason. We became arrogant, difficult, divisive, unwilling to learn. I know that is in my own heart, and I guess it is in your heart too.

And so this has *got* to happen (vv. 5–6) before God can make me effective and fruitful. He cannot trust me with fruitfulness, He cannot trust me with effectiveness, unless those couplets have become true in my life, at least in a measure.

Now what about the man who lacks these things? Well, there is a pitiful portrait of him here, in three little words. In the present he is *blind*: he simply doesn't see what is going on. Here is the Christian who has remained static. He goes to a church where there is no real ministry of the Word, and he has just fallen asleep in a sense. His eyes are shut. You want to say to him, "Look around you! Look at your own life! Can't you *see* the way in which you have fallen back?" But he doesn't see. We don't see when we have fallen back: we are the last people to see it. Sin blinds.

In the present he is blind; with regard to the future, he is *short-sighted*. You know what Peter means by that. A man who is short-sighted does not see the horizon, the Coming of Christ, and what this means. He does not see where world history is going; he doesn't see the whole picture; he is locked down in the present day with no picture of the whole will and purpose of God. You've got to have that picture before you; you've got to lift up your head. But he is short-sighted. He does not see that Christ is coming, that the wrath of God is coming, on that great day . . . He does not see these things. He is short-sighted: all he can see is the problems around him, the duties of just one day.

Then what about the past? "He has *forgotten* that he was cleansed from his old sins." He has forgotten his conversion; he has forgotten his first love; he has forgotten that house-party at Keswick when they did not want to go to sleep, so filled were they with the things of God, so thrilled were they with the experience that they knew. But all that has been long forgotten: the promises that he made, the Bible that he was given, the plans that he had, the friends, the fellowship. All that is forgotten. He has forgotten that he was cleansed. It is all in the past.

What a tragic picture! Blind, short-sighted, and having forgotten the past.

51

That is an exact picture, isn't it, of the backslidden Christian. It is an exact picture of the Christian who has not grown.

The climax (vv. 10–11): "Therefore . . . " yes, even Peter can write "therefore," like Paul. How Paul loves to build up his argument, and then finish with "therefore" and leave you with an irresistible conclusion. Peter does the same. "Therefore, brethren . . ." Now, are you ready for the conclusion with me? We have seen the facts. Now let us look at the conclusion.

"Therefore, brethren, be the more zealous," make more effort still, to secure your security, for if you do this by living a godly life, by growing in grace and knowledge, by a fruitful and productive life: if you do this, two marvellous blessings will be yours, blessings I covet for myself and I covet for you, and all whom you influence. First, here and now, *freedom from falling*. "If you do this you will never fall," Very simple, isn't it? And this in a sense is one of the underlying themes of this letter, because Peter had been such an unstable disciple. He always stumbled and tripped up all along the way. He had not understood the truth. He had put Christ right about His doctrine. He denied Him. He was always stumbling and falling, wasn't he? "When you turn again, Peter, strengthen your brethren!" And all through his apostolic ministry I believe that the one thing that Peter loved to do was to strengthen and stablish and settle—to use his own words—Christians. He wanted their feet to be on the rock. He wanted them to be immovable. He wanted them not to be at the mercy of every wind of doctrine, and every problem of worldliness. He wanted them to be those people, as in Psalm 15, who should never be moved. That is the godly man, the man who shall never be moved.

If you live in a developing, increasing, multiplying Christian life, that has these qualities, you will never fall. Do not fear backsliding. Some Christians fear it. "Oh, dear," they say, "can I keep this up?" While, of course, it is God who keeps *us* up. But our part is to make every effort to confirm our call and election. Then we *shall* never be moved; we shall have stability. We shall not stumble and fall.

That is in the here and now. What about the hereafter? Well, there will be *a glorious entrance into the eternal kingdom of our Lord and Saviour, Jesus Christ*. What a contrast with some of the other ends of Christian lives given in the Bible! 1 Corinthians 3:15, the man who is saved, but as by fire. Everything burnt up in his life: just a saved soul, and nothing more. But this is a very different picture. Here is a saved soul who has with him a Christian character, a fruitful life; and God steps down to welcome him. "Well done, good and faithful servant!" richly providing for him "an entrance into His eternal kingdom". Of course, the end of life is not marked "Exit" for a Christian: it is marked "Entrance"—entrance into the eternal kingdom of God; a rich entrance.

And, one last thought: there is a purposeful allusion between the beginning of v. 5, and v. 11. I am *richly* to supplement my faith with virtue, and then He will *richly* provide for me a glorious entrance on that day.

And so this chapter leaves us—as all Biblical chapters do—looking to the past, and looking to the future. Looking to the day when Christ called me, and empowered me, and equipped me, and sent me on my way—I've got to look back to that day, and recognise what Christ did for me, frequently. But also, with my eye on the future, to the day when Christ will welcome me as a growing, fruitful, stable Christian. And with eyes on both those pivotal points—and eyes, of course, particularly on Christ—I shall be an effective and fruitful Christian today.

The Tragedy of Permissiveness

By the Rev. Alan Redpath, D.D.

The Lord has led me, I believe, to speak to you on the tragedy of permissiveness. For a basic text, I ask you to turn to Ecclesiastes 2:10, "Whatever my eyes coveted, I refused them nothing nor did I deny myself any pleasure. Yes indeed, I got pleasure from all my labour, and for all my labour this was my reward. Then I turned and reviewed all my handiwork, all my labour and toil, and I saw that everything was emptiness and chasing the wind, of no profit under the sun" (*NEB*).

We are going to think for a few moments of one of the wisest and yet one of the most wanton men in history; a man who made shipwreck of everything. The very gifts and blessings of God became to him the source of temptation, and contributed to his downfall. I am so glad that the Bible never hides the defects of its heroes; it never smoothes out the wrinkles; it always paints a true picture. If I may say so, I would consider that the pitilessness of the truthfulness of the Word of God is one major argument for its inspiration. Nobody else, no other recorder, dare tell the truth as the Word of God does, in order that it may reveal the matchless power of the grace of God in the recovery of all of us who are prepared to meet God on His own terms.

Solomon's collapse is told with the same candour as are his wealth and fame. For the important thing is not Solomon so much as God dealing with him when his heart was turned away. Alexander Whyte, that great Scottish preacher, in his character study on Solomon says, "If ever a blazing lighthouse was set up on the way of life to warn every man, it is Solomon."

Let me ask you to think with me for a moment about—

I. THE PROMISE THAT HE SHOWED. If ever a young man proved the truth of our Lord's words in Matthew 6:33, it was Solomon: "Seek ye first the kingdom of God and His righteousness; and all these things shall be added

53

unto you." Solomon became king at about twenty years of age, and almost the first thing we read of him is, "Solomon loved the Lord, walking in the statutes of David his father . . . and the king went to Gibeon to sacrifice there: for that was the great high place" (1 Kings 3:3). Solomon used to offer a thousand burnt offerings upon that altar.

Yes, Solomon loved the Lord. And God met him in a dream, and gave him a blank cheque on the treasury of heaven. In v. 5 we read, "Ask what I shall give thee." In response, Solomon acknowledged his inadequacy. "I am but a little child: I know not how to go out or to come in." He was never quite as great again as when he admitted his littleness. God always reduces a man to a minimum in order that He might do through him His maximum. And here is a man conscious of his inadequacy, his bankruptcy, his unfitness for the responsibilities which had come to him. So he asked for an understanding heart, that he might discern between good and bad; and we are told in v. 10 that it "pleased the Lord that Solomon had asked this thing". And God granted his request—and added a bonus, simply because he asked something, not for himself, but for the good of other people. "I give you also what you have not asked, both riches and honour: so that no other king shall compare with you, all your days" (v. 13).

Solomon's response was to abound with thanksgiving; and he proved the genuineness of his thanks by building a house for the Lord (5:5). It took him seven years to build it; and in the course of the project he was encouraged by having the Lord's approval. We read in 6:11, "Now the word of the Lord came to Solomon, Concerning this house which you are building, if you will walk in my statutes and obey my ordinances and keep all my commandments and walk in them, then I will establish my word with you, which I spoke to David your father."

When the task was done, Solomon's prayer at the dedication of the temple is, I think, unequalled anywhere in Scripture for its discernment and understanding. Just glance at it with me for a moment. In 8:23 he recognises God's sovereignty: "O Lord, God of Israel, there is no God like Thee, in heaven above or on earth beneath, keeping covenant and showing love to Thy servants who walk before Thee with all their heart; who hast kept with Thy servant David my father what Thou didst declare to him; yea, Thou didst speak with Thy mouth, and with Thy hand hast fulfilled it this day."

He realised human sin: v. 33, "When Thy people Israel are defeated before the enemy because they have sinned against Thee, if they turn again to Thee, and acknowledge Thy name and pray and make supplication to Thee in this house; then hear Thou in heaven and forgive the sin of Thy people Israel." He rejoiced in God's mercy: v. 35, "When heaven is shut up and there is no rain because they have sinned against Thee, if they pray toward this place, and acknowledge Thy Name, and turn from their sin, when Thou dost afflict them, then hear Thou in heaven, and forgive the sin of Thy servants. Thy people Israel . . . and grant rain upon Thy land."

Further, he remembered the constant need of repentance. In v. 46, "If they sin against Thee . . . and thou art angry with them . . . so that they are carried away captive . . . yet if they lay it to heart in the land to which they have been carried captive, and repent, and make supplication to Thee in the land of their captors, saying, We have sinned, and have acted perversely and wickedly; if they repent with all their mind and with all their heart . . . and pray to

54

Thee toward their land . . . and the house which I have built for Thy Name; then hear Thou in heaven . . . and maintain their cause and forgive Thy people."

Oh, what promise Solomon showed. The language of Hebrews 6:4–5 describes him to a T. He was "enlightened", he had "tasted the heavenly gift", had "become partaker of the Holy Spirit", had "tasted the goodness of the Word of God and the power of the age to come". Surely that, all that, could not end in shipwreck. But God had warned him: He saw the dangers ahead; He knew Solomon far better than he knew himself. And He sought to come to terms with him in the language of 9:2, "The Lord appeared to Solomon a second time . . . And as for you, if you will walk before me, as David your father walked, with integrity of heart and uprightness, doing according to all that I have commanded you, and keeping my statutes and my ordinances, then I will establish your royal throne over Israel for ever. . . But if you turn aside from following me, you or your children, and do not keep my commandments and . . . go and serve other gods and worship them, then I will cut off Israel from the land which I have given them; and the house which I have consecrated for my name I will cast out of my sight; and Israel will become a proverb and a byword among all peoples."

In other words, "Solomon, you live faithfully under my orders, and if you do that my blessing will be upon your life. Or else, go your own way, wreck your own life and bring your country to ruin."

God's terms are just the same today. Like all His threatenings, they were issued to Solomon in order that they might *never* be carried out; and they came to him at a critical time in his life. He was about forty years of age. Goals had been accomplished; success had been achieved; he had reached the peak. And it all fell on deaf ears. And as far as I can see from my study of his life, God's warning was received in sullen silence.

Let me pause a moment. Can you reflect the freshness of early days? I can. How sweet their memory is! When Jesus was so real and so near. Can you recall the moment of your conversion? Perhaps you can't—it doesn't really much matter, as long as you know you are converted now. I can, because I was there when it happened! And I remember the day, I remember the place. I do not know that I have ever had such a spiritual moment since then. When I came to Jesus "and He made me glad", there were no reservations in my heart. All the barriers were down. I did not come to Him with qualifications: I came to Him with an empty heart, with a desperate need for victory in my life, for power. I was sick of myself, absolutely disgusted with myself. And I came to Him "weary, and worn, and sad".

How well I remember, two days after I was saved, going back home, confronting my parents, who did not understand; getting my new Bible out— and on a Saturday afternoon, of all things, when my father expected me on the golf course; and when my football club were waiting for me in the evening for practice training. I remember going to a field—it was a lovely, sunny day in August—I went past a little wooden gate and sat in the grass down by a stone wall, and bowed my head; and I read through the Epistle to the Romans, and it *lived*. The Word of God was alive. I'd never known that experience before. I found myself able to understand things which had been double dutch to me two days before. But within my heart was the One who could lead me into all truth.

55

What peaceful hours I once enjoyed;
How sweet their memory still:
But they have left an aching void
The world can never fill.

Is that your language this morning? It has been mine. And oh, to talk to Him in prayer; to find the Bible come alive!

But *now*, that is what matters. You talk about the temptations of youth: do you know anything about the temptations of middle age?—when the early glow has gone, when youthful vigour has left you; when you are not so strong as you used to be; and when you do not go up two steps at a time, running!

Do you know anything about the temptations of middle life? God has granted you success; goals have been accomplished; converts have come; you have made a name in the ministry; you are known for what you are as a man of God, in public—as an evangelist, as a preacher, as a teacher, as a minister, as a Christian leader, as a Crusader leader: you are known for this. Goals have been accomplished; success has been achieved in business life, in Christian life. And God has sought to come to terms with you over and over again, and reminded you that what matters most is that you put Jesus first, and that you keep Him first in every moment of your life. And he tells you—and He has told you over and over again in your quiet times, as He has told me—"You submit to me, and all will be well. You go your own way, and all will be ruined."

I met a business man in Chicago who came to me with tears in his eyes. It was after a morning service, and he said, "All that you said this morning was real in my life twenty years ago, but not now. It brought back to me a memory, an echo, of days when Jesus was wonderfully real to me. But, you see, I have a big business: three hundred men are under me now. Every day I leave my house at 6 a.m. I'm never back till ten at night. My family have grown up without ever knowing to have a father. It's been a huge success: seven days a week I have been working at it. I'm a millionaire ten times over." But I shall never forget that he broke down when he finished this statement, and said, "But my God, what a price I've paid."

That man was a successful failure, shipwrecked! Paul said, "I know how to be abased, and I know how to abound." And I'll tell you which is harder: learning how to abound. Yes, the promise he showed.

But how did it happen? Will you notice with me—

THE PASSION HE INDULGED. There seems to have been right from early days a fatal chink in Solomon's armour, and revealed early in his life. In 1 Kings 3, "Solomon made a marriage alliance with Pharaoh, King of Egypt; he took Pharaoh's daughter, and brought her into the city." That was the first step to disaster. It must have raised many an eyebrow in traditional circles; but it was allowed to develop until in chapter 11:1 I read, "Now King Solomon loved many foreign women: the daughter of Pharaoh, and Moabite, Ammonite, Edomite, Sidonian, and Hittite women, from the nations concerning which the Lord had said to the people of Israel, You shall not enter into marriage with them, neither shall they with you, for surely they will turn away your heart after their gods. Solomon clung to these in love."

56

This was deliberate disobedience. He was wise enough to know better, but he was not humble enough to obey. And once we allow Satan to get through one weak spot, he quickly fans out into every area of life. Look with me how Solomon revealed this *in his sexual life* (11:4). We read—and oh, how sad—"when Solomon was old his wives turned away his heart after other gods; and his heart was not wholly true to the Lord his God." Solomon's unbridled polygamy: he had seven hundred wives and three hundred concubines. It sapped his moral standards, blinded his eyes, darkened his spirit, turned all the promise of youth into an old age which had no dignity, no reverence, no authority. A wicked old man! His wisdom was not worth a thing, when he could not keep himself under control, or attain mastery over his passions.

An aeroplane is never in greater danger of being wrecked than when its captain and crew are threatened by hijackers. And a Christian is never in greater peril than when Satan has taken over in one area of his life: his sex life.

And his *spiritual life*. Perhaps you may disagree with me; perhaps you can put me right. But I cannot bring myself to believe that Solomon was ever *totally* committed to God. For although he offered a thousand burnt offerings in his youth, yet he burnt incense in high places: and on the other hand, I do not believe he ever abandoned altogether the worship of God. For 11:4–6 tell us that "his wives turned away his heart after other gods; and his heart was not wholly true to the Lord his God". So Solomon did that which was evil in the sight of the Lord his God, and he did not *wholly* follow the Lord.

And his *self-life*? Though he built a house for the Lord, yet he built one twice as large for himself, and it took him twice as long. I cannot escape the thrust and the pointedness between the conclusion of chapter 6 and the beginning of chapter 7—"In the eleventh year . . . the house was finished in all its parts, and according to all its specifications. He was seven years in building it . . . Solomon was building his own house thirteen years, and he finished his entire house." God's gift of riches had spelt this man's doom. How base can we be? But aren't we all like that? How we dissipate God's blessings and use them for our own ends.

One word sums up Solomon's life: *permissiveness*. This is not something new to this age and generation. But permissiveness cannot win. With Solomon nothing was black or white: it was all drift. And more people are lost by indecision than by decision. I pray God that heaven may take an X-ray of our hearts this morning. Maybe God has brought some of us to Keswick to say, "It's time to call a halt!" Examine your life: the door that was left open to Satan, with disastrous results. Review the areas in which he has fanned out, and seek the cleansing and restoration of the Lord Jesus.

I visited a city in Britain about six months ago, and oh, my heart was broken. I knew a young couple twenty years ago. I saw them get married; I saw their zeal for the Lord, their desire to win others for Him, their concern to put Jesus first. They began taking a leading place in Christian activities in this particular city. It was a lovely home to visit. When they had their little children it was lovely. I often met with them in family prayers, and it was such a refreshing to me. But in later years the teen-age boy became a rebel, and the parents were desperately concerned, and allowed permissiveness to come into their home. They started drinking with him, smoking with him, going to shows with him; because they felt, "Somehow we've got to keep hold of that boy. We've got to win him back." And they went along with him.

It has not worked. When I was at that home a few months ago, there was no family prayer: the family altar had gone. No testimony for Jesus. They are attending a church now which is absolutely dead, and where they hear absolutely nothing of the Gospel. My heart was sad.

The greatest temptations that face a Christian, especially in full time—so-called full-time service, are sex and money. And the Lord, while not expecting us to be paragons of virtue, does expect us to be consistent, *and blameless*, by His grace. The passion that Solomon indulged. And—

THE PRICE SOLOMON PAID. The slope became too steep. The brakes would not hold. He was on a collision course with God, and disaster struck. All that Moses, and Aaron, and Joshua, and David had won for their children at great price, was held for nothing. It resulted in suffering, defeat, and ultimate captivity. You know, every generation has to experience its trials and tests; and there is not any shipwreck of faith and holiness in all the world that is written more for us today than that of Solomon. He had wealth, he had wisdom, he had warmth of heart, he had women, he had false gods, until one day God's judgment struck.

A people that were ground down by forced labour to maintain the luxury of a court containing that disgusting crowd of women, was ripe for revolt. And when the power in Israel fell into the hands of a headstrong fool, discontent soon became rebellion, and rebellion triumphed. And it all flowed as naturally as possible from the same fountain as his idolatry, of which it was the punishment. The so-called natural consequences of our sin, even here and now, should alert us to the judgment of God in history, and in our lives.

Don't you see that in our beloved country today? We are eating the fruit, whatever we may say, of the injustices and the hardships imposed by class distinction in this nation, and injustice suffered by the workmen. And we are reaping it all now: families are reaping it; you and I are reaping it.

And the judgment of God is upon Britain today because of permissiveness. And where, in heaven's name, is there a voice in authority raised against it? Would to God that someone in authority would call this nation to halt! But what I am concerned is that God should call you to a halt, and call me to a halt, right now, before it is too late. Disaster struck in Solomon's life—and just imagine, oh, just imagine the words of 11:9, "And the Lord was angry with Solomon, because his heart had turned away from the Lord . . . who had appeared to him twice . . . Therefore the Lord said to Solomon, Since this has been your mind and you have not kept my covenant and my statutes which I have commanded you, I will surely tear the kingdom from you and will give it to your servant."

It is almost unbelievable that a man who walked with God had come to the point where God had to speak to him like that. His life of fellowship with God was in ruins. It did not exist any more. Spiritual horizons had disappeared. Solomon had ascended up the ladder of success before men, and he had gone down the ladder of humiliation before God. And God's anger is never inactive. You notice in 11:14, "The Lord raised up an adversary against Solomon." V. 23, "God also raised up as an adversary to him, Rezon the son of Eliada." V. 25, "He was an adversary of Israel all the days of Solomon." God was against him: an Adversary now.

One day his life was cut short. He had been promised wisdom unconditionally, and that promise was fulfilled. But he was also promised long life if—"If you will walk in my ways, keeping my statutes and my commandments, as your father David walked, *then* I will lengthen your days" (3:14). If . . . And God dropped the curtain when the man was only about sixty-two. Finished. What a terrific warning! That until the very end of life a fall is possible. The ship went down when the voyage was nearly over, when it was in sight of port. It touched bottom, and struck the rock. And that was not for want of warning lights, but through deliberately ignoring them.

What a pathetic warning in 11:4, "When Solomon was old his wives turned away his heart after other gods." My brothers and sisters, if Solomon can fall, which one of us is safe? Didn't John Bunyan say that he saw a door opening into hell, hard by the gates of the celestial city? I'm not saying anything about Solomon's final state in eternity. I'm not discounting what I believe, and what you believe, about the eternal security of a believer. But as we heard so trenchantly this morning, "Make your security secure." Solomon stands as a grave warning to watch it, that that permissive age does not erase the promise of an early faith, or make me cynically ashamed of the devotion of early years.

My friend to whom I referred a moment ago, said, "We don't believe as you do any more in our family." And there is no sadder sight, believe me— I've seen many—than that of an old man whose youthful enthusiasm for the Lord has withered, who has left his first love, and has become hard and cold and cynical. Better the early days when Solomon loved the Lord, and knew his desperate need of Him, than the latter days when success spoiled him.

Wasn't it this that Paul was afraid of when he wrote to the church in Corinth, in the language of *Living Letters*, "I am no shadow boxer. I do not beat the air. I buffet my body. I deal it blow after blow, lest, having proclaimed the rules to other people, I should be cast aside."

My dear friend who led me to Christ, six years after I was converted, found me wandering in a spiritual wilderness—a chartered accountant, going up the tree with ICI in London. And he just said this to me: "Don't forget it is possible to have a saved soul and a wasted life." Let that ring out as it rang in my heart that day. You can have a saved soul and a wasted life.

But I must add this: need it happen? Of course not. Then why did it happen? I have read through this story many times within recent weeks, and I find there is one thing lacking in Solomon's life: that is *repentance*. He believed in it—for everybody else. His prayer revealed that. But he never captured it himself: he was never a broken man, never a man with whom God came to terms, never a man who came back to the cross, broken. There was no thirty-second psalm in Solomon's life.

Listen to it: "When I kept silence, my bones waxed old through my roaring all the day long. For night and day Thy hand was heavy upon me: my moisture is turned into the drought of summer. I acknowledged my sin unto Thee, and mine iniquity have I not hid. I said, I will confess my transgressions unto the Lord: and Thou forgavest . . . my sin." That never happened to Solomon. Listen to Psalm 51, after the Bathsheba tragedy in David's life:

59

"Have mercy upon me, O God, according to Thy lovingkindness: according unto the multitude of Thy tender mercies blot out my transgressions. Wash me thoroughly from mine iniquity, and cleanse me from my sin. For I acknowledge my transgressions: and my sin is ever before me." I don't find that language in Solomon's life. No sin-offering, no blood of atonement.

Mind you, there was plenty of remorse, plenty of disgust with himself. Just listen to him: Ecclesiastes 2:1–17, "I said to myself, Come now, I will make a test of pleasure; enjoy yourself. But behold, this also was vanity... So I hated life, because what is done under the sun was grievous to me; for all is vanity and a striving after the wind." 5:10, "He who loves money will not be satisfied with money; nor he who loves wealth, with gain: this also is vanity." 7:26, "I found more bitter than death the woman whose heart is snares and nets, and whose hands are fetters; he who please God escapes her, but the sinner is taken by her." Masses of wordy grief! Masses of remorse! But no genuine repentance. He had gone too far. He could not be stopped, even though God's Word came to him that he was ruining his life and his kingdom.

How strange, beloved, how strange! But you know your heart and I know mine, that I put out my hands to grasp my sins, even though I have to stretch them across the very smoke of the pit to reach them; even though I have to go across the entrance to hell to get at them. Such is the sinfulness of my heart. I go after them.

Need it happen? No. For these words are still true: "If my people, which are called by my name, shall humble themselves, and pray, and seek my face, and turn from their wicked ways, then will I hear from heaven, and will forgive their sin, and heal their land." I'm sure of that, because of Calvary.

> *Plenteous grace with Thee is found;*
> *Grace to cover all my sin;*
> *Let the healing streams abound,*
> *Make and keep me pure within.*

I'm sure of that. The only question is, Is my repentance superficial, or is it solid right-away-through? Do I say, "I will arise and go to my Father, and say to Him, I've sinned! I'm no longer worthy to be called Thy son. Make me. . . ."?

Drs. Alan Redpath and William Culbertson

Righteous Lot

By the Rev. Dr. William Culbertson

I should like to talk to you about one of the lesser characters of the Bible—Lot, Abraham's nephew; and let us give him all the credit we can to begin with. 2 Peter 2:7–8 says, "God delivered righteous Lot, sore distressed by the lascivious life of the wicked; for that righteous man dwelling among them, in seeing and hearing, vexed his righteous soul from day to day with their lawless deeds." I am reading from the American Standard Version, and you noticed the repetition of the word "righteous". That is a correct translation of the original, and I like that threefold emphasis.

It is an important word, for as you read the story of Lot in the book of Genesis, it is a sad story. So it is a joy to read this New Testament evaluation of him, for without it we might have been more severe in our conclusions concerning him.

You are familiar with his story: briefly it is this. He left Ur of the Chaldees with his grandfather Terah, and his uncle Abram. Though there was nothing of the originality and the initiative of Abram in him, he did believe in Abram's God, and therefore accompanied Abram in his journey. Once in Canaan he was quite willing to leave Abram, choosing for his residence the fertile valley of the Jordan. Next we find him in Sodom, and from that wicked city he was delivered. In the concluding scene he is living in the rocky recesses of the mountains near Zoar; and that last recorded story of his life, the awful story of incest, and the birth of Moab and Ben-ammi, presents a dark picture indeed. And it seems from the Old Testament representation of the scene that his life was a wholly useless life.

But I remind you that Peter, by the Spirit of God, calls him "righteous Lot". So I take it he was saved; I take it that he knew the Lord, at least after a fashion. But there was much to be desired. Yet three times over in 2 Peter 2:7–8 the word "righteous" is used concerning him. So I take it that some of the lessons that we can learn from his life are the lessons which righteous people need to learn.

Frankly, I am persuaded that many Christians with far more light than Lot ever had, are living the same useless life which characterised him. I wonder how much that was wrong in his life, we shall find wrong in our lives today?

You read of him in Genesis 11:31, "And Terah took Abram his son, and Lot the son of Haran his son's son, and Sarai his daughter-in-law, his son Abram's wife; and they went forth with them from Ur of the Chaldees, to go into the land of Canaan." Now they did not know they were going into the land of Canaan, because Hebrews 11 tells us that Abram "went out not knowing whither he went". But God knew where He wanted him. So off they started: they made the journey from Ur of the Chaldees, and they got as far as a place called Haran, and there they stayed.

I think there was some importance to the way in which our fathers translated that first verse of Genesis 12, "The Lord *had* said unto Abram . . ." Not that at that particular moment He was saying it for the first time: He had already said this. Because, you see, Abram had not gotten to Canaan yet. "The Lord had said . . . Get thee out of thy country, and from thy kindred . . ." And I read in vv. 4–5, "Abram departed, as the Lord had spoken unto him; and Lot went with him: and Abram was seventy and five years old when he departed out of Haran. And Abram took Sarai his wife, and Lot his brother's son, and all their substance that they had gathered, and the souls that they had gotten in Haran; and they went forth to go into the land of Canaan." So Lot is before us, the nephew of Abram, and in the company of Abram.

Now what about it? Let me suggest four things. First, Lot was a *thoughtless* individual. Lot was indifferent to spiritual considerations; he did not value spiritual gifts and associations. He knew the Lord, or to use New Testament terms, he was saved. But he did not want to be a narrow believer; he was broad-minded, he had broad associations. This was Lot.

First, may I observe that this lack of understanding of the value of spiritual and eternal things, was shown in his willingness to separate himself from Abram. He ought never to have allowed separation from Abram. You see, he needed a friend like Abram. You know the story, in Genesis 13: "And Abram went up out of Egypt, he and his wife, and all that he had, and Lot with him, into the Negeb." And when they were there, you remember, there was a strife (v. 7) "between the herdsmen of Abram's cattle and the herdmen of Lot's cattle: and the Canaanite and the Perizzite dwelled then in the land. And Abram said unto Lot, Let there be no strife, I pray thee, between thee and me, and between my herdmen and thy herdmen; for we be brethren. Is not the whole land before thee? Separate thyself, I pray thee."

And so Lot made his choice, and he did separate himself: but as he did that, he was removing himself from the sphere of spiritual life that had nurtured and helped him up to that point. Listen to me. If God brings across your pathway some stalwart, strong, good servant of God, be very careful about letting anything come between you and that individual. For God does not bring strong people across our way just haphazardly: they can be an immeasurable comfort and strength and help to us in the hour of need.

True, Abram had his faults. Abram on occasion did what he should not have done. This is true; but on the whole Abram was God's man. And so I do not think it was wise at all for Lot to capitulate to this suggestion, even though Abram had made it. He might well have said, "Look, Abram, I need you! What there is of strength, what there is of spirituality, what there is of the evidence of God's blessing on my life, I owe in part to you! So let's settle this difference in some other way." That is the first observation that I would give to support the idea that Lot did not value spirituality.

But Genesis 14 tells us something else about this same characteristic of Lot's. He failed to learn the lesson of his captivity. He did not, when rescued by Abram from his captivity, say, "I've learned my lesson. I'm going to stick close to Abram . . ." You know the story. There were four kings in the Mesopotamian area, Amraphel, Arioch, Chedorlaomer, and Tidal; and they came against the cities of the plain, and overcame them. And for twelve long years the kings of those cities of the plain—Sodom and Gomorrah, Admah and Bela—served these foreign kings. Then they decided to rebel; and when the battle was joined, "The kings of Sodom and Gomorrah fled, and fell there; and they that remained fled to the mountain." And these kings of Mesopotamia ". . . took all the goods of Sodom and Gomorrah, and all their victuals, and went their way. And they took Lot, Abram's brother's son, who dwelt in Sodom, and his goods, and departed."

Then word came to Abram as he dwelt under the oaks of Mamre, and "When Abram heard that his brother was taken captive, he armed his trained servants, born in his own house, three hundred and eighteen, and pursued them unto Dan . . ." Think of that! To the extent of the land to the north he pursued these Mesopotamian kings. "And he divided himself against them, he and his servants, by night, and smote them, and pursued them unto Hobah, which is on the left hand of Damascus." Think of all the trouble that Abram went to; think of all that was upon his heart as he sought to rescue Lot from his predicament.

And "He brought back all the goods, and also brought back again his brother Lot, and his goods, and the women also, and the people."

Ah, wouldn't you think that Lot would have come to his senses. If he didn't know that he needed Abram before, certainly he knew it now. But, oh, no. He was so spiritually insensitive, so ungracious and so unthankful, that he didn't "make up". And his herdsmen, and the herdsmen of Abram, didn't get along any better than they did, even though Abram had rescued Lot and all that he had.

Then that memorable scene in which God dealt with Abram, and the story of Melchizedek, is told in the rest of chapter 14.

But these things are as little signs along the way, to say that though Lot was righteous, though Lot knew the Lord, he was not following hard after God. He was willing to separate himself from Abram; and even when Abram rescued him, he still chose Sodom to the presence of Abram. How about your choice? I wonder if your choices and my choices don't often tell more about us than we dream of.

A second thing I should like to observe about Lot is that he was *supremely selfish*. That comes out in Genesis 13. When Abram said to him, "Is not the whole land before thee? Separate thyself from me, I pray thee . . . if thou wilt take the left hand, then I will go to the right, or if thou depart to the right hand, then I will go to the left." Now notice: "And Lot lifted up his eyes, and beheld all the plain of Jordan, that it was well watered every where, before the Lord destroyed Sodom and Gomorrah, even as the garden of the Lord, like the land of Egypt, as thou comest unto Zoar. *So Lot chose him* all the plain of Jordan; and Lot journeyed east; and they separated themselves the one from the other."

Now, from the very standpoint of age, from the very standpoint of family relationships, I suggest to you that the right and proper thing for Lot to have done when Abram made him the offer, was to say, "Look, Uncle, you are the one to make the choice. I am here, as it were, as your guest. I am here tagging along, and reaping the benefits of God's blessing upon you. Surely it is your right to make the choice, not mine."

But that wasn't Lot! Lot could see only little Lot, and nothing else. So, supremely selfishly, he made his choice. And, you know—forgive me! I may

63

be wrong here—but I think this rankled Abram a little bit. And I must acknowledge I have enough of the old nature about me to hope it did! Look at the story. It says, "Abram dwelled in the land of Canaan, and Lot dwelled in the cities of the plain, and removed his tent as far as Sodom. But the men of Sodom were wicked and sinners before the Lord exceedingly. And the Lord said unto Abram, after that Lot was separated from him, Lift up now thine eyes . . ." Hm. "Lift up now thine eyes . . ." Would you agree with me that God would not tell him to do what he was already doing? And if he had to lift up his eyes, where were they? Oh, I can see him looking down at the earth and saying, "There, that's the kind of ingrate I have for a nephew! I give him the opportunity to choose, and he does choose; and he takes the best! And here I am . . ." and I can see Abram walking around in a circle with his head down, looking on the earth; and I think he saw a clod of earth, and I think he gave it a good kick! *There!*

God says, "Wait a minute, Abram! Lot may have made the better choice *now*; but you have made the better choice with eternity standing in view. Lift up now thine eyes, and look from the place where thou art northward, and southward, and eastward, and westward: for all the land which thou seest . . ." including where Lot was! " . . . all that land will I give to thee and to thy seed for ever."

So Lot was thoughtless, and Lot was supremely selfish. The third observation that I should like to make is this: That Lot *continually compromised*. We often ask the question, Where did Cain get his wife? Let me change it. Where did Lot get *his* wife? Well, it doesn't say in so many words in Scripture, as far as I know. But there is no mention of her until he lived in Sodom: and I wonder if there is not an inference here that that's where he got her. And if he did, I suggest to you he was marrying outside the will of God for him. At any rate, you will have to agree with this: Her heart was in Sodom, and she never got beyond it. She was turned into a pillar of salt for looking back, hankering, longing, yearning for Sodom, that wicked city. Lot compromised, probably, in connection with his marriage.

But there is an amazing story which shows his compromising spirit very graphically, in chapter 19. The beginning of the story is the time when God is about to destroy Sodom and Gomorrah and the other cities of the plains. And the Lord has dealt with this man Lot by sending two angels—these two men, as they are spoken of in different places in chapter 19. And they are vehement in their command to Lot: "Escape with thy life: look not behind thee, neither stay thou in all the plain; escape to the mountain, lest thou be consumed. And Lot said unto them, Oh, not so, my Lord!" Familiar words, aren't they? Do you remember when Peter said, "Not so, Lord!" Well, this is the attitude of Lot. "Oh, not so, my Lord. Behold, now, thy servant hath found favour in thy sight . . ." He was going to try to trade on the fact that God was merciful enough to deliver him out of the burning city. "I have found favour in thy sight, and Thou hast magnified thy mercy, which Thou hast showed unto me in saving my life; and I cannot escape to the mountains . . ." That is where he was told to go. "I cannot escape to the mountain, lest some evil should overtake me." Bless your heart, if God asks you to go to the mountain, the mountain is the safest place in all the world for you: you had better go.

But this unspiritually minded man, this worldly wise man: "That's not the place for me," he argues with God. "I cannot escape to the mountain, lest evil overtake me, and I die. Behold now, this city is near to flee unto, and it is a little one." I wish I could say it the way I think he said it! "It's a *little* one! No, it's just a little one—it's not a big one; it's only a little one! And my soul shall live!"

"And he said unto him, See, I have accepted thee concerning this thing also, that I will not overthrow this city, for the which thou hast spoken." And the city was Zoar. And you know what Zoar man means? Little. The compromising Christian: never going all the way with God. Holding back, and if need be, holding back just a little. But that is not the avenue to blessing.

I used to tell the classes at Moody Bible Institute a story about a man who came into the tabernacle of old, and the priest at the gate saw a bulge under the folds of his garment. So he said, "Nathan, what is it that you have under your garment?" "Oh, it is nothing, nothing. Just let me go in and worship!" "Oh, no! I am here as the guardian of the Lord's house, and you don't go in. What have you got there?" He said, "I have a—pig." "*A pig!*" "Yes, a pig—see, it's just a little one. It's cute, you know. It's just a little one!" And the priest drew himself up with all his power, and put his piercing eyes upon Nathan, and said, "But that little pig will become a big pig sooner of later." Oh, are you trying to bargain with God? Don't be a compromiser. That's one of Lot's difficulties. He continually compromises.

The last thing I want to say about Lot is that he was *worldly*: and that is always the result of compromise. You always go deeper and deeper. It has been called to your attention, I know, many times; but let me do it again, that the Spirit of God may emphasise His Word and bless it to our hearts. When Lot removed himself from Abram, Genesis 13:12 says, "he moved his tent as far as Sodom", or "he pitched his tent *toward* Sodom", as the King James Version suggests. Genesis 14:12, "They took Lot, Abram's brother's son, who dwelt *in* Sodom . . ." You see it beginning to work, little by little, more and more. Until finally in Genesis 19:1, "Lot sat in the gate of Sodom." And if I understand the Hebraism behind that, it suggests that he was a man of importance so far as the city was concerned. He sat in the gate of Sodom.

Perhaps the most tragic of all is this, that when he was told what was going to happen to Sodom, and when the angel visitants impressed upon him the importance of his departure, "they said, Arise, take thy wife, and thy two daughters which are here; lest thou be consumed in the iniquity of the city . . ." The first three words of v. 16 are devastating: ". . . but he lingered". Oh, how desperate can a man get; how foolish can a servant of God be! Here the fire is about to fall, *and he lingers*. He does not take to heart the explicit, meaningful words of the Lord. And you know, that living that way, though "he vexed his righteous soul", I cannot say I am too much impressed by that: although I suppose I should be. You know, all Lot had to do to get out of all the vexation of his righteous soul in Sodom, was to move out of Sodom. That's all he had to do. And he wouldn't move: he stayed there.

But his testimony was not accepted. Look at this: this is tragic. "And Lot went out, and spake unto his sons-in-law, which married his daughters— or who were about to marry his daughters—and said, Up, get you out of this place; for the Lord will destroy this city . . . but he seemed unto his sons-in-law like one that mocked." He had never talked that way before. He had never been anxious about their lives before. He had never been concerned about Sodom getting destroyed before. He had marred his testimony. That is the result of worldliness.

You see, Lot knew too much about Sodom to be happy with God; and he knew too much about God to be really happy in Sodom, and so he let his life be spoilt.

Well, these are the things that are on my heart. He was thoughtless, he was supremely selfish, he constantly compromised, he lived a worldly life. I suppose the language of Paul is descriptive of Lot: "Saved so as by fire." I don't want to be saved like that. I want to be saved: I am saved, by the grace of God. And oh, to have an entrance richly supplied unto the eternal kingdom. I like that word, "an abundant entrance" into the kingdom, that heavenly kingdom.

I wonder if God is saying something to you today. Are there some decisions being made that ought to be made? Preacher, I have been careless. Preacher, I have been compromising. Preacher, I have been worldly. And I begin to see that I ought to be living for the things that are not seen.

I like the words that J. Hudson Taylor used to say: There are two expressions that exhaust the vocabulary of every child of God: today, and that day. If you will live today with that day in view, you will be saved from the uselessness that characterised Lot.

Drifting is Dangerous

By the Rev. Michael Baughen, M.A.

A few years ago, in Manchester, we built a spanking new hall alongside our church, resplendent in its new brick and furnishings, and reckoned to be something that wouldn't give us any trouble for a very long time. However, after about two years something emerged out of one of the pieces of wood over a doorpost; something that looked remarkably as if we were growing mushrooms. It was a fungus, a dry-rot fungus in a brand-new building. And all this because of a little bit of drainpipe that had been badly fitted, and which overflowed. There was nothing deliberate about this trouble. It just happened. And the dry rot spread in a small cupboard, and it went over this doorway, and under the floor, and into the wall, and into the church, and round into the organ chamber: and it did all that in just under two years. What a pernicious thing it is! Yet, you see, there was nothing deliberate about it. It simply happened through neglect.

About the same time, the skipper of a large oil tanker was bringing his vessel up into the English Channel, and decided to take a short cut near the Scilly Isles. He wasn't on the bridge; he had left this to somebody else as far as navigation was concerned. And as the ship took the short cut it hit a rock, and the *Torrey Canyon* burst open. It wasn't deliberate. The skipper didn't intend to crash his tanker on the rocks. It simply happened through neglect.

A young Christian, sound, Bible-based, brought up in a Christian fellowship, and yet within his life a rot setting in, and a drift taking place, which brings him on to the rocks of disaster, not intentionally, not because he resolved to reject Jesus Christ and the Gospel, but simply because of neglect. It is the sin of neglect that I want to talk about; and I want you to turn with me to Hebrews 2:1. How does it happen? I suggest that the first stage of neglect is—

CARELESSNESS OF HEART. Hebrews 2:1 says, "we must pay the closer attention to what we have heard, lest we drift away from it". Now this is written to Christians. It is written to people who know the salvation of God. You can see this in v. 3, where the writer speaks about the drift that takes place. Again it is a seafaring term. The current, imperceptible to the human eye, beginning to move the ship in a particular direction—and the only way by which you can recognise that you are drifting away is by sighting something on the shore: the local pier perhaps is getting smaller and smaller, and you know that though you are resting blissfully in your rowing boat in the basking sun, yet your boat is drifting out to sea. You cannot see the current, but it is happening; you are drifting because you have laid back the oars, and are going with the current.

The same sort of thing happens with buildings. In some of the major ancient buildings of our land, where there is a tendency for the pillars to shift, or for something to move, they fix a glass sheet, or something of that kind, across the possible cracks, so that if there is a shift the glass will break, and people will know that it has shifted. It is impossible to see it with the naked eye, yet the shift, the drift, is taking place.

Some years ago, when I was working for CPAS, I was dictating a letter on one occasion to my secretary, and her biro ran out, and she said, "Do you mind lending me yours?" So I got out my biro which I had had for many years, and was a treasured possession. I gave it to her, and immediately she said, "Oh, isn't it wobbly!" I felt a bit offended, because my biro was very precious to me. And only then did I look at it, and see that it *was* wobbly The bottom of the case had broken away, and the thing was wobbling all over the place. But I had had it for so many years that I hadn't noticed that gradually, bit by bit, it was falling to bits. It was imperceptible to me because I was living with it; but when she showed it to me, I went out and spent two shillings on a new one!

Now the trouble is, in the Christian life, that this sort of drift, this sort of imperceptible change from the standards that we once knew, takes place, and unless there is some clear sighting to the truth of the Gospel of Jesus Christ and to the standards of God, we do not notice. And it sometimes needs someone to take us up short and say to us, "How do you stand before Jesus Christ now?" How does your love of Jesus compare with that you had in 1934? How does it compare with your love for Jesus in 1964, or 1970?

Has there been, in these years, a progression in love for Jesus and commitment to the Gospel of Jesus Christ? Or has there been, imperceptibly to us, a drift away from the standards of love and blessedness and wonder of Jesus that once we knew?

It is possible, my brethren, to sing the sort of hymns we sing in a Convention like this, and yet, in spite of the fact that we are living members of a Christian community, to sing these hymns and not mean them. For this is the danger of a careless heart that becomes familiar with the things of God; that can go into a church worship service and be casual about it; that can come out at the end of the service not having meant the hymns, not having prayed the prayers, not having been willing to obey the word. Have you done that? I am sure you have, unless you are an exceptional person. For the danger of familiarity grows into this carelessness. We become casual about the Word of God. It ceases to have a bite and an impact upon us, as we open it morning by morning. We become cool about salvation, and cool about evangelism. When did you last thank Jesus for saving you? This morning? The danger of familiarity.

This is something which has been true of the people of God through the centuries. The people of Israel were the same. Delivered from Egypt, brought through the Red Sea, given the law, given the manna, all the things that God had done so tremendously for them. And yet, familiarity. In Numbers 11:4 they say, "O that we had meat to eat! We remember the fish we ate in Egypt for nothing; the cucumbers, the melons, the leeks, the onions, and the garlic. But now our strength is dried up, and there is nothing at all but this manna to look at." Nothing but this manna! And yet this was God's provision. Without it they would have died. They forgot the taskmasters, the making of bricks without straw; they forgot the incredible way in which God brought them out and delivered them from Egypt. All they could do was to grow familiar with what God had done, and grumble.

How many Christians become like that! We grumble about Christian fellowships, services, meetings, prayer gatherings; grow careless about these things by the sheer familiarity of them, and forget that through Jesus Christ we have been delivered from hell and judgment, from darkness and blindness, from separation and condemnation, from the kingdom of Satan. That we have been delivered to forgiveness, to peace with God, to blessings, to His faithfulness, to answered prayer, to His grace, His joy, His love, to the glorious inheritance of the people of God, and to a wonderful eternity ahead. We grow familiar with these wonderful things that Jesus Christ has done for us as the people of God.

So I ask you, firstly, Is there in you and in me a carelessness of heart over our salvation? This text says we are to pay the closer attention to what we have heard, and the force of this phrase is that we are to grasp it, and to prove it in its power, this salvation which we receive from Jesus. But if we see here a carelessness of heart as one result of neglect, we also see, as we turn on to 3:7-8, a—

HARDENING OF HEART.

Carelessness about salvation leads to hardening about God's voice to us.

Last week I had a tragic letter through the post. It was from someone who once had been a keen Christian worker, but who had imperceptibly begun to slip from God. Carelessness about Jesus Christ and salvation had crept into her life. She had slipped and had an affair with a man. He had been divorced as a result of it, and she was now married to him as a non-Christian. Married because she thought she ought to, and not because she wanted to. She wrote of her utter despair, married to a non-Christian, not allowed to go to Christian meetings, afraid even to speak of Jesus Christ. She even said, "If you reply to this letter, don't reply to this address." And all this, because she had slipped from Christ by carelessness, and slipped into a tragic mistake.

How often this story can be repeated. The hardness that comes into our heart when we hear God's voice and do not obey. Mind you, it is difficult the first time. The first time a Christian, born again of the Spirit of God, has lived in fellowship with the Lord, comes to this beginning of hardness, it is difficult to disobey; but when you have done it once, it becomes easier, and the next time you can do it, and the third time it is easier still, until in a very short space of time we have no compunction about disobeying the clear word of God. Satan bolsters up our excuses. Our conscience is deadened. We can sit through a hundred sermons and remain untouched, though we can always see how it applies to someone else.

Hebrews 4:12 describes the penetrating effect of the Word of God as something which is living, active, and sharper than any two-edged sword, piercing to the division of soul and spirit, of joints and marrow, and discerning the thoughts and intentions of the heart. That is what God's Word does to us, isn't it? We are exposed by the Word of God when we face up to it as Christians; and only a hardened, disobedient heart can be exposed to the Word of God and do nothing about it. Only someone who no longer has a fear or reverence for the living God can ignore the Word's exposure. And yet tragically it is possible to have been keen, fresh, alive, Jesus-sent and Spirit-filled, and yet to sit here tonight with a heart that is hardening to the voice of the living God.

You have fallen out with someone. You know it is wrong. You know you ought to put it right. You know the Word of God condemns it, and yet you shove it to one side, because you do not want to face the issue that God has touched in your life. You know the standards in your office, perhaps, which you fit into; and that you are not known as a Christian in that office. You know this is wrong, yet you shove it to one side and say, "No, I cannot face this."

We think of the time that we waste instead of serving Jesus Christ. Or it may be the way in which we use our money. We know that this is wrong, and we are convicted by the Word of God; and yet we say, "No, I do not want to face this issue. I'll have God's will in everything else, but not this." We know that God is wanting the dedication of our life, and we resist it, and say, "No, I am going to hold on to my life, and I am going to run it my way." We know it is wrong. We will join in the fellowship, we will sing the hymns, we will pray at the prayer meeting. But over this issue we resist the living God in His conviction in our heart and spirit. We know that there are things in our life, selfishness, self-centredness, and we refuse to allow God to deal with them. We put up a sign and say, "No admittance. God, keep out. And, God, if you convict me aboutt his from your Word, I am going to shut my ears and I am not going to listen." And God writes across the life, "hardened". This heart is hardened to the voice of the living God.

Friends who are older here, it is possible that you have grown hardened to the Word of God. I think your life will show to other people which way you are going, because it seems to me that with older people, if they are really the Lord's, they grow in sweetness, and if they are not, they grow in sourness. I think it is one or the other if you are getting on in years, and your reality of Christian commitment and love and communion with Jesus Christ shows unmistakably in your life.

If the careless heart is one of the results of neglect, the hardened heart is the second; and the third is the—

UNBELIEVING HEART. We find this in Hebrews 3:12. "Take care, brethren," says the writer, "lest there be in any of you an evil, unbelieving heart, leading you to fall away from the living God." An unbelieving heart in a Christian! Yes, an unbelieving heart in a Christian. For this was true of the people of God after their deliverance after Egypt and the Red Sea; this was true when they had the challenge of entering into God's inheritance and promise as they faced the promised land and the spies came back with the report, as you remember, and it was at this moment that the people of God failed in faith. The people who had seen so much of God's deliverance and wonderful intervention. The spies come back, and Caleb and Joshua say, "We can go up and overcome it. The Lord is with us." But the others say, "We can't." Caleb and Joshua see God, and the difficulties. The other spies see the difficulties, and God somewhere in the background; but the difficulties loom so large that they say, "We can't do it." God writes His verdict across it, the verdict of unbelief. The result was thirty-eight years' delay in the fulfilment of God's purpose for His people.

And us? Well, I am amazed sometimes that some people who are evangelical, committed to the Word of God and to the saving grace of Jesus Christ, act as if the living God doesn't exist. We are prepared, perhaps, to read books on faith, to read books about the wonderful acts of faith of people down through the years; but when it comes to something in our personal lives, or in our church or chapel situations, then we fail. There is human calculation. We say we cannot do it. We say this is impossible. We say we can see the need, but we cannot meet it.

But why not? Is God unable to work in our generation? Do we serve a dead God, or a living God? Is He the God of the impossible? Is He the God who is able to do exceeding abundantly above all that we ask or think, according to the power that works in us, or isn't He? I believe it is a terrible tragedy that very often believing Christians do not live by faith in this way, who restrict God to these human calculations, are not prepared to say to the living God, "Lord, we trust you. We believe you have led us to this thing. We believe you are in this thing. We believe you can do it, though humanly we cannot see how."

I long to see many, many more churches and Christians committed in faith to a living God. And He never fails us when we do this. The world may oppose us; unbelieving people in our church circles may oppose us. Indeed, Joshua and Caleb were stoned for it. But if we trust God with this sort of faith, we will see great things, and prove the Lord in power. But take care, brethren, lest there be in any of you an evil, unbelieving heart. Something which does not trust the living God.

Three things that spring from neglect: the careless heart, the hardened heart, the unbelieving heart. But this section of God's word speaks also of mercy. Turn lastly, if you will, to 4:15, for here we have this glorious record of a high priest, who is not like a human one. He is able to sympathise with our weaknesses, and in every respect has been tempted as we are, yet without sinning.

What a wonderful thing this is about our God! He isn't someone so detached that He does not understand. He is someone who has come and lived in our flesh, and borne the temptations and trials and pressures. He has known what it is to be inflicted with the temptation to be careless or hardened, or even unbelieving. This is the high priest to whom we can go. The high priest who is ready with mercy, if we come with repentance and seek His forgiveness and cleansing.

And so in 4:13 we are reminded that we are "open and laid bare to the eyes of him with whom we have to do". Although we may hide it from our neighbour, we may hide it even from our marriage partner, we may hide it from our church elders, we may hide it from our friends and family, we cannot hide from God. If there is in us a careless heart, or a hardened heart, or an unbelieving heart, God knows, even if no one else knows. And if you know this is true in your heart and mind tonight, then I bid you to take hold of 4:16, where it says, "Let us then with confidence draw near to the throne of grace, that we may receive mercy and find grace to help in time of need."

Thou art the Man!

By the Very Rev. James Dunlop, M.A., D.D.

God has been speaking to us in this meeting, and I believe is continuing to speak in the word that has come to me for this evening. 2 Samuel 12:7, "And Nathan said to David, Thou art the man!" The man of careless heart, the man of hardened heart, the man of unbelieving heart; and yet withal, the heart of a Christian.

Let us notice, as we come to this word of Nathan to David, first—

THE MAN WHO HAD SINNED. We know the circumstances under which Nathan spoke this word to David, and they were very serious. David was a man of God, who had proved and experienced God through many years. The man who had established the ark of God and the worship of God in Zion. The man who delighted to walk in his house before God with a perfect heart; the sweet, inspired psalmist of Israel. And yet this man David came

71

to a day, at the age of fifty or more, when he deliberately committed adultery, caused an innocent man to be murdered, practised despicable and cunning duplicity, and violated all the laws of kingliness and godliness.

The terrible blot that came on David's life is set down in detail in Scripture without extenuation or without excuse. David had come to a period in his life when he could enjoy hard-won peace and prosperity. He had been successful over his enemies. He was rightly enthroned in the affections of his people; and he was settled in Jerusalem, the city of God. But in that perilous period of ease and accomplishment there came ominous signs of his drifting spiritually from God and His standards.

For example, in direct violation of the law of Moses, which forbad the multiplication of wives on the part of the Hebrew kings, lest their hearts should turn away, we are told that when established in Jerusalem David added more and more wives and concubines to his household, sowing the seeds of heart-burning and jealousy and quarrelling and crime of which the harem must ever be the prolific source; fostering in himself the habit increasingly of sensual indulgence.

It would appear also that at this time David was coming to yield to a fit of indolence, unlike the martial spirit that had characterised him hitherto; allowing Joab and his soldiers to do what fighting had still to be done, while he tarried at Jerusalem. And one sultry afternoon he rose from his siesta, and was lounging on his palace roof, when he saw Bathsheba washing herself and, to adopt Nathan's subsequent phrase, a traveller came to him, a truant thought, to satisfy whose hunger he went down into the home of a poor man and took his one ewe lamb, although his own folds were full of flocks. We need not try to extenuate his sin by dwelling upon Bathsheba's willing compliance, or her despisal of her plighted marriage troth to her husband absent on active service. The record of Scripture lays the burden of this sin on the king alone, before whose absolute power, indeed, Bathsheba may have felt she was compelled to yield.

David sinned, and sinned deliberately. A man of God. One brief spell of sensual indulgence, and his character blasted, his peace vanished, the foundations of his kingdom imperilled, the Lord displeased, and great occasion given to his enemies to blaspheme.

How true to life these Old Testament stories are! When David knew that the results of his sin could not be hidden, he resolved to try to veil his sin. Uriah, the husband, must come home and be with his wife; but this soldier husband, though he came, refused to tarry with his wife while the war was in progress, although the first night David sent him a special mess of meat from the king's table, and on the next night made him drunk. This was David, the man of God. And so the king decided Uriah must die. There was no alternative. Dead men tell no tales; and if a child was to be born, his lips at least could not disown it. Accordingly his death warrant was sent to Joab— how his eyes must have glistened when he read it, for it put the king pretty well into his power.

"Set ye Uriah in the forefront of the hottest battle . . ." and the thing was done. Uriah was left to die. And the word was sent to David, and nobody knew a thing about it, presumably, except Joab and himself. He had managed it well. Seven days later Bathsheba was taken into David's home as another of his wives.

But there was one fatal flaw in the whole arrangement. We read, ". . . the thing that David had done displeased the Lord". David and Bathsheba were indeed to hear more of it. But oh, the tragedy that he who was God's anointed, the psalmist, the king, should trample everything in the mire, in one dark sin.

We need not dwell in detail on the days that followed. The baby was born, and was soon to die. The consequences of David's short season of sinful pleasure began to reveal themselves. At first he wrapped his sin in his bosom, pursed his lips and refused to confess; but his peace had gone. Sin always hinders and breaks a man's intercourse with God. It hinders prayer, and it hinders usefulness and service for God. And David now knew all that. Conscience made him sullen, uneasy, and unwontedly cruel in the treatment of others at this time. If you read the narrative you will see. No sweet sounds come from this period of David's life. No sounds until his great outburst of confession in Psalm 32 and Psalm 51. And the former of those, Psalm 32, reveals how he felt: "His bones waxed old through his groaning all the day long." He was parched with fever-heat day and night. God's hand was heavy upon him until, I believe, Nathan's advent on the scene at last was a positive relief.

One day this old friend made his way to the palace and desired a private interview with the king. He told David what seemed to be a real and pathetic story of high-handed wrong; and David's anger was greatly kindled against the man who had perpetrated it. Then, like a lightning flash, came the brief, awful, sudden, stunning sentence, "Thou art the man!" And David was revealed to himself in the mirror of his own judgment, and driven to his knees. Nathan reminded him, faithful friend and servant of God as he was, of the past, particularly dwelling upon God's unstinted mercy and condescension to David. "But," he said, "thou hast despised His word, thou hast slain Uriah, thou hast taken his wife." And David's only answer: "I have sinned against the Lord." And on that brief confession came a flood of hot tears, and in an instant his scorched heart found relief; and when Nathan had gone, he beat out that confession into the fifty-first Psalm, one of the greatest penitential utterances in all literature.

But before we go on to consider that, let us pause for a moment. I have been outlining the sin of one man of God. It may be that some here in this great tent are saying, "But that really doesn't represent me. I haven't sinned like that. I am a new creature in Christ Jesus, and I couldn't be guilty of that." Do you think, then, that only those who pray and confess after the manner of David, only those who have sinned after the similitude of his transgression and then pray and confess, "Lord, create in me a clean heart, and renew a right spirit within me," only they need to say such things?

The Bible is full of the anomaly of sin in the believer; of the tragedy of that fact. A great deal of the Bible is about that; and concerning this, God has constantly to speak to His people. Of what may He have to speak to you, thou man of God? If not David's actual sin, though God knows it may be, or something like it, what form does your sin take? Pride, self-righteousness, jealousy, ill-temper, envy, covetousness; sins of the flesh or of the mind; sins against others or against yourself? And remember this: it is not the sins that we commit, but the sin in us that makes us commit them; that is the serious fact. If we say we have no sin, we deceive ourselves, and the truth is not in us. We are new creatures in Christ. Yes. But our evil hearts are still evil; and although in Christ we have received a new obedient heart, yet too often the old nature is allowed the victory that brings us down even to the level of our former sins. And then defeat comes, the defeat of the end and object of our new life in Christ.

Is that the position with you, whatever has caused it? We lose intercourse with God, than which surely there can be nothing more grievous for the Christian. You see, we are dependent upon God for this intercourse. And so does sin hurt Him that He withdraws the sense of His near presence, and there is instead the sense of isolation from Him. The Holy Spirit will not share your heart or mine with sin. The veil comes down again. You can't keep an unclean thought in your mind, and harbour a spite, without grieving the Holy Spirit.

And sin hinders prayer, as I have already said. The approach to prayer is blocked. There is not the true desire to seek God; nor is there the power to speak to Him with the assurance that He is hearing. Be honest about it, fellow Christian. Prayer hindered, real prayer stopped. What a tragedy for a Christian! And sin hinders usefulness and service. It is possible to continue to do work for Christ out of custom or convention, or for reputation with men, or just because it is expected of us. But the zest has gone. The joy has gone. Yes, and the usefulness has gone, for that depends entirely upon the power of the blessing of God with whom we have lost touch.

Whatever the failure in your life, you must be honest and real enough to face it, and confess it, and have it put away. If God is speaking to you about it, and revealing it as sin, saying, "Thou art the man who has sinned," though a child of God, you will accept and acknowledge it, will you not?

Let us notice, next—

THE MAN WHO REPENTED. And he is the same man, David. And let me say that he showed that he was a true man of God by the fact and the manner of his repentance. He has put it all down into this intensely personal fifty-first Psalm—a psalm that is almost too sacred for us to transgress upon, as it gives the inner revelation of this man's soul, a soul that is spiritually real. And at the top of it we notice that David dedicated it to the chief musician, that all the world might read it and put it to music if they would; it is set openly for us in Holy Scripture for our instruction and our help, and it is a truly precious guide to God's people everywhere who have in all earnestness been made conscious of their sin, and have sought God for its removal. Will you let it be such a help to you?

What are its chief notes? By the confession of one sin and many transgressions. The confession of evil done against God. The confession of inbred evil. The consciousness of the unclean heart. The loss of joy. The fear of forfeiting the Holy Spirit. The broken and the contrite heart. And then the cries for the multitude of God's tender mercies. Nothing less could erase the dark story from the book of remembrance, and rub out the stains. To be clean, because purged with hyssop. To be whiter than snow, because washed. To have the song restored, and to sing aloud, because delivered from blood guiltiness. To be filled with the Holy Spirit. To be able to point other transgressors to the Father's heart. These are the petitions of that sin-weary heart laid upon the altar of God. There is no doubt of the genuineness of David's repentance.

74

Are there like marks to our repentance? For here is a pointer to all men in their personal dealings with God against whom they have sinned. This psalm rings true to the New Testament experience of the man who knows God through Jesus Christ, and to the experience of the saints in all the ages. It means that all sin must be judged, and thoroughly judged. No glossing over it; no calling it by any other name. And after that, it means a seeking of the right source for forgiveness and cleansing. And after that, it leads to Spirit-filling with joy and power and service and worship.

Let us dwell upon this all-important matter, for I think this is where perhaps some of us are found tonight. The need of forgiveness clearly recognised, because too often, and not least in these present days, men are inclined to rush on to a profession of a new life, to make a new start as it were, without a proper comprehension of the enormity of sin in God's sight. And without having it definitely forgiven and put away by His grace, we have no right to go on. We have no encouragement from Him to go on, even to a life of apparent uprightness and service to Him, unless we have had His cleansing and His personal seal of acceptance once more. So let us not slur over this. We must come to the place of personal forgiveness and cleansing; to this humble place, if God has been speaking to us and saying, "Thou art the man."

Let us notice David's repentance. It involved *a confession to God that hid and would hide nothing.* Nor must ours. God, of course, has known all about our sin from the beginning. As we have been reminded, we may hide our uncleanness and our failure from other people, we may hide its greatness from ourselves, but we can never hide our sins from God.

Oh, what a solemn, what a humbling thing that is. Our sins are utterly open to our holy God. The broken vows, the coldness that really is in our hearts when we profess so much in Christian circles, our self-pleasing, our backsliding, our sin, open or secret, which is a blow against God whom we profess to love. He knows our sin; He knows it exactly: and He wants us to acknowledge His omniscience, and His hatred of our sin, by coming to Him and confessing it as such, recognising that it has been primarily committed against Himself, "Against thee, thee only, have I sinned, and done this evil in thy sight." Thus humbling of heart and life has to be faced; and it must be real. And let us not overlook confessing to Him our particular sins. For from our particular sins we must repent. And I have found that very often this whole matter comes down to one or two particular things.

But David went deeper than that. He confessed that his nature was from the beginning corrupt in God's sight. He confessed his need of a clean heart and a right spirit; and he wanted this thing to be dealt with at its very roots. And his prayer, you notice, was for a clean life coming from a cleansed heart. He prayed with full purpose of, and endeavour after, new obedience. Not just for a judicial cleansing, but for the practical holiness of life following on that. Here is a man who cannot bear the thought of remaining in, or returning to, his sin. That is repentance. Is that the mark of your repentance? It must be. Art thou this man, the man who is truly repenting, who is now repenting?

Then let us see, in the third place—

THE MAN WHO WAS RESTORED. For David's prayer was answered. He returned to his fellowship with God. He became God's man again, in the infinite grace and mercy of his God and Father. Oh yes, he had to bear the consequences of his sin; and they were very costly. His child died; and it wrung David's heart as he thought perhaps of the innocent little one suffering for his crime. Certainly he was the reproduction in his own family of his sin. His worst features appeared in his sons; and then he had to suffer Absalom's rebellion against himself and his throne, and be turned out of Jerusalem by the people who once loved and revered him. David went through hard times as an old man. But he knew God again. He walked with God again, and he thrived again as he was enabled to reflect God to men in many many ways. He found the unspeakable blessings of forgiveness and restoration; and so may we, my dear people. God, the God who delights to restore in His sovereign grace, waits and longs to restore us; and our repentance gives Him full sway to do so.

I remind you that all restoration must be on a firm and just basis, of course. He has appointed and provided a way of forgiveness and full return for the penitent—a way revealed in measure to David, when he prayed that he might be purged with hyssop, with its reminder and suggestion of the blood of the passover lamb and of the cleansing of the lepers in Israel. The way that finds its complete fulfilment in the blood and water that flowed from the riven side of our Saviour, for all sin and all uncleanness, which is fully efficacious to wash whiter than snow and cleanse from all sin. It is on that basis that full restoration is ours if we return in genuine repentance and faith.

But what I want to point out is that the restoration God gives is full and complete; and I would dare to say, in the name of my Lord, the words that Nathan said to David: "The Lord has taken away thy sin." He loves and He longs to do so, for His love, infinitely pure and hating the sin, never ceases in its yearning over the prodigal son; over you, over me. Our sin and uncleanness never staunches that love which waits eagerly for the confession and the genuine repentance, that it may wash and restore the soul.

David had sinned grievously. David had to bear the results of his sin; but God's love for him did not change, and would not let him go. And so it is with you and with me. This is the God with whom we have to deal. Our God and Father through Jesus Christ. His love will not be frustrated. We may well nigh have lost ourselves in the labyrinth of our sins. But He has made full provision for our restoration, and if we confess our sins He is faithful and just to forgive us our sins, and to cleanse us from all unrighteousness. Let Him, then, say of us in this regard, Thou art the man—the man who fully confesses and returns; and He will say, "Thy sins, which are many, are all washed away. Go in peace, and sin no more." And those words are not just an assurance to us, but are full of His divine power, and they bring full restoration. He says to you, "Him that cometh unto me, I will in no wise cast out."

Tuesday July 13th

10 am Bible Reading

The Way to Christian Stability
(2) The Foundation for Christian Truth and Knowledge
(2 Peter 1:12–21)
Rev. R. C. Lucas

TAPE NO. 291a

11.50 am Forenoon meeting

Conscience
Archdeacon H. W. Cragg

TAPE NO. 303

3 pm Afternoon meeting

Invitation to Live
Rev. Peter Coombs

TAPE NO. 303a

7.45 pm Evening meeting

The Christian's Threefold Peace
Rev. K. A. A. Weston

TAPE NO. 300

Out of the Depth
Rev. R. C. Lucas

TAPE NO. 300a

Call to Submission

A major change in the Convention programme this year was the introduction of a second meeting for ministers. The customary gathering, in the Methodist church on Tuesday, at the same time as the morning meeting in the tent, has always been regarded as a key event, since blessing received by ministers is multiplied in their churches. Keen interest was evoked, therefore, by the announcement of two sessions—the second on Thursday morning; and the change of name to "Ministers' Seminars". It had been thought that this might indicate a change in the character of the meetings, introducing discussion and perhaps questions-and-answers. Indeed, it was noised abroad that the first "seminar" would be devoted to Keswick's message in this permissive age; and the second, of a more practical nature, on how to get that message across.

It didn't work out like this, however; in fact, we had two meetings of the traditional fashion. Perhaps the glorious weather on Tuesday accounted for the fact that attendance was well below the usual: but the body of the church was virtually filled. The Rev. G. B. Duncan spoke upon the question of David, "How can the ark of God come to me?" (2 Sam. 6:9) and its present-day counterpart in many hearts, How can the presence and power of God become the supreme reality in my church, my ministry?

On Thursday the Rev. R. C. Lucas, from the record of our Lord's temptation in the wilderness, educed lessons on the temptations of ministers—to be sub-spiritual, semi-spiritual, or stupidly spiritual. That is: over-occupied with "bread"—social concerns; with "power and authority" and unworthy means to proper ends; and spectacular demonstrations of "trust in God" which in reality are putting Him to the test. Our sure guide in all matters relating to Christian life and ministry is the Word of God.

It is a custom at Keswick for the leaders of the young people's meetings to give one address each in the main Convention. On Monday evening the Rev. Michael Baughen had done so; on Tuesday afternoon the Rev. Peter Coombs, vicar of New Malden in Surrey, gave a lively message on "Invitation to Live".

Year after year one marvels at the manifest ordering of God in the dovetailing of the two evening addresses; and this was particularly marked once again. For instance, on Tuesday the Rev. Keith Weston, vicar of St. Ebbe's, Oxford, a new speaker, brought an assuring word from Romans 5:1, "Being justified by faith, we have peace with God through our Lord Jesus Christ." In a complementary message, from Psalm 130, the Rev. R. C. Lucas counselled any who might be in the depths to cry to God (v. 1); to wait for Him (v. 5); and to hope in Him (v. 7). Thus the call to submission to God, and glad acceptance of all His good, perfect and acceptable will, was sounded forth.

The Way to Christian Stability

2. THE FOUNDATION FOR CHRISTIAN TRUTH AND KNOWLEDGE (2 Peter 1:12–21).

By the Rev. R. C. Lucas, M.A.

Our subject today, 2 Peter 1:12–21, The Foundation for Christian Truth and Knowledge. I should like to begin by looking back to the passage of yesterday, 2 Peter 1:1–11, in order to identify again the great themes of this short letter. The themes which are clearly on the mind of Simon Peter, "servant and apostle of Jesus Christ", are as follows: "The knowledge of God and of Jesus Christ our Lord." That *knowledge* is what we are introduced to, by the grace of God; and to be a Christian is to have that knowledge. V. 3, "Through the knowledge of Him who called us . . ." Vv. 5–6, "We are to add to our virtue knowledge, and to knowledge self-control." In other words, a *growing* knowledge of God is ours as Christians. Again, in v. 8, not to be "ineffective or unfruitful in the knowledge of our Lord Jesus Christ".

Peter is very clear about the importance of this knowledge. It is for lack of this knowledge of God and Jesus Christ—today especially, when the churches and the world seem to have lost touch with this knowledge so often—that life is meaningless to so many people. To be a Christian is to know God and His Son Jesus Christ. But this knowledge is not a static thing. On the basis of this knowledge, we are urged to grow in our experience of God, and in further knowledge of Him. And this *growth* is another theme of this letter. I believe that this theme of growth unifies both the epistles of Peter. You find it, for example, in verse 1 of 1 Peter 2, "Like newborn babes, long for the pure spiritual milk, that by it you may grow up to salvation," and that theme of growth in knowledge goes right through the first letter and the second letter as well.

Such growth is a sure guarantee of *stability*. This is another of the great themes of Simon Peter. He wants us to be those people who do not fall and stumble (see 2 Peter 1:10), but have grown to a maturity that gives us stability, so that we stand firm like a rock among our fellow men. This theme of stability is very dear to his heart, I think, partly because of his own experience as a disciple of Jesus, when he was by nature as unstable as water; and then because of the instructions he received in Luke 22:31, "Simon, behold! Satan demanded to have you, that he might sift you like wheat, but I have prayed for you that your faith may not fail; and when you have turned again, strengthen—stabilise—your brethren" and make them secure. "When you have learnt stability, Simon, then I want you to make it your business to teach others Christian stability: to settle your brethren firmly."

That is an undoubted theme of these two letters. Glancing back into 1

79

Peter 5:10, "After that you have suffered a little while, the God of all grace, who has called you to his eternal glory in Christ, will Himself restore, establish, and strengthen you." And in the second letter the theme of stability comes even more to the fore.

So in 2 Peter 2:12, you see he is at this business again of stabilising Christians. "I intend always to remind you of these things," he writes, "though you know them and are established in the truth that you have." They are already established Christians: they already have a measure of maturity. But he says, "I am going to go on reminding you of these things, that you may become yet more stable and rock-like in your discipleship."

Before we plunge into our passage, I want you to look at the end of the letter because—as so often happens in letters in the New Testament—all the strands of thought in the letter are drawn together and summarised in a pithy sentence or two. This is particularly the case in the second letter of Peter. If you wanted to summarise all that I have to say, the words of 3:17–18 put it perfectly: "You therefore, beloved, knowing this beforehand, beware lest you be carried away with the error of lawless men and lose your own stability. But grow in the grace and knowledge of our Lord and Saviour Jesus Christ."

You see that Peter tells us that in this letter he is really doing two things. Negatively, he had a warning job to do. New teachers have come into the church, very subtle, apparently rather spiritual: but they are unsettling everybody. And Peter feels he must warn the young Christians about them. Positively, he urges them that the best way not to slip back is to go on: and that is always so in the Christian life. You can't stand still: to stand still is to go back. So he says, "Grow in the knowledge and grace of our Lord Jesus Christ, and then you won't be carried away, then you won't lose your stability."

Like a wise pastor, he deals with the positive side first—1:3–11 is the classic passage in the New Testament on Christian grace, on positive advancing in grace and knowledge. But also, like a wise pastor, he is not afraid to warn against erroneous teaching, and expose it—as he does in chapter 2. That is never a popular thing to do; it is never an easy thing to expose false teaching, especially when some of the finest and best Christians in the congregation are being tempted to be ensnared by it. And this is not outside the congregation, but within the congregation. I have sometimes been tempted to say, "Never mind: they'll learn." But I have been most interested to see that Peter does not take that rather *laissez faire* attitude. He doesn't say, "Never mind, they'll learn in the experience of life as a Christian." No, he feels it is incumbent upon him to tell them exactly where they stand, and what is happening, and why they should not listen to these new voices.

Now this New Testament emphasis on true and false teaching leads to the inevitable question, How do you know what is the truth? How can you be so sure? And so I think it is inevitable that Peter should pay some attention to the foundation of Christian truth and knowledge. That is what he does now, and that is why it comes so perfectly in its context. He has explained that the Christians are to grow in the knowledge of Jesus Christ. He is going to warn them very soon about the false teaching. But before he does that, he makes sure they understand the foundations upon which their knowledge is built, the foundation of the apostolic testimony and the prophetic word—or, as we should say, the New and the Old Testaments.

So let me with no more ado go straight through vv. 12–21 and try to allow them to speak for themselves. I would call vv. 12–15, *Peter's anxiety*. "Therefore I intend to remind you of these things, though you know them and are established in the truth that you have. I think it right, as long as I am in this body, to arouse you by way of reminder, since I know that the putting off of my body will be soon, as our Lord Jesus Christ showed me. And I will see to it that after my departure you may be able at any time to recall these things."

As I say, his readers already are fairly mature and established; nevertheless Peter intends to remind them: and the theme of this section is, *Constant reminder of the truth*. In vv. 13–14 he says that he will remind them as long as he is alive. He will become a bore, if you like, in this. He will persistently do so. He will go on and on, while he is alive.

Secondly, in v. 15 he says he will make arrangements to see that when he has departed from this earthly scene, they are still reminded of what he has to say. He is certainly a persistent teacher, isn't he? He says, "I'm going to go on reminding you while I'm still with you as your leader and apostle. But after I have departed—and our Lord has told me that this may be very soon . . ." This letter was certainly written right at the end of his life—"after my departure, when you no longer have me in the flesh, I'm going to make very careful arrangements that you still hear what I have to say".

Now, some people think it likely that v. 15 refers to this second letter itself; but it more likely refers to the Gospel of Mark, which from the very earliest days of the church has been regarded as an interpretation, a writing down, of Peter's preaching, Mark being a disciple of Peter. So it is very possible that v. 15 refers to the fact that Peter is going to see that this is all written down before he goes; and in John, Mark perhaps, he finds the man who will write it down.

So here is a teacher who certainly is not unstable: he is very determined. He is determined that they shall not forget these things, if he has anything to do with it. Now why is this? Is it simply because truth bears repetition? Well, there is, I think, some truth in that. Every teacher knows, from Sunday-school onwards, that memory work is essential if ever people are to learn anything. Every preacher repeats himself: it may or not be obvious, according to how skilful he is; but he will be saying the same things over and over again, because he knows that is essential if they are to lodge and to stay in people's minds.

It is said of one of the greatest brains of his time, Erasmus, that one of the reasons why he was so learned was that he had an almost perfect memory. Most of us have a most imperfect memory: I know it goes for me! Therefore we need to learn the truths of Scripture, familiar though they may be, over and over again. And yet I do not think this is really an explanation of the force of Peter's words, true though it is. It is, perhaps, that we need to be reminded of truths that saved us? Now that is a great New Testament theme. Many a church leader today needs to be asked that question: What were the truths that brought you redemption? What were the truths that brought *you* out of darkness into light? Are you still preaching them? Are you living by them? Are they the meat and substance of what you preach? And very often it is not so. People have gone on: they have left these things behind. Isn't that so?

81

One of the things that both Paul and Peter are anxious to do, is to remind people of their foundations, of the truths that saved them.

Now I do not think it is necessary to rule out any of these interpretations as to why Peter is so keen on repetition. I think he knows that the truth will bear repetition; that he must repeat in order that people will remember; and that people need to remember the truths that brought them to salvation in the first place, that they may pass those apostolic truths on to others. Ah, now, there's my clue! I think that the real force of vv. 12–15 is often missed. What Peter is really saying, I should think, is this: "I want to make perfectly certain that you have not just the facts, but my version of the facts."

That may sound to you rather conceited. But remember who he calls himself at the beginning of the letter. He is a servant and an apostle of Jesus Christ. It is his apostolic testimony to these truths that they needed to know, and that they needed to know for ever. Others could continue the work of teaching and reminding. That is what we are doing at Keswick, by and large, from this platform. But what we cannot give is the apostolic testimony. For no one today is an apostle. Only one can build that foundation—the apostle. And what Peter is saying here is, "I am going to make very certain that when I have departed from the scene you have my apostolic testimony, so that you can go back to the foundation, and know what the true foundation is on which you build. That is why I am going to repeat. That is why I am going to remind. That is why I shall see that it is written down."

Now when he had gone, of course, the building of the foundations was over. There were other builders of those foundations: one of them was Paul. And if you will glance to the end of chapter 3 you will see a fascinating little passage: "So also our beloved brother Paul wrote to you according to the wisdom given him, speaking of this as he does in all his letters. There are some things in them hard to understand, which the ignorant and unstable . . ." —notice, the unstable—". . . twist to their own destruction, as they do the other scriptures." He already recognises that the writings of the apostle Paul are *Scripture* for the church; and I am beginning to be convinced by vv. 12–15 that Peter is already recognising the fact, as he is about to depart, that his own testimony will be Scripture for the church, because he is an apostle. And these two brethren, Peter and Paul, are indeed the foundation-builders of the church, because they are the writers of the New Testament.

Let us look, then, at what he says about his *apostolic testimony* (vv. 16–18). Peter's anxiety (vv. 12–15); the apostolic testimony (vv. 16–18). He changes from "I" in v. 15 to "we" in v. 16, clearly thinking of himself and the other apostles; and thinking in particular of that inner three who went with Jesus to the Transfiguration. "We did not follow cleverly devised myths when we made known to you the power and coming of our Lord Jesus Christ, but 'we' were eye-witnesses of His majesty. For when he received honour and glory from God the Father and the voice was borne to Him by the Majestic Glory, 'This is my beloved Son, with whom I am well pleased,' we heard this voice borne from Heaven, for we were with Him on the holy mountain." Now he says that, "We apostles, we who were in that circle with Jesus, did not and do not follow cleverly devised myths when we teach you the Gospel."

The implication is that these new teachers *do* follow mythical stories. I think it is important to realise what "myths" really means. A myth, to us, is something which is just patently untrue. I do not think the false teachers would have got very far if they came along with things that were patently untrue. The word "myth" in theological circles today has come up in the world, and is, I think, a little bit nearer today to what it meant in those days. That is to say, a story which might be imaginary or speculative; a story which might very well not be true, but which enshrined a great truth. What the false teachers of those days—and these days—say, is that the story need not be taken too literally, but the meaning of the story is what matters.

Now that can be taken very far, and *is* taken very far; and sometimes it puzzles and bewilders Christian people very much. They hear, for example, on "Meeting Point" on television, or on radio, some eminent church leader say that he does not worry too much about the *literal* meaning of the story of the resurrection, whether Christ's body *actually* broke through out of the tomb and appeared *physically* before His disciples. They say that is not what matters. What matters is the truth that is enshrined in it all, that Christ conquered death. If this distinction is too subtle for you, maybe it is a comfort to you to know that it is too subtle for me; and perhaps it is a greater comfort still to know that it is too subtle for the New Testament writers!

In order to make that quite plain, I must give you another cross-reference, because I think this point is so important. I would ask you to turn back to 1 Corinthians 15:17, where we have one of the most clear statements in the New Testament, to guide us through these rather difficult areas which puzzle people today. At any rate, here we know exactly what he means. "If Christ has not been raised . . ." first, "your *faith* is empty"—you have no faith: faith is not something that we produce from ourselves. You know, people come up to you and say, "You're so lucky: you have faith!" It depends on the resurrection. If the resurrection did not take place, your faith is futile and pointless. Secondly, your *forgiveness* is futile and pointless. It is not there: you are still in your sins.

"Then those also who have fallen asleep in Christ have perished" (v. 18). Don't imagine for a moment that those Christian friends, parents, of yours, are at home with Christ. That is meaningless if Christ did not rise from the dead. "If Christ has not been raised", none of these things are true. So if the story was not true, then the sooner the Convention Council pull down these tents, and sell this very valuable site for building, the better. Because there is no point in talking to one another, and trying to encourage one another, unless there is a foundation underneath it.

That is exactly what he is saying, as we come back to 2 Peter 1:16, "We did not follow cleverly devised myths. We were not telling you stories of which the truth does not matter very much. We were not just telling you of some abstract thought about God. We were telling you of things we actually saw, that happened, 'when we made known to you the power and coming of our Lord Jesus Christ'."

Now it is very interesting to notice what he "made known to them". He made known to them something which, in a sense, you might say the early apostles could not possibly know—the glorious coming and power of Jesus Christ. After all, the Jesus Christ they knew had been born in the humblest possible state. He came from no particular class. He was despised and rejected by the leaders of His day, and then ultimately died a shameful, weak death: and after His resurrection departed and left them. It would be very difficult, wouldn't it, to convince a Roman citizen of the first century that your King was a very powerful king, if that was all that you could say about Him. And you would try to say to him, "Well, He is actually coming again." And the Roman citizen would say, "Well, that's a jolly good story! But it is not a very impressive thing that He died like that, and allowed people to defeat Him."

No; you see, the early disciples, the early apostles, needed more. They needed a clear revelation in the incarnate life of Jesus, that what He said about Himself was true; and that hidden behind the meekness, hidden behind that ordinary human life, there was the power and majesty of God. And that is the reason for the story of the transfiguration, that we study far too little. At that unique moment God drew aside for one moment the curtain. He allowed Peter and James and John to see for a moment a glimpse into reality—that this Person in front of them was the King, even although it might seem, as far as the eye could normally see, that He was not.

Turn back to Mark 9:1, and you will see exactly what I mean. You will have noticed and been puzzled so often by this verse that comes before the story of the transfiguration: "Truly I say to you, there are some standing here who will not taste death before they see the kingdom of God come with power." And that has puzzled us. Surely they did not see the kingdom of God come with power before they died? But, yes they did! They saw the authentic anticipation of that great coming in power. They saw the truth of it all in the transfiguration. Now they knew that He was indeed the King of the universe; that the power of God was behind Him and in Him: therefore the fact that His victory would come was no longer a matter of dispute or doubt. Peter and James and John saw the coming of God's kingdom in power and glory, just for that moment, to assure them that what they were taught about Jesus was no myth, but reality.

So come back to v. 16: "We did not follow cleverly devised myths when we made known to you the power and coming of our Lord Jesus Christ, *but we were eye-witnesses* of His majesty." Now we are on such sublime ground here that I hope you will not mind if just for a moment I rest your minds with a rather ridiculous illustration of the importance of an eye-witness.

When I was a boy at school in my early teens, we used, every week, one afternoon, to play at soldiers. It was something that was quite popular in some ways, and with some boys unpopular. And one term I discovered that my name was not down on the register. This was a marvellous opportunity! And so every Wednesday afternoon in that term, when the register was called out, and my name was not called out, I obviously was not there! Just before they went out in their uniforms on to the parade ground, I slipped out of the gate of the school and on to a passing bus, into the nearby town where there were untold delights of second-hand bookshops, and what used to be called in my youth "Picture palaces".

On one of these journeys in a bus—and pocket money went a long way in those days—I was, as boys usually are, on the top of a double-decker bus, on the front seat. And a car came, alas, driven by a woman! and went slap into the front of the bus. We stopped, and the police came, and I was the only person who had seen the accident—apart from the driver; and so the policeman, of course, wanted to know all that I had to say: and I thought I was very important, and it was rather a thrilling occasion.

Until two days later—because I, like most people, only saw a day at a time—I was doing my lessons when I was called into the headmaster's study. And I saw to my horror, standing beside him, a policeman. Of course, I had not realised it would lead to that! But I was the only person who could give evidence, because I was the only eye-witness. And so the truth came out, to my consequent shame and suffering!

Now that, if we may leave those childish games behind, is what is important about this little paragraph. "We were eye-witnesses: we *saw* it." Then look at v. 17: "When He received honour and glory . . . and the voice was borne to Him by the Majestic Glory . . . we *heard* this voice . . ." We saw; we heard. An eye-witness, and if we may call it so, an "ear-witness". "We saw with our own eyes; we heard with our own ears. Of course we did, because we were actually there with Him on the holy mountain."

This, then, is a first-hand account. Now this is a unique privilege: it is not given to us; it is not given to anybody else. A unique privilege given to the apostles: to see the glory of God. You will remember that the apostle Paul, "born out of due time" as an apostle, was given his own special revelation of the glory of God—again, not given to ordinary Christians. We do not have the privilege to have seen the glory of Christ as the apostles did. We therefore depend upon their unique testimony to what they saw and heard.

May I say something about the reliability and truthfulness of this testimony? Here we have men whose sincerity and truthfulness really cannot be questioned, who solemnly tell us that they saw certain things, and heard certain words; and again and again tell us these things, and are willing to seal these things with their blood. Now I believe that the scepticism that is so rife today, that disbelieves their testimony, that just tosses the New Testament on one side, proves too much. Because such scepticism would make any historical record worthless. It would mean that it was quite impossible to write any kind of record. Some people do not seem to realise that. They are willing to toss aside the record of these men of what they saw and heard, though it is given by many of them in different times and different places, and sealed by the testimony of their lives of integrity, and by their sacrifice. They toss that on one side, and yet they will believe so often what they read "in the paper" today, without so much as trying to verify it. That is surely an unreasoning scepticism.

A proper doubtfulness about everything we hear, is certainly a Christian virtue. To search for the truth is something, of course, which we have to do. A student said to me yesterday that he had been troubled with doubts. Well, yes, that is something that happens to us all. From those doubts, as we look into them, and search for the truth, we shall come to surer foundations. But there is a scepticism that is unreasonable; and I think there is much of it today, which would make any writing of history, any writing of any story, an impossibility.

But, of course, we have an added reason for trusting the apostles. Not only have we the reason for trusting them for their own truthfulness, and for their own first-hand encounter with the Lord: but that they also have the help, the specific help, of the Holy Spirit of God. John 14:26—a very important cross-reference, which is often misunderstood in Bible studies today. The disciples were complaining to our Lord at His imminent departure; and one of the reasons for their complaint was this. They said, "You've taught us so many wonderful things; we shan't be able to remember it all. And we feel there are many things You still have to teach us." John 14:25–26, "These things I have spoken to you, while I am still with you. But the Counsellor, the Holy Spirit, whom the Father will send in my name, He will teach you all things, and bring to your remembrance all that I have said to you."

Now you see, this has a specific reference to the apostles. It cannot have a specific reference to you and to me. Has Jesus ever brought into your mind, into remembrance, all the things that He said? There is no need for that. You have the Gospels in front of you. The Holy Spirit was not sent to bring to *your* remembrance the things that Jesus said: He was sent to bring to *their* remembrance the things that Jesus said, in order that they might testify and write them for our perpetual learning. This verse, then, does not apply generally to Christians, but specifically to these disciples; that the Holy Spirit will lead them into the truth of Christ's teaching, so that they could give an authoritative apostolic testimony, on which the church of Christ could be based. We do not find the truth of God by being led by the Spirit in that sense: we find the truth of God by reading and understanding the apostolic testimony which was given by the leading of the Holy Spirit of God. Jesus has built His church upon Peter and Peter's teaching, upon Paul and Paul's teaching, upon the apostles and the prophets.

That is why Peter is so anxious in these verses—12–18—to tell us that his testimony is reliable and true. He wants us always to know what he had to say; he wants us to know about his witness to the power and the coming of the Lord Jesus Christ. He wants us to know that he was there. He wants us to see through his eyes and to hear through his ears: he was there, and he passes it on to us. And our faith in the power and coming of Jesus rests upon this apostolic testimony.

Now vv. 19–21: Here he goes on to show us the further grounds of our knowledge, *the prophetic word*. And I should say that "the prophetic word" was a current expression of the day, embracing the whole of the Old Testament, and not simply the prophets in particular. Let me then read it: "And we have the prophetic word made more sure. You will do well to pay attention to this as to a lamp shining in a dark place, until the day dawns and the morning star rises in your hearts. First of all you must understand this, that no prophecy of Scripture is a matter of one's own interpretation, because no prophecy ever came by the impulse of man, but men moved by the Holy Spirit spoke from God."

V. 19a: The Authorised Version and the Revised Standard differ in a rather interesting way. The Authorised Version says, "We have . . . a more sure word of prophecy." In that case, Peter would be saying, "This is my testimony: but if you don't believe me, go back to the Scriptures. They will support it." The Revised Version says, "We have the prophetic word made more sure"—in other words, "What I am telling you is supported by the prophetic Scriptures; but, in fact, my apostolic testimony endorses and makes them even more sure." Grammatically both are possible, and the commentators will no doubt continue to argue until the last day. But I think I personally shall follow the Revised Standard Version. I think it is more likely that Peter would say that his apostolic testimony makes the prophetic word more sure. In other words, he is adding his apostolic seal to the Old Testament prophetic anticipation. A good case can be made out for both, and of course there is a sense in which both the Old and the New Testaments endorse one another and support one another.

Now I want to leave the rest of v. 19, which has a very important application, for a little while; and go straight on to vv. 20 and 21, where he tells us about the authority which lies behind the prophetic word, the Old Testament. He says that this is a matter of the first importance, which is what he means in v. 20: "First of all you must understand this . . ." It is of the first importance that you should understand the authority of the Old Testament Scriptures. Yes, it is, indeed, still today. We badly need the Old Testament to come back into our churches and into our preaching. Is it authoritative? Is it true? Now let us see what he has to say.

Now v. 20 is a very difficult verse. It is probably one of the most difficult verses, in some ways, that we shall deal with, just because I think the popular interpretation is the less likely of two possible interpretations. Literally it means this—"First of all you must understand this, that no prophecy is of a man's own unravelling." "Is of a man's—or one's own—unravelling." But better, "a man's own unravelling"—or untying; that is literally what it means. "No prophecy is a matter of a man's own unravelling"—his own solution, in other words.

There are two ways of understanding this, both possible. The first is to suppose that this refers to the reader, the recipient of the prophecy. No prophecy that he receives or reads is a matter of his own unravelling. He cannot interpret it just as he wants. He cannot read into it: he must not be guilty of what the Rev. Alan Stibbs often calls imposition, rather than exposition. That is starting from a text, and then telling what you want to say—and perhaps very kindly coming back to the text at the end, as a matter of form! May God deliver the church increasingly from that kind of preaching!

But it may also refer to the writer or author of the prophecy. "No prophecy is of a man's own unravelling." "A matter of one's own unravelling" means that the writer, the author of the prophecy, was not making his own solution; was not unravelling the problems, but was simply saying what he was given to say. Now when I studied this, I could not feel happy about the normal interpretation of this, as shown in the Revised Standard Version, that no prophecy is "a matter of one's own interpretation"—that this was really a matter of saying, "You shan't interpret Scripture as you like." It seemed to me that the real reason against this popular way of understanding the verse, was the context. For Peter is not talking about interpretation: he is talking about authority and inspiration. He is talking about the reliability of the Word. He is saying that the same God who spoke through Jesus at the transfiguration, spoke through the prophets. The Word that was borne to Him on the mount of transfiguration, was borne to them by the Holy Spirit. And v. 21 appears to me to clinch this. "No Scripture is a matter of one's own unravelling—a man's own unravelling, a man's own solution; because no prophecy ever came by the impulse of man." Now that makes sense: that flows naturally. But rather "men moved and borne by the Holy Spirit spoke from God".

I wrestled with this for several days, and came to the conclusion that that was what was meant. Then I turned to the commentators whom I have learned to trust; and I found that with no exceptions this was the view that they took. That is therefore the view which I believe to be the more likely of the two possibilities.

So what he is saying is this: When Isaiah prophesied, he did not have a solution of what he had to say. He could not unravel what he was saying. He spoke from God. Indeed, much of what he was saying was a mystery. It did not seem to apply to his own day. He did not altogether understand his own sayings. He did not understand the problems of God; he did not understand the purposes of God. He could not unravel all that God was going to do. But he gave us the word that God gave him to speak.

That this is the right interpretation is I think very probably substantiated by looking back to 1 Peter 1:10–12, where he says very much the same thing: "The prophets who prophesied of the grace that was to be yours searched and inquired about this salvation; they inquired what person or time was indicated by the Spirit of Christ within them when predicting the sufferings of Christ and the subsequent glory." They wondered what it was all about: they searched and inquired. And "it was revealed to them that they were serving not themselves . . .'—they would not understand; it would not be in the first place something that would serve their own generation—". . . but you, in the things which have now been announced to you by those who preached the good news to you through the Holy Spirit sent from heaven, things into which angels long to look."

So the prophets were not always aware of the full importance of what they had to say. Of course they spoke to their own day: they had a word for their own people. But in their prophecy, in their preaching and teaching, was something of God that was going fully to come to completion of its meaning in the future, when Christ should come. Didn't I say yesterday, "All the promises of God are yea and amen in Christ"? None of the Old Testament can finally make sense until Christ comes.

So vv. 20–21 really are very simple; and usually the simplest interpretation is the best. The apostle is simply saying that it is of the first importance that you realise that the Scripture is not human in its origins. It is a matter of the Holy Spirit moving men to speak from God. That is what the church has always believed, down two thousand years: that the Bible is not like any other book; that it contains the apostolic witness, which is unique, and the prophetic testimony which is unique, because it is given by the Spirit of God.

Now then, let us look at the application, in v. 19: "You will do well to pay attention to this." Why should you pay attention to this? Because you are living in a very dark place. What is that dark place? It is the world. The world is still dark until the coming of Christ in glory. Therefore, if I am to go through this dark world and see where I am going, I must have a lantern in my hand. What is the lantern I have in my hand, to see where I am going? I don't need to tell any Scripture Union member that: I ought not to need to tell any Christian that. For two thousand years the church has always said, when it is true to itself and its origin: the lamp in our hands is the Word of God. When the church has lost that lamp, it has wandered off into the dark; and when it has got that lamp back again, it has come back into the light. Isn't that so of the local church, as well as of the church universal?

How do I find my way? There is "a lamp for my feet, and a light for my path". It is the Scriptures. How, then, am I led through life? Not primarily by the church, great as the witness and example of Christians can be. Not primarily by the Holy Spirit, but by the Word. We should distrust those who tell us that their lives are led by the Spirit, unless they can give a good account of themselves in their leading from the Word of God.

When can I dispense with this lamp; when can I put it on one side, so to speak, and let it be blown out? Well, this verse tells us. You should "pay attention to this as to a lamp shining in a dark place, *until the day dawns*". You need a lamp all night-time; but when the sun comes up in the morning, you turn your light off. You don't need a lamp in the daylight. When does the day come; when does the day dawn? Why, that is quite obvious from this letter: it is the coming of Christ in power and great glory. Until that, we are living in a dark world. It is still night in the universe. But when Christ comes in power and great glory, the sun will dawn, "the Sun of Righteousness will arise". Then you won't need this lamp any more.

But he goes even further. This, I think, is a very wonderful touch. At the moment the truth is external to us: we always ought to distrust the idea that the truth can be found in us by searching our own hunches and feelings. The truth can only be found by searching the Scriptures. It is external to us. When Christ comes again, you might say He will be external to us. Yes, that is true: we shall have to look to Him. Yet Peter adds something which is very wonderful. When "the day dawns and the morning star rises in your hearts". What that means is that the light, part of the light—if you like, the reflected light—of the glory of God will be not only external to me in the coming of Christ—I shall not only see Him—but that light will dawn in my heart, so that I then have an immediate knowledge of God, which I cannot have now.

I believe that one of the problems in evangelical Christianity is an attempt to have here and now what can only be ours then. There are certain things that we have to wait for, and one of those is an *immediate* knowledge of God. Our knowledge of God at the moment is mediated to us through the Scriptures, through the witness and testimony of Christian people, through circumstances: through all these things. Then, we can put all those things on one side: we shall need them no longer—our Bible, and the testimony of Christian people, will no longer be needed when Christ comes and the sun rises, and "the morning star rises in our hearts". What a grand idea! What a magnificent thing to look forward to! An immediate knowledge of God!

Now may I draw together, with some applications, this tremendous passage on the foundation of Christian truth and knowledge. What a wise pastor Peter is, to build these foundations in, before he goes on to the rather difficult and troublesome business of dealing with those who have wandered from those foundations, in chapter 2.

May I repeat what I have said—in good Petrine manner! First, we are not to be guided by any inner light now. I am always interested in the Quakers, because my forefathers were Quakers. It was a movement, like so many movements that have begun, through the grace of God, when the church has been very dead—the church institutional: it began with a real movement of the Spirit of God. So real was it that they "quaked" at the presence of God. And we shall only know revival in our own country when people begin to fear God again: that is the mark of revival. Not enthusiasm, fear—fear of God. Now a hundred years ago there was a great dispute among the Quakers, at any rate in the London area, as to whether they should follow "the inner light" or the Scriptures. In this dispute some people went one way and some another; but generally the movement went in the direction of "the inner light", as being superior to the word of Scripture. And so the testimony, the Scriptural testimony of Quakerism, died.

I think that any student of church history, and any student of the church today, will see that: that unless the church stands by the Word of God, in the end the testimony of that church or movement will die. When I was in South India, following in the steps of Mr. George Duncan in ministering to the Mar Thoma church, there was a clear example of this. That very live, evangelistic community in South India is the result of a Biblical reformation that took place a hundred years ago; and the churches from which they came out a hundred years ago are but a shrivelled stump today. Were they going to follow the Word of God? Many chose to follow the Word of God, and as a result a keen evangelistic witness has been maintained by those Christians in South India.

I think of a young fellow who came to talk with me about a fortnight ago, and has caused me a great deal of anxiety. He is a very fine young Christian man: he has a lifetime of great service ahead of him. He wants to undertake a course of action that I could not myself reconcile with the Scriptures. When we were talking about this, he said to me: "But surely the Bible is only a record of experience. I, and many other Christians also, have experience; and should not our experience be put alongside that of the Scriptures?" Now that was sincerely meant: but you see the thin end of the wedge. You see the danger. If we can put the inward leading of the heart alongside the authoritative word of Scripture, we shall be led away in the end from the foundation. I believe that every course of action that we take should be able to be reconciled with Scripture, and consistent with Scripture.

Now finally, two cross-references, which I think endorse and underline all that we have been thinking about. Ephesians 2:19–20, "You are no longer strangers and sojourners, but you are fellow citizens of the saints and members of the household of God, built upon the foundation of the apostles and prophets, Christ Jesus Himself being the chief corner-stone." Of course, by "the apostles and prophets" he does not mean upon their human lives, but upon their testimony and their teaching. That was what founded the church: and they, of course, all point to the corner-stone, Christ.

Peter's concern at the end of his life is that we should not forget this; and I find it very moving and very interesting that at the end of *his* life and testimony, Paul felt exactly the same. So my final cross-reference: 2 Timothy 4:1–5; and I only discovered this recently, that at the end of their ministries both Peter and Paul were concerned about the same issue, the issue of foundation truth, the preservation of the Gospel deposit, the preservation of the authentic testimony to Christian truth. And at the beginning of 2 Timothy 4, "I charge you in the presence of God and of Christ Jesus who is to judge the living and the dead . . . preach the Word" (v. 2). "The time is coming when people will not endure sound teaching, but having itching ears they will accumulate for themselves teachers to suit their own likings, and will turn away from listening to the truth and wander into myths. As for you, always be steady, endure suffering, do the work of an evangelist, fulfil your ministry" (vv. 3–5).

And how will he do that? Well, you have only to glance back again to chapter 3—it is such a pity, I always think, that there is a chapter division here. How are they to carry on that testimony to the truth, when so many people wander away to more—apparently—attractive teaching? "As for you, continue in what you have learned and have firmly believed, knowing from whom you learned it, and how from childhood you have been acquainted with the sacred writings which are able to instruct you for salvation through faith in Christ Jesus. All Scripture is inspired by God and profitable for teaching, for reproof, for correction, and for training in righteousness, that the man of God may be complete, equipped for every good work" (2 Tim. 3:14-17). There is the foundation of the Christian church, and there is the foundation for any Christian ministry.

Conscience

By the Ven. H. W. Cragg, M.A.

A short phrase out of 1 John 3:21, "If our hearts do not condemn us, we have confidence before God." The confidence of the Christian heart before God is one of the most treasured and valued possessions of the Christian life. Is it not your experience that day by day as you look up into the face of your heavenly Father, you may know that there is no cloud between you? And is it not also your experience that when there is a cloud, you find your confidence is gone, your sense of peace and rest in His presence, your sense of assurance about your salvation, and about the answers to your prayers? Confidence before God is one of the most gracious gifts of the Spirit to us: and are there not moments when the awareness of it, and the sense of it, and the blessing of it, slip away? Why? Because of some cloud between.

"If our heart does not condemn us, we have confidence before God." By the word "heart", as you know, the New Testament means the meeting place of the will and the affections. It is the place where we react to things and to people and to God, and by that reaction steadily build up character. In the writings of St. John the heart is the whole moral nature of man, and includes the conscience. The *New English Bible*, recognising this, translates our text as follows: "If our conscience does not condemn us . . ." Our subject, then, is very plain to begin with. It is the importance and provision of a clear conscience. So we might read, "If our conscience prick us not . . ."

I want, as we approach this theme, to say three general things about conscience which are inescapably true, and which we ought constantly

91

to have at the background of our thinking. The first is that *conscience is built into every man*. It is not a gift at conversion: it is part of God's creating work. It is built into every man. You will see precisely what I mean by this point, in Romans 2:14–15, "When the Gentiles who have not the law do by nature what the law requires, they are a law to themselves, even though they do not have the law. They show that what the law requires is written on their hearts, while their conscience also bears witness and their conflicting thoughts accuse or perhaps excuse them."

Conscience is built into every man. It is the safety-valve of the moral and spiritual life. It is the arbiter of ethical conduct. So the man who violates his conscience sins against his Creator, and damages himself. And this applies universally, whether that man is a converted man or not.

But if this is true—and it undoubtedly is—then in the second place it is important to add that *conscience is not an adequate guide, left to itself*. It needs to be educated in order that it may function aright. How often we have said, "I did what I did because at the time I felt it was right, only to discover that what I did—and felt it was right—was not right. Between the moment I felt it was right, and the moment I discovered it was not right, I have been learning something. And what I have learned has sought to educate my conscience, so that in the second instance I know better than I did in the first."

I took my car one day to Croydon. I was aware that there were places where I was not allowed to park, and I was hopeful that there might be places where I should be allowed to park. I spotted a road where I noticed that one side there was "No Parking", clearly marked. So I parked on the other side, and went away for an hour to do some shopping, and when I came back my conscience was entirely clear—until I saw a policeman almost sitting on the bonnet. And the moment I saw him my conscience became anything but clear! The reason was that there was a different style of marking—and much less obvious—on the side of the road on which I had parked. And I was guilty: my number was taken; my name was taken; my licence was inspected; I got a letter to which I replied; and that was the end of it, of course! When I first left my car I had a clear conscience: but I was wrong.

To be a proper guide, conscience must be educated; and therefore the simple business of learning what is right in God's sight, and what is wrong, is part of the inner education which will govern conscience. But there is a third preliminary which needs to be said. What I have said already applies to any man and to every man, wherever he may be. But the converted man shares in the regenerating work of the Holy Spirit, and therefore his *conscience functions according to new standards*. He has a higher, deeper, richer, finer education of his conscience than any unconverted man could ever have. He is a regenerate man. He is not just saved for heaven from hell: he is a new man in Christ; and the conscience which was part of him originally, now becomes part of his new creation.

In the light of the New Testament this will give him two things. It will give him, first, *a finer sense of sin*, making him see wrong in what did not seem wrong before, and which is not wrong in the mind of the unconverted man.

You remember the little man up the tree? When Zacchaeus came down from the tree to the feet of Christ, one of the obvious marks of what had been achieved in him by God was that he said, "If I have taken anything from any man by false accusation, I restore him fourfold." This is something he would never have dreamt of doing until he met the Saviour. But when he met the Saviour, immediately there was awareness within him that what had been his common practice was all wrong. He would begin to make restitution. A finer sense of sin in the regenerate man.

But with a finer sense of sin, a regenerate conscience gives a man *a great sense of responsibility*, giving him to see what God is calling him to do. It is not just that he is keener and finer and sharper in his judgment of what is wrong: he is broader and grander and greater in his judgment of what is required. Isn't this why the name of William Wilberforce is the name we always attach to the abolition of the slave trade? Like so many of his day, and many since, Wilberforce had a conscience, but not only a conscience about what was wrong in slavery, but what was right in liberation. I wonder how your conscience has changed since you were converted?

Now, in the light of this, and with the New Testament in our hands, I want to say two things about the conscience of the Christian man. And the first is that—

THE CHRISTIAN LIFE REQUIRES A GOOD CONSCIENCE. Then we have confidence with God. A good conscience is not an option; it is not a luxury; it is not a special bit of blessing. It is required of every converted man. In Hebrews 10:22 we read about the attitude of the Christian worshipper in relation to his conscience: "Let us draw near—that is to God—with a true heart in full assurance of faith, having our hearts sprinkled from an evil conscience, and our bodies washed with pure water." "Our hearts sprinkled from an evil conscience" through the blood of Christ, as we enter the presence of God. Just as in Old Testament days the worshipper was sprinkled as he entered, so the conscience of a Christian man must be sprinkled as he enters into the presence of Christ. This is why the way into the holiest of all is by the blood of Jesus, which alone can cleanse the guilty conscience and make it clean as we confess our sins to Him. "Draw near to God with a clear conscience."

Isn't that why I don't draw near to Him when my conscience is not clear? Isn't this one of the reasons for the fall-out in the prayer life? Isn't this one of the reasons for the lack of liberty in prayer? Isn't this one of the reasons for the subservience of prayer to other activities? It is easy to *do* when I am not right; but it is not easy to pray. Draw nigh to God, having your heart sprinkled from an evil conscience.

In 1 Timothy 1:19, where the apostle Paul is writing to young Timothy, and we have this striking phrase about warring a good warfare: "Holding faith and a good conscience . . ." and he goes on: "By rejecting conscience certain persons have made shipwreck of their faith." Hold your faith and a good conscience. If you reject a good conscience, you make shipwreck of your faith, so that your faith becomes like a piece of dereliction, an old wreck lost on the rocks, because conscience never kept sides with it, so that they could go happily together.

If I preached heresy, some of you could put me right. If I stand here with a bad conscience, none of you know anything about it. Paul said to young Timothy, "Hold these tight together"—your doctrine true, your conscience clear. Wreck your conscience, and your doctrine becomes powerless. The Christian life requires a good conscience.

I should like to remind you how much a good conscience was cherished by the apostle Paul throughout his public ministry, from the day of his conversion right on to the end of all records of that ministry. I think, for instance, of Acts 24:16, where he is making his defence before Felix, the governor. And in that defence he has this to say: "So I always take pains to have a clear conscience toward God and toward men." This is his defence: his conscience is clear. Let them accuse him of what they will, his conscience is clear, and he has taken pains to keep it clear. It has not just happened automatically. He has not always found it easy. But he has put himself to the task, to keep a clear conscience, so that he can look up into the face of God with confidence, and look out upon his fellow men with confidence.

Can you look God in the face today? Can you look everybody you meet in the face today? There is nothing I find more embarrassing in personal contact with men and women, than to stand on the edge of a pavement on a corner of a street, talking to a man—and all the time we are chatting together he is looking at the ground and shuffling his feet about; and he only looks me in the face when first we meet, and when we say goodbye. And I say to myself, "Didn't quite like that somehow!" Is this how we meet our fellow men? Is this how we meet our God? Paul said, "I take pains to have always a conscience void of offence before God and before men." The upright is clear, and the outright is clear in the downright Christian life.

In 1 Corinthians 4:4, where Paul is writing specifically about the Christian ministry, he has this tremendous statement to say: "I am not aware of anything against myself. I know I am not thereby acquitted," he adds. "It is the Lord who judges." "I am not aware of anything against myself." Could you say that? He was not claiming perfection: he never did. He was not claiming that God could not have anything against him: he never did. But he said, "As far as I am aware—that is to say, by the artbiter of my inner conscience—I know nothing against myself."

Why? Because whenever he discovered anything against himself, he put it right quickly. I find it impossible to enter the pulpit on a Sunday if I know anything against myself. On the few occasions I have tried it, it has not worked. May I ask you again lovingly: Do you know anything against yourself? Just a few weeks ago I said something to a friend of mine, a man of roughly my own age. When I reflected on it later the same day, I came to a rather disturbing conclusion: that in his ear it could have meant what it did not mean in my mouth. And I wasn't happy about it. So I sat at my desk and wrote a little note: "If I gave you this impression, please forgive me."

Discovered anything against yourself? Put it right, right now. Don't wait. There used to be an old story from Keswick—I don't know to what extent it is verifiable, but there must have been a large area of truth in it— that one year at Keswick the local post office sold out of postal orders, because sitting in the tent all sorts of people became conscious of debts unpaid!

Paul says, "I don't know anything against myself." Oh, how happy is the man who could look up into the face of God and say—and write, "God helping me, the way is clear. And whenever it has been cloudy, I have put the cloud away by an immediate act of repentance and restitution."

Just one more from this pen: Romans 14:22, concerning all matters of uncertainty. "The faith that you have, keep between yourself and God; happy is he who has no reason to judge himself for what he approves."

Have you been approving something lately, and—now as you sit listening to the little pieces of this composite study on the one word "conscience"—you know that you have been approving things that, well, you are not happy about them now?

You know the story of the boy who was upstairs getting ready to go out with his mother, and it took him quite a while, and Mother was surprised. He was usually ready very quickly. When Mother called upstairs he said, "Well, Mother, I've just been looking at my collar. I'm not quite sure whether it is clean enough to go out with you." "Well," said Mother, "if it is doubtful, it's dirty." I find to my sorrow that all sorts of Christians nowadays can be terribly doubtful, but they won't let it be called dirty. I find that is a sure guide. To me, if it is doubtful, it is dirty.

I picked up a Bible belonging to a friend of mine one day, and as I picked it up a little bit of paper fell out. On it were five lines:

> Whatever impairs the reason,
> Hardens the conscience,
> Clouds the sense of God,
> Spoils the relish for spiritual things:
> That to me is sin.

Christian life requires a clear conscience.

Now, briefly, the second truth—

THE CHRISTIAN GOSPEL REPAIRS A BAD CONSCIENCE. This immeasurable blessing is not to be denied the man who has never known it: or having once known it, lost it. 1 John 3:20 has this splendid statement: "If our heart condemn us, God is greater than our heart, and knoweth all things." I find that the commentators are divided on this verse. Some would be very rigorous, and say, "If our heart condemn us, then it is very bad with you indeed, because God knows more than your heart recognises; and if you judge yourself, think of what God must say! How serious must be God's judgment. He knows everything, the things you have forgotten, the things you do not account important: He knows the lot. And if you judge yourself, how much more severe must the judgment of God be."

There are other Bible commentators who say it just means this: If your heart condemns you, God is greater than all your condemning heart, and in His merciful pardoning grace, He can swallow it all up. You guess which commentators I go with! I have looked at this hard, and I'm going with the second batch! "If our heart condemn us", all that condemning heart can be bathed in the blood of Christ, and the pardoning love and mercy of God, bigger and bigger, with all that condemning heart needs or ever will need. To lose myself in mercy, is the answer.

The prodigal got a conscience in the far country, and burdened with a guilty conscience he came home to tell about it. But he didn't get his telling "telt". No sooner had he started, than father smothered it up; the arms around his neck and the kiss upon his face, and the quick order for the best robe and the fatted calf, and the merriment of a boy come back. "Where sin abounded, grace did much more abound."

Oh, who is the man here with a guilty conscience? Who is the woman here with a guilty conscience? My friend, bring it to Christ: He is bigger. So it is that God gives grace to clear the conscience, and with the grace, the strength to overcome the weakness you feel, and before which you fell. God's pardon for your sins; God's presence to overcome yourself; and God's power for every situation. "If our heart condemn us, God is greater . . ."

Just two practical thoughts, and then I'm done. First, *don't drown conscience*. Paul writes to Timothy about having a conscience seared with a hot iron. You take the lovely leaf from the garden flowers, and you put it on the ironing board. You put the iron on top. What have you done? You have made a nice little book-marker: but it has no life. And there are people—and we could all become people—who have so dealt with conscience that it begins to lose its life, its keen edge, its God-appointed ministry. Don't drown conscience.

Second, *keep short accounts with God*. Rule up the ledger every night, and take no debit balance over to the next morning. "If we confess our sins, He is faithful and just to forgive us our sins, and to cleanse us from all unrighteousness." And this is not a cheap, easy salvation, which means I can sin and sin, and sin, and then get forgiveness, forgiveness, forgiveness. The man who plays with the Gospel like that is only half a man: and he isn't at all a Christian. The forgiveness of Christ is for that sinful breakdown, that accident, that short-coming, that omission, that commission. But rule off the ledger every night: "Let not the sun go down upon your wrath, neither give place to the devil." Put your head on your pillow with your heart right with God. Keep short accounts with God.

Oh, the rest and the joy and the strength and the usefulness and the ministry, if our heart does not condemn us!

Invitation to Live

By the Rev. Peter Coombs

When last, I wonder, did you go to a wedding, and to the wedding reception that followed? It may have been the marriage of a friend, or of a son or daughter: why, it may even have been your own wedding—if there are any newly-weds here. Well, now, whenever that wedding was, may I ask you a question about it? Was it a joyful ocacsion, marvellous food, good humour, witty speeches? I am sure it was all those things, set in the context of a happy family reunion. Why, that's what weddings, and wedding receptions, are all about!

Jesus said the kingdom of heaven may be compared to a king who gave a marriage feast: in other words, not only wedding receptions should be joyful things, but the kingdom of heaven as well. The Christian life is, too, for you and for me, to be a time of great jubilation, according to the New Testament. At least, I take it that is what Jesus meant by this parable: otherwise why compare God's kingdom to a wedding reception if He did not mean that (Matt. 22: 1–14)? Why not compare it to a board meeting, or even to a funeral, as He could have done had He chosen?

This is not the only place in the New Testament where response to the call of God is seen in terms of a banquet. To become a Christian, and to be a Christian, is something to be happy about: it calls for great jubilation. I sometimes wonder, however, just what the kingdom of heaven looks like to the outsider, to the man in the street. I have no doubt at all that to most people these days the kingdom of heaven does in fact seem a very serious business indeed—a sort of endless church service, with dark suits and dreary hymns and dismal faces. I am quite sure that that is the impression that a lot of Christians give!

But how wrong that is. Sometimes when I go around my parish, not in a suit and a clerical collar, but a sports jacket and one of my more psychedelic ties, the simple fact of going round a parish like this causes people to comment on it. In these folks' minds this is not normally how a parson dresses; unless they are dressed up like undertakers on duty, they are not doing their job properly! So a lot of good folk think these days.

A fortnight ago I attended the centenary thanksgiving service of a local primary school. The mayor was there; the education officer was there. It could have been a very solemn and stuffy sort of occasion. But during the service, during one of the hymns, half the school children stood up: they got out of their pews and they danced, country style, up and down between the aisles of the church, as the rest of the school sang a hymn. Well, of course, people commented on the fact that children were dancing in church. But I did not see it as dancing in church: I saw it as the offering to God of healthy bodies and youthful enthusiasm and joyful spirit. Why not, in church, jubilation?

"The kingdom of God may be compared to a marriage feast," said Jesus. May I tell you why Christian people can be happy and rejoice? There are many reasons. Because God is still on the throne; because Jesus lived and died and rose again to be our Saviour; because His Holy Spirit is in your life and mine, if we belong to Him by faith; because we can know the forgiveness of our sins day by day, our eternal destiny is secure, and we are on the winning side. And who else but Christian people can say all that? *Jubilation* for the Christian.

But of course, according to this parable there can only be jubilation, on the part of the guests, because there has been first, on the part of the Host, *preparation*. Here I am looking at v. 4: "Behold, I have made ready my dinner, my oxen and my fat calves are killed, and everything is ready." Here is preparation. Picture the host flinging wide the ornate doors of the banqueting chamber to welcome his guests to the feast. Yes, but before you picture the doors flinging open wide, and people flocking in to enjoy the good things set before them, spare a thought for all the hard work that has gone on by way of preparation.

T.K.W.—D 97

We men don't often do that at home, do we? We come in from work; we sit down at table; we say grace; we enjoy our meal; we may give a hand with the tea-towel afterwards. But how little thought we so often give to those hours spent at the shops, and at the kitchen sink, and at the cooker, to make that simple meal possible. And if one simple meal involves all that preparation, how much more a banquet. And if one banquet involves all that kind of preparation, how much more preparation was needed for the reality of which this parable is but a picture.

The king said, "Everything is ready," and he meant it quite literally. For the Christian, everything is ready. This whole world is ready, the whole universe of which our earth is but a tiny part. And that wasn't done overnight: the whole world prepared by God to be the home of life and living things. The world is ready; the human race is ready. Here it is for each one of us to take our allotted part within it. God, having prepared the world, places men and women within the world to have sovereignty over all its parts. And here we are, either a son of Adam or a daughter of Eve, prepared by God to do His perfect will on earth.

But more important, of course, our salvation is ready: for we are sons of Adam and daughters of Eve in more than one sense, not only sharing our forbears' life, but also sharing their lostness, not only sharing their sovereignty, but also sharing their sin, and their need for a Saviour from sin. And what preparation was needed for that! The whole sweep of Old Testament history was needed to make ready the Holy Land as the cradle in which the sinless Saviour was to be born. And by that very same sweep of history, involving the very same people and the very same places, making ready the cross on which the sin-bearing Saviour was to die. From sinless Baby to sin-bearing Saviour, the only sinless Person who ever lived was made on the cross the depository, the refuse dump if you like, for the sins of the whole world. The Son of God, who had never had a moment's separation from His Father from all eternity, tasted there the utter desolation of orphanhood. This, and nothing less than this, was the price required by the Father for our eternal salvation; and this was the price—willingly offered and willingly paid—by the Son. As I say, from the cradle to the cross, from sinless to sin-bearing, one small step for the Man Jesus, but one gigantic leap for mankind: for by it, sinners as we are, we come right into the presence of a holy God.

There was no other good enough
To pay the price of sin;
He only could unlock the gate
Of heaven, and let us in.

And when He cried out on the cross, "It is finished!" He was proclaiming to you and to me that the gates were open, the banquet was ready. Preparation had been done.

Jubilation in this parable; preparation; and following hard on this we have the *invitation*. The invitation was extended three times, in vv. 3, 4 and 9, to the potential guests. Even then they made light of it. They found their excuses. "Too busy," said some. "Not enough time," said others. Yes, we can all find an excuse for not doing something we don't want to. And folk today still make their own excuses for not accepting the most generous offer this whole world affords. Those who neglect salvation, choose not to

98

choose, forgetting that to choose not to choose is, in fact, to choose, as those who never went in to the feast found to their cost.

But let us see what happened to those who accepted, because I read that in the end many did throng into the gates: and "the wedding hall was filled with guests" (v. 10). And for them, have no doubt at all, there was *satisfaction* —the satisfaction of being in the presence of the king. For what is basically an invitation to a wedding? It is not just an invitation to eat sausages on sticks, or to listen to witty speeches. An invitation to a wedding is an invitation to come into the presence of the host, and to meet him, and to get to know him better, and to have fellowship.

This surely is why the offer of the Christian Gospel in 1971 is so attractive. At the heart of the blessing of the Christian Gospel today is the fact that we are invited into the presence of the King, that King who just loves to have fellowship with His people. Why, this is what the Christian faith is all about— fellowship with the King.

We have an overseas friend staying with us at the moment, and last month I took her to Windsor for an afternoon's outing: I wanted to show her the castle, and the royal apartments. So we drove out of London along the M4 toward Windsor, full of anticipation, until we turned a certain curve in the road about three miles out of the town where the castle looms majestically before one on the road. "Nearly there," we thought, as the castle came into view. But as I saw Windsor Castle my heart sank, because on top of the round tower the Royal Standard fluttered in the breeze, and I knew at once—and I had to explain this to my overseas friend—that if the Standard flies on Windsor Castle, the Queen is in residence: and if the Queen is in residence, the state apartments are closed to visitors. And sure enough, our trip to Windsor was a most disappointing affair. It was all "No admittance", "Authorised persons only", "Keep off the grass", that sort of notice.

I thought at the time, "Well, fair enough. Her Majesty has her own private life to live." But how unlike the Christian and his Sovereign. If He is in residence, then we are invited in, to be right with Him in the heavenly places, to enjoy fellowship day by day—not only us with Him in residence, but He in us in residence. And the Royal Standard, of course, has a place in our lives, hasn't it? Isn't it said that joy is the flag that flies in the heart of the Christian man or woman when the King of kings is in residence? I wonder whether we all know that deep, unconquerable joy when He is there.

Some little time ago I was chatting to the former Bishop of Stepney, and he told me of a visit he once made to an East End tenement. He had business on the second floor of a house, and he was about to go down to the ground floor and wend his way home, when something told him to go upstairs to the attic, and to knock on the door. Not knowing quite why he was going upstairs instead of down, he did this: he knocked on the door, and a very weak voice said, "Come in!" and the Bishop went into what he described as the most dark and dingy room he had ever entered. An abattoir next door shut out all the light; and in this room he found a bed and a chair and a table, and sitting in the chair an elderly lady, completely crippled with arthritis, and on the table, a couple of feet in front of her, her lunch, untouched.

The lady told the Bishop that her daughter had left that meal early that morning, before she had gone off to work, and usually the home help came in to feed the lady with the meal left by the daughter; but that particular afternoon the home help had failed to turn up. When he heard that, the Bishop knew why he had been sent upstairs, and who had sent him. He took the meal and fed the lady; he made her comfortable; they chatted together. And he found there, he told me, a Christian lady, full of faith and hope and joy. He had prayer with her, and before he left he promised to put her on his prayer list.

But the dear old soul said to the Bishop, "Please don't bother to put me on your prayer list. You're a Bishop; you are a busy man; you're far too busy to remember me. Besides," she said, "*I've got everything*." And, of course, in a sense she had everything that mattered, for the King was in residence. Satisfaction.

Jubilation, preparation, invitation, satisfaction, and a parable that contains so much joy and happiness concludes in a most dramatic and startling way with an episode that we can best summarise as *destination*. For here at the feast is a man with no wedding garment. Now some folk suggest that eastern practice was that royal hosts used to provide their guests with outer garments in which to attend their banquets. Well, this may be; or it may be that the man simply turned up in unsuitable clothing. At all events, it is clear from the parable in v. 12 that the man was speechless. In other words, when he was challenged he knew that he was in the wrong. He had nothing to say. He could make no excuses. He stood self-condemned.

The meaning is surely this, that although we come to God as we are, as sinners, when we have dealings with Him for the very first time, we cannot go on standing before Him as sinners, to enjoy fellowship on a real and lasting basis. No: having come to Him as sinners, we must then be clothed with the wedding garment of the righteousness of Jesus Christ, by which and in which alone we can stand in the presence of a holy God.

In other words, none of us can enter and enjoy the kingdom of God dressed in the ordinary clothes of our own righteousness. Why, the quality of our own shabby lives is quite enough to keep us out of the kingdom of heaven. For our lives, however good and moral and upright and helpful they may be, still lack that perfect righteousness which is the demand of a holy God. We need that perfect righteousness.

All of us are a bit like the little boy who saw his father working hard in the yard one hot summer's day, and decided to quench his father's thirst. So the little lad went into the kitchen; he got a chair and put it by the china cupboard, and climbed on the chair, and got out a nice, shiny, clean glass. He got off the chair and pulled it over to the sink; climbed on the chair, turned on the tap, and filled his glass with clear, crystal water. Off the chair he got, down the garden to where his father was busily working, holding the glass so carefully in both hands. And he presented it proudly to his father.

But what the little chap did not see was that his own thumbs were both in the glass—filthy, dirty thumbs, from his own little gardening in his own plot. The water was a dirty, cloudy colour when it was handed over to his father.

You see what had happened: the lad's intention was perfect, ten out of ten for wanting to quench his father's thirst. But his achievement was far from being perfect. And his father, thirsty though he was, and loving father that he was, just couldn't drink that offering.

You know, that is so like us—perfect in intention, ten out of ten all of us, for wanting to live a good moral, upright, and helpful life; but in achievement, falling far short of what pleases the heavenly Father, and is acceptable to Him. "All our righteous deeds," as Isaiah reminds us, "are as filthy rags." Yes, but in Christ, and through faith in Christ, the Father looks upon the perfect life of the sinless Son. The life of Jesus was both perfect in intention and in achievement, and the Father accepts us in Him. Christian people are "accepted in the Beloved", clothed with the wedding garment of Jesus Christ. And on being clothed in that, as our parable says, hang eternal issues, our destination.

Eternal issues, yes; but also very down-to-earth and practical issues as well. For what freedom and joy become ours when we wear the garment of Christ's righteousness. Gone all the strain and the stress of trying to please God by the quality of our own lives; trying to please God for the wrong reasons. Gone the need for self-justification, to try to get into God's good books by our own efforts. Why, we are in His book anyway, and He has written our name in the book Himself—His book of life. Yes, there is a tremendous joy and freedom to be had in wearing Christ's garment.

But something else, too: for it is not a freedom to do just as we please as we go through life. The Christian life is not a joy ride in the wrong sense. We have freedom and joy, yes. But those come to us together with a new incentive to live a holy and a purposeful life for Him. And I'll tell you why joy and freedom come with this new incentive. It is because there is something about new clothes, isn't there, that does something for us? We put on that dress, that hat, that suit, and do you know that imperceptibly we change within. I've seen this happen in people: I have seen it happen in myself. We get a little more poise with that new hat on; a little more confidence in that fresh suit; a little more grace—don't ask me why: it happens. No doubt the psychiatrists can tell us. But the nicer we look the nicer we are, and the nicer we tend to become.

Yes, but it is not human clothes that we are thinking about. This is a divine garment. It is Christ's clothing we are wearing. And this means that we, too, should change imperceptibly in its wearing, not so much in the direction of poise as in the direction of purity; not so much in the direction of new confidence as in the direction of more Christ-likeness, becoming like the one whose garment we wear. And this is the Christian target for human life. This is our life's work before us in the realm of Christian character. But, why, this is no sacrifice to have this as a target; to have a life's work of that nature. Whoever thought it was a sacrifice to get out of our working clothes, and to put on something special for a wedding? That is no sacrifice: for we are all going to a wedding; that is our destination.

At least it is for those who are properly dressed. We are all going to a wedding, and we are going to have a marvellous time.

The Christian's Threefold Peace

By the Rev. Keith A. A. Weston, M.A.

From Romans 5:1, I would like to pick out the phrase, "peace with God through our Lord Jesus Christ". Surely this ranks as one of the most thrilling statements in the New Testament. The leader of the Crusader Bible class in which I was a small boy, once told us of his own childhood, and of how, as he had been put to bed regularly by his mother, he was allowed to stay awake until his father came home from business, and he would tell us of the family nightly ritual. The key in the front door, the greeting for Mother, the noise of the umbrella going into the umbrella stand, the bowler hat on the peg, and then clump, clump, clump as Father came up the stairs to the boy's bedroom. And then, with Father sitting at the bedside, the joy of telling him all the things that had happened that day, a hug and a kiss, and goodnight, lights out.

And, said that godly man, one day, when the french windows were open on a lovely summer evening, he kicked a football straight through the open window, and it struck the grandfather clock. It smashed the glass, and the clock stopped. The horror of what he had done shook him deeply, because he had often been told by Father that if he wanted to play football he could by all means play football, but not in front of the french windows. And he had often heard Father tell Mother of the history of the grandfather clock; how it had belonged to the family for many years, and had never stopped. And there it was, the glass smashed and the clock stopped for the first time in centuries.

"Mother, I think I would like to go to bed." "Why, darling, it is very early. It is not time for bed." "I am not feeling too well. I think I'd like to go to bed." And he went upstairs as quickly as he could, pulled the bedclothes over his head, and tried as hard as he could to get to sleep.

Then he heard the key in the door, the umbrella in the umbrella stand, the greeting for Mother, the bowler hat on the peg. Clump, clump, clump. I can never remember how the story ended!

But are there not people like this in the world today? If I may turn a rather stupid illustration to sublime truth: the Lord is coming again, and every eye shall see Him, and everyone shall stand before His judgment throne. And how many will stand there with peace in their minds and hearts and lives? St. Paul says here: "We have peace with God through our Lord Jesus Christ." We shall face Him one day, and by grace call Him "Abba, Father" through the Spirit, because we are at peace with our God. Being justified by faith we have this peace here and now; and if the Lord were to come tonight, we'd rejoice at His coming.

But tragically there are many people who will face that day with no peace in their heart. "Is it really possible," we ask, "for me, with my past, to stand in the presence of the Holy God with peace in my heart? Can it really be true that I can have a conscience void of offence before God? I, whose life, if I am honest, is a trail of sin and rebellion against God. Can it be true that I can be at peace with God, when He knows, and I know in my heart that He knows, the hidden depths of sin in my life that even my nearest and dearest do not know about, and which, if I am honest, I would be truly ashamed for them to know?"

If there is any doubt in your mind, read and ponder again this thrilling phrase: "Therefore since we are justified by faith, we have peace with God." It is a statement of fact for the Christian: "we have peace with God through our Lord Jesus Christ". And through Him we have obtained access to this grace in which we stand here today, with all the problems of the world, and its sinful pressures upon us. We stand. We are not bowled over. We have peace in this sinful world. And what is more, the thought of sharing the glory of God fills us with joy. Paul says that, when one day we stand by grace before his throne, we rejoice. We have peace through our Lord Jesus Christ.

I would like you to look closely at this passage, so that we can answer two questions. First, *What is the source of this peace?*

May I draw your attention to two vital phrases which flank the statement. "Therefore, *since we are justified by faith . . .*" is the first vital phrase. Not everyone has peace with God. Only those who are justified by faith have peace with God. Now that is a difficult theological word for many of you, so may I remind you of what your Sunday-school may have taught you long ago. "Justified" means just-as-if-I-had-never-sinned. God can look at the Christian person who has put his trust in the Lord Jesus Christ, and see him as one just-as-if-he-had-never-sinned. You see, it is my sin that robs me of peace. Deal with my sin, and you will restore peace. It is those of us who are justified who know peace with God.

But, you ask, secondly, *How can my sin be dealt with?* How can God look at me as though I had never sinned? Because that is an incredible thing for me to believe.

The other vital phrase that flanks this glorious statement is—"we have peace with God *through our Lord Jesus Christ*". It is not of my deserving that God can look at me like that. It is not of my doing that God gives me peace in my heart. It is His doing, and His alone. It is through Jesus Christ our Lord that we can have peace with God; because, you see, He has done something about the sins which destroy our peace.

Now may I remind you that there are no chapter divisions in the original, and therefore we must read these verses in conjunction with the last verses of the previous chapter. 4:25 reads, "He, Jesus, was put to death for our trespasses, and raised for our justification." The Lord Jesus Christ brings us peace because He was put to death for our sins, and raised for our justification. We have, therefore, as Paul puts it in Colossians 1:20, "peace through the blood of his cross"—and that is the only place where a sinner can find peace with God: at the foot of the cross. You see, He is spoken of here as the Saviour, first whose death puts right what was wrong; and secondly, as the Lord who is alive to apply to sinners the fruits of His death. He was put to death for our sins, and raised again for our justification. The Lord who died on Calvary's cross, that He might win peace for sinners, is the one who is about His business in this great tent, applying the fruits of His saving death, that we might be justified.

Now St. Paul, I believe, spells out this tremendous truth in the following verses, and I would like to draw your attention to three similar phrases, in vv. 6, 8 and 10. Note the connection between our sins and their effect; and our Saviour and what He has done for us.

v. 6: While we were yet helpless, Christ died.

v. 8: While we were yet sinners, Christ died.

v. 10: While we were enemies, we were reconciled to God by the death of His Son.

In three succinct phrases Paul puts before us the appalling facts about our sin and what it does to us, and the glorious truths of what the Lord Jesus Christ has done for us when he died upon the cross: while we were helpless, while we were sinners, while we were enemies, Christ died. And so through His death we may have peace in each of these situations.

May I draw the truth out for you? Because Christ has died, there is—

PEACE FOR THE HELPLESS. That is what v. 6 says. The word "helpless" means utterly incapable of helping ourselves. Utterly incapable of our own salvation. The Authorised Version says, "When we were yet without strength . . ." We were totally impotent to help ourselves. And you will notice that this feature, our helplessness, as a result of our sin, is equated in that verse with ungodliness: "While we were helpless, Christ died for the ungodly." To be ungodly, is to be a helpless person. To be in a state of ingodliness, is to be in a state of hopeless helplessness; and it was while we were in that condition that God, praise be to His name, did something about it.

Some years ago our youngest child, Mary, contracted measles. She was terribly ill, and for a whole fortnight, if my memory serves me aright, she ran a very high temperature, and just lay hot, covered with spots, totally helpless. One couldn't raise a smile from her, not even an opening of her eyes. It seemed that she had lost all sense of wanting to live. And I tell you, we were very worried about her. For a whole fortnight she just lay there, her little frail body totally weak, without any strength at all. Thank God she revived, and she is perfectly fit and well. But I remember sitting on her bedside trying my best to get a smile out of our Mary, who is a cheery little girl. Totally no response.

The Lord Jesus Christ saw us like that, in our ungodly state. That is what the poison of sin does to a life. That is the kind of thing that Satan is doing to a life which is ungodly—sucking the very strength of life away, until that person is bound and helpless in his sins; and while he was yet helpless, Christ did something about it. He died for the ungodly. "He took the cup of bitterness," says the Scripture, "and He drank it to the very dregs." I wonder if this could be likened to the drawing of the poison of the system of the person who is helplessly strengthless in their poisoned sinfulness? And the Lord didn't shudder at that fact. He came and sucked that poison away, until there was none left; and He died that we might live. There is peace for the helpless because Christ has died. And this Saviour lives today to apply to your heart and life the fruits of His saving death. He wants to give life to the lifeless, help to the helpless. He wants to conquer the effect of sin in your life.

Notice again, in v. 8, that Paul furthers his argument—". . . while we were yet sinners". I want to put a title to this, and explain why I put it. Because Christ has died, I say, secondly, there is—

PEACE FOR THE HOPELESS. Now I am quite sure that you will not need me to remind you that the word "sin" means "a missing of the mark". A classic expression of this is in Romans 3: 23, where sin is equated with falling short of the glory of God. And if we fall short of the glory of God, what hope is there for our eternity? We face a Christless eternity because we fall short of the glory of God, and nought that defileth shall enter into heaven. And if we fall short because of our sinful defilement, we are indeed hopeless people. There is no hope for eternity, and death will be a tragic experience; and I hate to think what Scripture speaks about a Christless eternity.

But "while we were yet sinners"—those who fall short of God's standards for heaven—"Christ died for us". And so for the hopeless there is hope. For those who have no peace in their hearts, because they know deep down that their situation is hopeless, Christ has died, and brought peace to them. While we were still like that, Christ died. He didn't wait for us to turn to Him. Long before ever we thought of Him, He had thought of us. Christ has stepped down, so to speak, and has allowed Himself to be condemned in our stead, and to bear in His own body on the tree, in perfect obedience to the will of God, all that that fearsome condemnation means for us. And Christ died for sinners. "He was wounded," says the old prophet, "for our transgressions." Not His own. He had none. But He saw you and me as hopeless sinners, our lives stained and marred at every point: and Christ was wounded for our transgressions; bruised for our iniquities.

There is peace, then, for the ungodly, hopeless sinner, because Christ has died in his place.

Thirdly, because Christ has died, there is—

PEACE FOR THE HOSTILE. "While we were enemies, we were reconciled to God by the death of His Son" (v. 10). I think this verse tells me that I must never be trivial about my sins, because it describes the state of the sinner as being an enemy of God. Its effects are so devastating that St. Paul says "While we were still enemies, Christ died for us."

Sin brings the sinner into a state of war with God. Let us not mistake that truth. "While we were enemies." "Well," you say, "I was not an enemy of God. I didn't bear Him any evil thoughts." No, but the sin in your life brings you into a state of war with God whether you realise it or not, and you are an enemy of God if you are not justified by faith. Jesus said, "You are my friends if you do what I command you." Now put that round the other way. If you do not do what Christ commands you, you are His enemy. You cannot have it two ways. "Those who are not with us are against us." There is no halfway mark. You are either for Christ, a friend of Christ, because you keep His commands, or you are against Him because you fail to keep His commands, or rebel against them.

"Enemies of the cross of Christ" is a telling phrase of the apostle. James wrote that to be a friend of the world is to be an enemy of God. And how often the friendship of the world creeps imperceptibly into our hearts and lives; and hardly realising what we are doing, we accept the world's standards and the world's motives and the world's desires, and we become friendly with the world. And, says St. James, that hard-hitting apostle, the friendship of the world brings you to become an enemy of God.

I say again, let us not be trivial with our sins. For the sins which we so often treat trivially, and try to shrug off, bring us into such a relationship with God that we are actually in a state of hostility with Him. We are against Him. We are His enemies.

Now will you notice the wonderful truth that "while we were yet enemies" —if we can take the same phrase—God still loved us. It is the very person who is spitting hostility against God, that God loves. It is in the very place where we blaspheme against God and rebel against Him and say, "We will not have this Man to rule over us," that God says "I love you." While we were enemies, God went about the reconciling of these people to Himself through the death of His Son. Isn't that glorious?

I have said that we need to be very careful not to underestimate what sin does to us. May I put the contrary thought? We must not underestimate either what Christ did when He died upon the cross. "You who were once estranged and hostile," writes St. Paul to the Colossians (1:21), "He (Jesus) has reconciled by His death." Then there follows, in 2:15, "For in His cross He disarmed the principalities and powers, and made a public example of them, triumphing over them in it.'

Now I wonder if you have noticed that verse, Colossians 2:15, in your Scriptures? It tells us that the cross is not the greatest tragedy of history. It is in fact the greatest victory of history. Do not underestimate what Christ was doing when He died upon the cross; for when the Lord went to the cross, He went to war with principalities and powers, and Satan, the prince of this world. And I believe that the reason why the Lord Jesus Christ in the garden of Gethsemane sweated great drops of blood was not the physical pain of the cross: it was the thought of this all-out confrontation and warfare with Satan that was to happen on Calvary. Behind that passage in Colossians is the thought that the whole powers of evil, Satan and all his dominions, principalities and powers, massed their strength against the sinless Son of God; and while men watched the cross on the hill called Golgotha, without their ever beginning to realise it, in the spiritual realm a mighty battle was being waged, and there the sinless Son of God disarmed principalities and powers, and made a public example of them, and "triumphed over them in it", which is one translation which is perfectly reasonable of that verse. He made His triumph over them in it, that is to say, in the cross: for that is what he is speaking of.

The cross was not a tragedy. It was a triumph. There the Lord Jesus Christ wrought victory for His people; the greatest triumph and victory the world has ever known. While we were on the wrong side, enemies, Christ died; and in His death He defeated Satan and all his powers, and led captivity captive. That is to say, He came to you and to me in our sinful hostility; He took the shackles off our arms and legs, off our souls, and led us who were captive to Satan and on the wrong side, to be captives of the Prince of Peace. That is what the Lord Jesus Christ did when He died. The world saw and never understood. Have you seen and understood?

So there is peace for the hostile through His cross; and the victorious King offers peace to those who were once enthralled in Satan's dominion. Do you see why I say I think this is one of the most thrilling passages of Scripture? Listen again: "Being justified by faith, we have peace with God through our Lord Jesus Christ." Peace through His cross for the helpless sinner. Are you a helpless sinner? Do you feel the strengthlessness which sin has wrought in your life; powerless to do what you know to be right, powerless to serve God, powerless to do what your conscience tells you is right? Look to the cross, then, where He wrought peace for the hopeless sinner.

And there is peace for the hostile. Does that include you? Do you sometimes find yourself opposed to God in your life? Have you realised what sin does to you? The Lord has won the victory, but you are still marching with the wrong army? Let Him lead you to His own captivity.

May I finish by drawing your attention to those glorious words from the Psalm which St. Paul quotes earlier in this same fourth chapter: "Blessed are those whose iniquities are forgiven, and whose sins are covered; Blessed is the man against whom the Lord will not reckon his sin" (vv. 7–8).

Do you know what that word "blessed" means? It means, "supremely happy". A state of supreme spiritual well-being, deep down in your soul. Christ died that you might have that. Blessed indeed is the man whose iniquities are forgiven. Are yours? Blessed is the man against whom the Lord will not reckon his sin, because Christ died.

Out of the Depth

By the Rev. R. C. Lucas, M.A.

From Psalm 130, I will read the first phrase only: "Out of the depth I cry to thee, O Lord."

I love the Psalms, and I am sure you do; and I value them beyond price, because they have a unique place in the Bible, and also a unique place in the ministry for a Christian believer. The Bible, I suppose, we might call simply the Word of God for men. It is inspired, and therefore it is reliable; and it tells us how the real God speaks to His people. The Psalms, of course, are part of that great revelation; but in a special sense they contain the words of men to God, inspired just the same, and therefore reliable, telling us how a real believer speaks to God. Now this is a very important distinction, and the Psalms in fact give us a God-given standard by which we may know if our experience is true Christian experience, and pleasing to God. In them, as you will have discovered as a Christian by now I guess, you will have found that Christian joy finds perfect expression; that Christian penitence finds perfect expression in the penitential psalms; that Christian longing for revival finds uniquely powerful words; and that Christian bewilderment and despair also find a perfectly apt expression as we bring our hearts to God.

107

And so I turn to Psalm 130 as one of the penitential psalms, because I think it is a God-given word for those who have been, or are at this moment, in the depth. How comforting it is, isn't it, straight away to know that this is a place recognised by God. He knows that His people will sometimes find themselves in this place. Often, of course, it is through our own fault. Sometimes not so, because of the familiar slings and arrows of life. It is, of course, a common experience for unbelievers to find themselves in the depth these days. You will know how, outside in the world, depression and frustration and loneliness are all too common. But we Christians live in the same world, and we are not immune from these things. And it is possible, as a Christian believer, to find ourselves in the depth. I won't list all the reasons why this may be so in our experience. It can be bereavement, that can just take our breath away. It can be a disappointment, a bitter one; a childless marriage; an opportunity that we have missed that we know will never return. It can be in our work and witness for God, or indeed in our daily work as we seek to stand as a Christian; opposition and misunderstanding, which we feel to be terribly unfair. It can be simply the pressure of the spiritual battle. And all these reasons for depression, for going, if you like, into the depth, are aggravated all the more by our own weakness and our own frailty and our sin.

Now this Psalm 130 comes especially to all who are in the depth, and shows us how to come out of the depth. Actually it puts words into our lips. It is not only the word of God to us, but it gives us the very words to speak; and sometimes that is such a help, isn't it? Because we hardly know how to express the deep need that nobody else seems to be able to plumb or to understand.

And so this psalm, in a very wonderful way, is going to put into your lips words that are true and wise and adequate and healing for the position in which you find yourself. This is one of the four psalms that Luther regarded as the greatest of them all. He called it a Pauline psalm, because it is so full of the grace of God; and he consoled himself by reading it repeatedly when in great pressure, pain or peril. I call this a psalm of increasing and growing trust; and as growth is so much a theme of our thoughts this week, let us think of growing trust in God, as we come perhaps out of the depth. Even if you yourself have not had that experience, I hasten to say you will certainly have this experience in the future, and you will certainly have to help other people have this experience. What have you to say to them? Well, I would turn to this psalm.

First, we see that we are *taught to cry to God.*

"Out of the depth I cry to thee, O Lord.

Lord, hear my voice: let thy ears be attentive to the voice of my supplications.

If thou, O Lord, shouldest mark iniquities, Lord, who could stand?

But there is forgiveness with thee, that thou mayest be feared."

Now, we can do one thing from the depth: we can pray. Indeed, it is often said that only when we have had experiences that lead us into the depth, that we begin really to pray again. I am afraid the shameless truth is that were it not for opposition and temptation, and were it not for the need to stand in the world as a Christian witness, we would very seldom really pray, any of us, because we are not, even when renewed by the Holy Spirit, really

108

dependent upon God. And God has to bring experiences into our lives, and sometimes knock us right over by these experiences, in order to cast us, not down into the mud, but down on to our knees. And if God has dealt you some heavy blows, one of the reasons in His mercy and grace is that He might bring you to your knees, that you might again begin truly to cry to God. Every one of us can tell each other to pray to God. The difficulty is to do it; to continue to do it, and to cry from the heart to Him, with reality and truth.

Now you notice that as this man begins to pray, he is no longer an enemy of God. The unregenerate man is an enemy of God, and when he finds himself in the depth he is full of annoyance with God, and immediately he puts God in the dock. "Why," he says. "Why does He do it? That is the kind of God you Christians believe in! I wasn't to blame. I don't see that I have done anything wrong." But, you see, we know that we are listening in these verses to a Christian, to a believer. For him it is quite different. Finding himself in the depth, he knows himself to be in a sense in the dock. For it is in his experience of the depth that he has learned much in a very short time that he would never have learnt before. He has learnt about that false zeal, those unholy ambitions, mixed motives, a deceitful heart, pride and fear: things that he never dreamt were in his heart, God has taught him through this. Most of us learn more about our sinful hearts after we come to know Christ than we ever knew before. It is part of the education of Christians, to be shown what is really in their hearts. Nevertheless, despite the increasing realisation of the weakness and sinfulness of his heart, this Christian believer continues to pray. For prayer, as you will have discovered, is the only refuge of the helpless.

Now what happens when in this experience we begin really to pray? We press into the presence of God again. We wait upon Him, and we wait for His word. Well, a new calm begins to descend upon us. We find that some of the burdens already begin to be lifted; and what is more, a new boldness comes into our voice, a boldness that the Bible demands of us. It tells us to go to the throne of grace with boldness in our need. And do you see what the psalmist does in vv. 3 and 4? He begins to reason with God. Some of the most wonderful chapters and passages in the Bible are when the men of God, who know God, begin to reason with Him on behalf of sinners.

Do you remember Moses? Was there ever a man who knew how to reason with God as he did? "O Lord," he says, "you cannot let your people go. If you let your people go, the heathen will say. . . ." What wonderful arguments he had with God, pressing upon God the reasons for the exercise of His grace. And that is what the psalmist does here. "Oh Lord, I know that I cannot stand before thee; if thou shouldst mark iniquities, Lord, who could stand? With us is wickedness, but with thee is forgiveness."

I wonder if you see that a very wonderful thing is beginning to happen as this man comes out of the depth. He is beginning at last to forget himself. How miserable we are when we are full of ourselves! We can even be full of ourselves in the Christian life; wrapped up with our spiritual troubles and pains. It is a wonderful thing if our eyes are gradually taken off ourselves and our own misery, and we cease to buttonhole everybody about our difficulties and our problems, and our eyes begin to go to God Himself. You see, he is no longer thinking about his own sin—that indeed made him miserable— but he is fixing his eyes upon God; and he says, "Well, I know this about you, that with you is forgiveness." He is beginning to glimpse again the immeasurable wonder of the God of grace.

One of the things that I discovered after I had been a Christian for some time was that I had forgotten that God was a God of grace. It is part of the deceitfulness and wickedness and perverseness of our hearts that, when we begin to grow as Christians, when we learn to please Him more, when we learn some of the first lessons of Christian holiness, we begin—I hardly dare to say it, and yet you will recognise this as the truth—we begin to feel that we have a claim upon God. We begin to feel that we can approach Him no longer simply as a sinner, but as someone who has made some progress in the Christian life. But we never shall possess any holiness which gives us any claim upon God. And sometimes it needs an experience of being brought into the depth, the depth of despair, or the depth of sin, before we realise that this is so.

I think it was Dr. Barnhouse who used to say, "We think we have fallen from grace, only to find that we have fallen into grace." Yes, it is from the depth that we begin to discover what kind of a God we are dealing with. The whole of our life is simply one long discovery of the grace of God. We didn't really know that we needed that grace when we first came to Him, perhaps when we were young. I know I need His grace now; and you are just discovering it. It may be you discover it only after one term on the mission field, and you come back and you say, "Now I know that I above all need the grace of God."

We have thought this evening about the blessedness of Bible forgiveness. It is a very wonderful subject, isn't it? I am sure sometime you have taken your Bible and gone through many of the ways in which forgiveness is expressed for the Christian. How God says He will not remember our sins. That is a tremendous truth, isn't it? One that I believe we have to have wrought into our own lives. It was something that God taught me in my first years in the ministry. When you hear so many things said against Mrs. Brown, Mr. Brown, everybody else, and yourself. These things that are going round, darting round corners. And I learnt very soon in my ministry to forget the lot. To forget everything that was said against me, and tell other people who came to me and said what had been done to them, "Forget it." And to find the joy and liberation of simply taking that thing and forgetting it. And then to look up into the face of God and say, "That, Lord, is how you dealt with me. Thank you." I have forgotten. I will not remember. He has blotted out our sins as by a cloud. I often think of that now if I go up in a jet aircraft—something that I am not particularly fond of. But one of the good things is to leave London Airport in the usual drizzle, and then to rise above the cloud and suddenly find yourself amazingly in the blue, and all that rain and dismal mist and dirt and so on forgotten, blotted out by roll upon roll of cloud. It is a wonderful sight. So God has blotted out the misery.

Notice what he says at the end of v. 4. This is the language of the Christian believer: "There is forgiveness with thee, that thou mayest be feared." Here again is the lesson of a mature believer. This is something we only learn as we continue in the Christian life. We learn that the mercy of God is not to be presumed upon.

It is very possible, when we are young Christians, to have an idea of God as though He is just one of ourselves; almost to bring Him down to our

110

level. But, the more you grow in the knowledge of God, the more you see the greatness of God, and the more you see the condescension of His forgiveness; and the more careful you become not to grieve Him, the more you fear to grieve Him, and the more you fear His chastening. We shall never be kept in a happy or holy position before God unless we fear Him. That is a very simple lesson. It is so simple that I fear many of you may miss it. But I do ask you not to miss it.

If you have an experience of being in any sense in the depth, the first lesson that God will teach you is to cry to Him. It may be that you have not really been praying in this sense from the heart for a very long time.

Now there is a progression in this psalm, and as we go on to v. 5, we see that the second thing God teaches us is to *wait for Him*.

"I wait for the Lord, my soul waits, and in His word I hope.

My soul waits for the Lord more than watchmen for the morning, more than watchmen for the morning."

One of the lessons we have to learn as we continue in God's grace, is that His time is not our time, just as His ways are not our ways. He does not, as far as I can see, immediately reveal either His presence or His plans to those who cry to Him. Not always. We long for Him, but we have to learn to wait for Him.

Let me, if I may, give you some rather trivial illustrations. I speak almost as a fool, and yet they have made it plain to my own mind. I take you to the city from which I come, and I imagine the office boy going to call upon the boss to sharpen his pencil, or to do some trivial act, to brush his shoes. He goes to the boss, and waits in his waiting room. The secretary says, "Wait there until he wants you." I cannot imagine that the office boy would go straight in the door without knocking, and say, "I've come to do your shoes, are you ready?"

Now turn it the other way round. Let is say that the boss is going down to the basement to the office boy. Do you suppose that, taking one look into the office boy's cubby hole and seeing him halfway through his tenth chocolate biscuit, he waits tentatively in the corridor and says, "It's perfectly all right, I'll wait." No, of course not; he goes straight into the cubby hole and says, "I want you to take this message across the road to another office." He doesn't wait.

It is the inferior who waits for the superior; not the other way round. It is not God, so to speak, who is waiting for us. It is we who are to wait for Him.

Sometimes you will have discovered that you have to go to prayer and to penitence, and you have to go to the waiting room. You have to wait on God, and nourish yourself in His Word, as the psalmist tells us to do here in v. 5, and to wait for God to reveal Himself to you in a new way, and to answer the problems and the difficulties that you bring to him.

Another illustration. Again I speak foolishly. One can get the impression from some people that the situation is like this: that I am sitting at a table, and that I feel the need of something, and I ask God for it, and He will get it for me immediately, as though God is a waiter, walking round the table bringing me exactly what I want. When I hear some talk, some prayer, that is the impression I get. But that is nowhere to be found in the Bible. In the Bible it is God who is seated at the table. It is I who am waiting upon Him. It is He who asks me to do things for Him. He is the one who commands; and

I wait upon Him and bring Him what He wants. God is not going to answer your prayers exactly as you want and when you want; and I thank God for it. We have to wait. It is part of the humility of being a creature. It is part of the humility of being a child of God. It is a lesson that takes a little time to learn, first to cry to Him and then, when we have cried, to wait.

Now notice the progression in vv. 7 and 8. After He has taught us to wait for Him, as the watchman waits for the dawn, He teaches us *to hope in Him*. I think I would rather put this, "be confident in Him", because that is what the word "hope" means. Let me read vv. 7 and 8.

"O Israel, hope in the Lord: for with the Lord there is steadfast love, and with him is plenteous redemption.

And He will redeem Israel from all his iniquities."

Now I trust that nothing I have said will give you a harsh view of the God we Christians love and worship. But while my expression of these truths may have been inadequate, I have taken this psalm as a guard against a false sentimentality of God which belittles our almighty Father.

Our happiness as Christians—and we must learn this soon—our happiness as Christians lies in God doing what He pleases, when He pleases. Our misery is in God doing what we please, because we will have no other. We have got to learn as Christians to let God be God.

Now it is a tremendous thing when we Christians can take our hands off the tiller, and trust God to be God. Does that seem a shocking thing to say? No; so great is the pride and wickedness of our hearts, that we imagine we can do these things more wisely and better than He can. What a tremendous relief it is, and what a joy it is, to let God be God. And as an old writer says on this psalm, "We can afford to let God be God, because He has three wonderful companions with Him." His first companion we have already met: "With thee is forgiveness." The other two companions are mentioned in v. 7: "With the Lord there is steadfast love"; and with Him is His third companion, "plenteous redemption". That is a delightful phrase; but I think here the New English Bible puts it rather more powerfully. Listen to the New English Bible describing these two friends: "For in the Lord is love unfailing, and great is His power to set men free."

That is the message that God brought to my own heart, I believe, to pass on to you from vv. 7 and 8. When I have cried to the Lord and waited upon Him, I can be confident in Him that He will deliver; for if there is one thing that is said about God from the beginning to the end of the Bible, it is that He is a great deliverer. After all hope has gone, again and again in the Bible story, God comes down to deliver; always beyond belief, and yet He comes. And I want to urge you to be confident in Him to deliver. Not to be confident in anyone else, for here in v. 8 the emphasis in the sentence is on the word "He". *He* will deliver; no one else. I believe He can deliver our nation; and that is not a glib thing to say. With this psalm in front of me, I can believe no other, nor can you. "O Israel, hope in the Lord. He will redeem all iniquity."

He can deliver you, I believe, from your situation on the mission field, where you have found yourself, maybe, at cross purposes; maybe entwined in a situation not of your own choosing, but which has cast you into the depth. God can deliver. He can deliver you in the present crisis in your own life here at home. He can deliver you from the sin that besets and plagues you.

112

I have sat on a hard seat in this tent listening to talks wondering if God really could deliver. Wondering if what the speaker said was true, or whether it was something he had just got up and had to say. I am rather touched by this myself, and it seems almost now as if the psalmist is giving a testimony: that he is no longer thinking of himself, that he is turning to others, and he says, "O Israel, do be confident in the Lord, because I know that He can deliver." By the grace of God I can say that to anybody who is sitting on a seat as I was years ago at Keswick. I can say, *He does deliver.* I can testify with sober reality that the Lord can redeem us from our iniquities, and set us free from the sins that plague us. He can. No one else can. And part of our Christian happiness is learning to be confident that He will and can.

Glance back, then, at these three stages in a man who travels out of the depth. He is taught, first, to cry to God; to take his place once again at the throne of grace—a forgotten place—to persevere and to press into that seat of mercy. He is taught, secondly, to wait for the Lord; to be humble, to know that he has no claim upon God, but that God will reveal Himself when His time comes, and that the light will dawn in the darkness of his situation when it pleases our loving God. And then he is taught to be confident in the Lord. When he has waited, that confidence grows; and that is the secret of a happy life on the heights, taken out of the depth to live on the height with God, confident that if at the moment He has not yet appeared to deliver, He will; for "He will redeem Israel from all his iniquities."

The refurbished Moot Hall, after whitewash had been removed, revealing the pleasant grey-green Cumberland stone.

Below: A picturesque corner of Keswick, just off Main Street, with Skiddaw in the background.

114

Wednesday July 14th

10 am Bible Reading

The Way to Christian Stability
(3) False Teachers (2 Peter 2:1–22)
Rev. R. C. Lucas

TAPE NO. 292

11.50 am Forenoon meeting

Bringing the King Back
Rev. James Dunlop

TAPE NO. 304

3 pm Afternoon meeting

The Spirit-orientated Life
Rev. K. A. A. Weston

TAPE NO. 304a

7.45 pm Evening meeting

The Key to Fruitfulness
Rev. Alan Redpath

TAPE NO. 391

The Lordship of Christ
Rev. G. B. Duncan

TAPE NO. 301a

Call to Sanctification

An outstanding feature of Keswick in Convention week for those privileged to attend, is the Reception for missionaries and overseas visitors, following the Wednesday afternoon meeting, in the small tent, at 4 p.m. After a period of informal fellowship—a grand opportunity of meeting folk from all parts of the world—a roll-call revealed that seventy-two countries were represented; and the chairman offered prayer for our less-favoured fellow-Christians behind the iron and bamboo curtains. A Brazilian folk-song in Portuguese was sung by the Glass family—the Rev. David and Mrs. Glass, of the Rio bookshop, with their three sons and one daughter: bearers of an honoured name in the story of missions in South America. In a brief, appropriate message on the woman who broke her alabaster box of ointment over the feet of Jesus, the Rev. R. C. Lucas said she did something more beautiful, more important, and more lasting than she knew. So do all who render sacrificial service which is an expression of love.

Incidentally, in the meeting which preceded the Reception—in the large tent—the Rev. Keith Weston had enlisted the aid, as "devil's advocate", of the chairman, Canon Alan Neech, general secretary of BCMS, and a recently appointed member of the Convention Council.

Wednesday evening's meeting was one which very many will long remember. It is customary for the Convention to reach its culmination on Thursday, with a call to complete commitment to Christ. The issue of His Lordship in the life of every listener was so clearly presented this evening by Dr. Alan Redpath and the Rev. George Duncan, however, that manifestly for great numbers the hour of decision had come.

Dr. Redpath prepared the way for the challenge through Mr. Duncan, with a powerful address on the key to a fruitful life. From 1 Peter 3:15, Mr. Duncan urged that the Lordship of Christ in the life of the believer is the supreme issue of our day. He presented his challenge under three headings—*the rights on which His claim is based*, as Creator and Redeemer; *the reign in which His will is done*—and Mr. Duncan indicated practical aspects of His Lordship, in the submission of our will to His, our whole life to His plan and purpose for us; and *the room in which His throne will stand*—our hearts: not "on our lips" or even "in our lives", but, says Peter, "in your hearts reverence Christ as Lord" (*RSV*).

In the hush of the manifest presence and probing of the Spirit of God, Mr. Duncan presented his final, personal challenge to every hearer—"What does the Lord want with *your* life?" And in that solemn moment, response was made as heads and hearts were bowed in prayer.

Doubtless this was the climactic moment for very many: a never-to-be-forgotten confrontation with the Lord, determining the entire pattern and character of life in the future. It was a clear call to sanctification of heart and life.

116

The Way to Christian Stability

(3) FALSE TEACHERS (2 Peter 2:1–22)

By the Rev. R. C. Lucas, M.A.

The subject for this morning is—The False Teachers. I want to start with two introductory words, to set the scene for this chapter. First, l want you to notice the strong, even passionate language that Peter uses about these false teachers. I think I am right in saying that this is rather too highly flavoured for our sensitive modern palate. But the reason why Peter uses such strong language of condemnation concerning these false teachers is because, on the human level alone, he feels very deeply about it. I do not think he knew anything of that false version of tolerance that we have in our day, when tolerance is sometimes just another word for indifference. He was not indifferent about the truth of God; therefore when men mutilated that truth, altered or destroyed it, he felt strongly. But there is more than his human feelings. He is also an apostle of Jesus Christ; therefore he is revealing to us the divine viewpoint. And to God, such teaching as these men brought was offensive, because it was poisonous to His people. Therefore we can be sure that Peter is giving us a true picture of these men, of what they are doing, of the harm they are bringing, and, indeed, of the motives of these men—which we should not dare to judge; and from this warning, we must be advised to take warning in our own day.

Let me quote from Michael Green's commentary: "Doubtless such stringent condemnation as Peter's appears to twentieth-century readers as inappropriate, because we have largely lost any sense of diabolical danger of false teaching, and have become dull to the distinction between truth and falsehood in ideas, as we have to the distinction between right and wrong in behaviour." That, I think, helps to explain to us something which makes this chapter rather strange and even unattractive to us—the frank, and even passionate feeling with which the apostle writes.

The second word of introduction is a question: Were these false teachers outside the church, or inside? And the answer to that, of course, is in v. 1, "False prophets also arose among the people, just as there will be false teachers among you"—that is, within. What he is talking about in this chapter is a party or parties within the visible church, not sects without. This is nearly always the case in the New Testament; and after all, nearly every New Testament epistle is written over against a background of controversy with false teaching. Yet I believe this is almost as persistently evident today. One commentator on 2 Peter regards the false teachers of this chapter as being rather like the theosophists of today. Now if in fact this false teaching

117

is just equivalent to the theosophists or the Jehovah's Witnesses or what you will, it would be very easily recognisable, and it would be hardly worth while for Peter to spend so much time defining and denouncing them. Every well-instructed Christian knows that these movements are not at all Christian, either in their beginnings or their end.

No, the men we are dealing with here—and this is what makes our study so important—were professing Christian teachers. Furthermore, they were often more successful in their results than the ordinary orthodox, true teachers of the faith. How, then, are we to interpret this chapter? Well, it is impossible to know exactly what was the false teaching that the apostle was attacking. I think this is by the Spirit's ordering and inspiration. If we could easily label these false teachers, we should put them in a docket; we should say, "Well, we'll avoid that!" and we should read the danger signals no more.

I believe by the Spirit's wisdom we are given here many symptoms of false teaching. We shall not find all these symptoms in any one particular brand of false Christian teaching: but we shall learn from such a chapter as this how to recognise the significant symptoms of men taking the wrong turning. So this is an immensely important chapter. It is not talking about people right outside; it is talking about people who profess to be Christians, who are acknowledged as Christian teachers, and often acknowledged as Christian leaders.

Now in vv. 1–3 the Christians are alerted to this danger. The chapter division, again, destroys the connection between 1:21 and 3:1. 1:21, you remember, was talking about the inspiration of the true prophet: he spake "from God. *But* false prophets . . ." not moved by the Holy Spirit: that is the implication ". . . also arose among the people . . ." in the day of the prophets ". . . just as there will be false teachers among you." The plague of Isaiah and Jeremiah and other great prophets was the false prophets, who often stood alongside and said things that were much more attractive, and sometimes much more compelling, and which many more people would listen to. And the plague of his own day, said Peter, was the new teachers who were insinuating their teaching upon the Christians, and drawing people away.

Now in these first three verses I want to notice a number of factors. I am going to put them under five headings.

(i) *The church*—the church local, that is—*is divided*. This is the meaning of the words, "destructive heresies", for the word "heresies" originally simply meant "choices". It comes from the idea that certain people pick and choose the doctrines that they are going to emphasise. From that it comes to mean a school of thought that emphasises a certain side of Christian truth. And you will know that most heresies start with an exaggeration, or a false emphasis on one side of Christian truth. A choice is made; a school of thought is formed; and so a division is caused in the body of Christ. The church local is divided.

Very frequently this is associated with a man, and becomes a personality cult. We get this throughout the New Testament. In 11 Corinthians 1, you remember: "I belong to Apollos, I belong to so-and-so." And the answer of the apostle is that, if they are true Christian teachers, you don't belong to them: they belong to you. The true Christian teacher does not have people belonging to him, on his apron strings, over whom he is lord: he belongs

118

to them, he is their servant. But these people do tend to be lords; they tend to have dominion, they tend to have people following them. Somebody said to me two days ago in Keswick, The mistake we made—talking about a certain Christian movement—was that we followed a man. The church local, then, is divided. Secondly—

(ii) *The Lord is denied.* "They secretly bring in destructive heresies, even denying the Master who bought them." A very telling, almost pathetic phrase, isn't it, from the pen of this writer. Now it is not possible fully to know all that he intends by this phrase: but in some way the false teachers denied the authority and Lordship of Jesus Christ. This can be done in a number of ways. One of the ways is to deny the authority of His teaching. It has often struck me as very interesting that in Mark 8:38, Jesus says we are not to be ashamed of *Him and His words.*

When I was a Christian at school, I remember being tempted to be ashamed of Jesus. When I became a theological student, I was tempted to be ashamed of His words. It is easy enough to see that those are different sides of the same thing. The Christian is committed not only to the authority of Christ the Person, but to the authority of Christ as a teacher. To him the Lord's teaching is the last word—the first and the last. Of these teachers, it is true that they often denied the Lord in this way. The church is divided; the Lord is denied. Thirdly—

(iii) *The many are attracted.* "Many will follow their licentiousness" (v. 2). This reminds us that success pure and simple, in terms of numbers, is no proof of truth. A big crowd at meetings is no certainty that God is at work. Many people follow these false professing Christian teachers, and many people are attracted and drawn to new teaching. There are some people who are always looking for new things. These are common experiences. V. 14 of this chapter says of these people, "They entice unsteady souls." Do you see, there is our theme again? Unstable people. It is the mark of the very young Christian to be unstable, naturally. He has not yet begun to get that solidity of experience and understanding. And it is they particularly who are drawn after the new teachers. The many are attracted. Fourthly—

(iv) *The way of truth is reviled* as a result of this. "Many will follow . . . and because of them *the way of truth* will be reviled." This is a common way of describing Christianity. In the Acts of the Apostles the Christian faith is called "the way" six times, also "the way of the Lord", also "the way of salvation"; and here, in Peter, "the way of truth".

When the false teachers have done their work, and standards have been lowered—as we shall see later on—and Christians are becoming exaggerated and excited in a way that does not bring honour to God, shrewd men of the world outside the church see the results and are naturally critical. The cause of Christ is discredited. Peter is very sensitive to this. I have not time to look at some of the cross-references in 1 Peter, but you will see there that he is very sensitive to this matter of criticism from the outside, and he warns young Christians not to imagine that all criticism is due to their faithfulness. Some criticism is due to our foolishness. And he tells us in 1 Peter 4 to "examine ourselves", to make up our minds which is which. The way of truth is reviled.

Fifthly, about these false teachers in this preliminary note, which alerts the Christians: *Christian people are exploited.* "In their greed they will exploit you with false words" (2:3). I must turn to a cross-reference which is very striking, in 1 Peter 5:2. Here is the mark of the true leader, the true under-shepherd. "Tend the flock of God that is your charge, not by constraint but willingly, not for shameful gain but eagerly, not as domineering over those in your charge, but being examples to the flock." Now there you see what it is to be a true shepherd. We are not to do it for gain, or for prestige and power. The Lord's people are sometimes exploited, not for money so much as for the power and prestige they give to the people they follow.

This was the case of poor Balaam, in v. 15. These false teachers followed "the way of Balaam". It is an extraordinary story: this true prophet of God, who knew very well what the truth was, and how Balak came to him with very extensive fees, his cheque book in hand—and a royal cheque book has always been something, even in those days. And poor Balaam was in an awful tizzy. No doubt he had his wife also behind him, saying, "We could do with this extra!" And Balaam said, "Lord, I'd very much like to go and prophesy against the people of Israel, and curse them. I know I oughtn't to; but look at this money! We must be practical." But He refused.

And then the king sent people of importance and influence to Balaam. This has always been a weak point among Christian teachers! We are all of us susceptible to the world's blandishments; and money is not so powerful, in winning our allegiance, as people of influence, people of importance. Many a man faced with this begins to waver. He wants—we all want, don't we, in our hearts?—recognition, power, influence. Let us be frank about it. We know the wickedness of our hearts; and if we are Christian leaders we have to watch this very carefully. And the mark of the man who has gone along the wrong road, is that he begins to yield to these things: and this always leads to this exploitation of the Lord's people.

This alerting, therefore (vv. 1–3), is one of the most powerful passages in Scripture, to my mind, in showing us, almost by hints, what is the result of beginning to leave the pathway of Christian truth. The church local is divided; the Lord is denied; the many are attracted; the way of truth is reviled; and the Lord's people are exploited. So the Christians are alerted to the certainty of the appearance of false teachers among them.

Now we turn to the next paragraph, vv. 4–10. Here the Christians are reassured, and the certainty of the judgment of these false teachers is made plain to them. As Principal Kelly has said in his recent commentary: "When the wicked are successful, and their misdeeds go unrequited, men tend to imagine that God is asleep. But His apparent inactivity should not be mis-understood." When this kind of false teaching takes place, and many are drawn away, the true teachers tend to despair, and wonder whether God is asleep; if He is looking after His people. And so Peter is anxious to show us that God indeed is watching over them.

Now in vv. 4–10 there is this tremendous sentence repeated: "If God did not spare..." First, "If God did not spare the angels that sinned" (v. 4). Then, "If God did not spare the ancient world" (v. 5). Finally "If God did not spare the cities of the plain" (v. 6). I am not going to look into the details of these verses as stories, except just to say—since in these days people grow up without an extensive Bible knowledge, and misunderstandings can easily arise—that when Peter says that God did not spare the angels, and the an-cient world, and the cities of the plain, because of their sin and the error and evil of their ways, he is not saying that God is a vengeful God. Actually throughout this letter Peter emphasises the amazing patience of God; His forbearance that waits (3:9). In 1 Peter 3:20 he talks of God's patience in the days of Noah.

The mark of God in judgment is that He is patient and forbearing, and slow to anger. But in the end, if men will not turn from their ways of evil and error, God must judge. It is God's strange work; but it is work that He will do. Without that, of course, the moral foundations of the universe would collapse. In case you have been taught to see a division between the Old Testament and the New Testament in the picture of God, turn to Exodus 34:6, when God proclaimed His name to Moses; and this proclamation has never been abrogated, and is still as true today. It is true that the revelation of God in the Old Testament is not complete, until Christ comes, but it is not incorrect; and I would ask you whether you know any description of God anywhere else, greater than this. Moses had asked God to reveal Himself to him: and "The Lord passed before him, and proclaimed, 'The Lord, the Lord, a God merciful and gracious, slow to anger . . .'—this phrase is repeated time after time in the Old Testament—'abounding in steadfast love and faithfulness, keeping steadfast love for thousands, forgiving iniquity and transgression and sin, but who will by no means clear the guilty, visiting the iniquity of the fathers upon the children and the children's children, to the third and fourth generation.' And Moses made haste to bow his head toward the earth, and worshipped." So may we do; for there is a picture of the true God, a God merciful and gracious: but if men presume on that mercy, if men flout the authority of his love toward them, then in the end He will not clear their guilt, and the results of that condemnation and judgment will be seen for many a succeeding generation.

Now that is the truth that is in 2 Peter. It is not a vengeful God, but a patient God, who in the end cannot clear the guilty; and the result of this condemnation lasts, as I say, for many generations, as it did in the ancient world, and on the cities of the plain.

But Peter, like every New Testament writer, can never stop long on the theme of God's judgment. You notice the way in which his logic in a sense takes the wrong turning. You expect him to say, "If God did not spare . . . if God turned the cities to ashes, then He will condemn the false teachers." But suddenly you find him talking about the rescue of His people: for that is what really interests the apostle. He is talking to Christians, and the question that deeply concerns him is this: when judgment comes, what becomes of the innocent? What becomes of God's people? This is a tremendously important question, because God's judgment is still visited upon nations. What becomes of God's people when judgment is visited upon a nation? This is a situation that might very well be relevant. What of our own nation here? And the answer in this wonderful paragraph is that when God visits men in judgment, He preserves and keeps His own church. ". . . but preserved Noah" (v. 5); "He rescued righteous Lot" (v. 7). He keeps His people: He preserves them, and He rescues them. This is a great and glorious truth indeed, isn't it, for people in many parts of the world? God's people cannot be destroyed, either by false teaching, or the consequence of it, the terrible judgments of God. When God visits His enemies with judgment, He visits his people with preserving and keeping power, that they may live through the judgments.

121

Notice the mark of the people of God. One of them, Noah, was a preacher. Even in that ancient world when everything was against it, and years went by and no sign of God, yet he went on preaching the righteousness of God. There is the mark of the people of God: they are active. Lot, well that's a different story, isn't it? If we read the Old Testament alone we might think that Lot was one of whose salvation we are in doubt: he was so hopelessly compromised. And yet three times Peter here tells us that he was "righteous Lot", he was a justified saint. Even though he was compromised, he was a justified man. And we see the fact that he was a believing man, a regenerate man, by the fact that he was "greatly distressed by the licentiousness of the wicked" (v. 7); that he "vexed his righteous soul day after day with their lawless deeds" (v. 8).

That is the mark of the people of God. Even if his testimony is not as bold and bright as Noah's, yet he is a true believer; and compromised as he is in that awful place, he is vexed, and grieved, and shocked by what he sees. It is very easy, isn't it, honestly to lose the sense of shock. I think many of us find that; I find that. It is possible, isn't it, to sit down in front of a television programme which is frankly very funny at times, and not to realise that one is just bypassing things that ought to shock one. If they were on the cinema screen, you might forbid your children to go to them. It is very easy to become rather lax in these things, and to say, "Oh, well, that's just how things are today. And we Christians must not be square. We must not show ourselves to be old-fashioned and shocked, and show ourselves to be grieved, or we shall lose touch with people." It was to Lot's credit, although it may not have been true of members of his family—and perhaps that was part of his trouble—he himself was deeply grieved.

In this paragraph, then, the Christians have been reassured that God knows what He is doing. They can wait for God to act. He will act in judgment, but in that judgment His own people will be preserved and rescued. "He knows how to rescue the godly from trial", and to keep them in peace, as well as how to keep the unrighteous under punishment.

Now I want to turn to the false teachers, and come to closer grips with them. I want to ask two questions which have highly significant answers. The first question is, *Who are these men*, who cause such damage in the church of God, and will receive such condemnation from the hand of God? In v. 10, Peter comes out into the open at last. We have been waiting for him to do so, and he tells us in plain language what these men are. He gives us a description which is a key to the whole chapter: "Especially those who indulge in the lust of defiling passion and despise authority."

The mark of the false teachers, then, is that they indulge their passions, and they despise God's authority. What is particularly interesting is that both these descriptions can be comprehended by one word, and when I discovered this I felt that I had found the key to the chapter. That word is to be found at the end of v. 8: "He was vexed in his righteous soul day after day with their *lawless deeds*." "Lawless" is the word: it is also to be found in 3:17, "Beware lest you be carried away with the error of *lawless men*."

It is quite clear that to Peter, *the* thing to say about these men, *par excellence*, is that they are lawless: they indulge their passions and break God's law; they despise authority, which means they challenge God's law. These are the two sides of lawlessness: "I will not keep His law, and I challenge His right to lay down the law. The actual precepts of God, and the authority of God, I hold in small regard." Now I wonder if this rings any bells in your mind? Surely this is a mark of the society in which we live, and alas as a church, an institutional church in which we live. It is certainly a mark of the society in which we live. People are increasingly lawless in the sense that they break the laws of society with shamelessness, and often impunity; and they despise the authority that society lays down, seen, perhaps, in a particularly despicable way in the attacking of the policemen—as an illustration of this revolt against authority. One of the things on which we pride ourselves in this country is that the police are unarmed. One wonders sometimes how long that is going to go on. Only just outside the church where I work a man was gunned down in Cornhill, the other day: gunned down in front of the church, and a family left without a father. That is not only to break God's law, but it is to flout His authority. We live in a lawless age.

But what worries me is that this lawlessness has invaded the church. We have lived through an extraordinary twenty years. We have heard, for example, through the exponents of the "new morality", that the old laws of the Bible are not necessary to Christian living today; and that many of them have to be re-translated, made more flexible. But even worse, we have been told that this is a time when the authority that men took for granted— the authority of the Bible—cannot any longer be taken for granted. We have got to search for new ways to compel men's belief and set their standards. The Bible is often set aside, sometimes explicitly, but more often implicitly, in a welter of language. We have got to the stage now where we do not really know where we are, because so often the leaders, in trying to paper over the cracks, to produce statements which can hold everybody happily together, produce a mass of ambiguous language, and we do not really know what is being said. But the one thing that can almost certainly be said is that underneath it is the spirit of lawlessness. There are people who will no longer keep the law, or deny God's authority to give it.

Now this rejection of authority in our own day is described in gripping language in vv. 10b–16. There is a mysterious allusion in v. 11 concerning the "pronouncing a reviling judgment" upon the angels "before the Lord". This is an illustration that Peter gives concerning the despising of recognisable authority. But in vv. 12–13 there is much plainer language, much easier to understand, where lawlessness is simply said to lead to animal behaviour. "These, like irrational animals, creatures of instinct, born to be caught and killed . . ." for after all, animals have no brains ". . . will be destroyed in the same destruction with them . . . They count it pleasure to revel in the daytime." Whereas normally people only live an animal life at night-time, now they are so shameless that they will do this in the daytime: they don't mind people seeing it. Isn't that a sign of our times? "They are blots and blemishes . . ." Unlike the man of God, they have blots and blemishes. ". . . revelling in their dissipation, carousing with you. They have eyes full of adultery, insatiable for sin." They are never satisfied: and they are determined that we shall never be satisfied, and they inflame all our baser passions, and they feed them, and they arouse them. It is an extraordinary thing that publishers can produce pornographic literature, one magazine of which costs a pound an issue, and find that they are taken up readily. When one used to think of a magazine as expensive, it was a shilling or two. This, then, is the result of the rejection of authority.

Now I think we can spend too long on this: because we need to see the positive answer, the Christian way; and I want you to see how clearly this opposite is marked out. These men accept no authority and break God's commandments. What is the Christian? Well, the Christian is the man who by definition has a Master who bought him (2:1). A Christian, therefore, is a man under authority; *under* the Lordship of Christ. I know this can become a sentence, easily said. But to be under the Lordship of Christ means to be a disciplined man, a discipled man, a man who does what he is told.

How difficult it is, incidentally, if children are brought up in a family where discipline is not insisted upon, when they learn that the heavenly Father does insist upon No being No, and Yes being Yes. That is why parents have such a tremendous duty in bringing up Christian leaders. Christian leaders will come, by and large, not from late converts, but from children of Christian homes, who have been taught authority through their parents, so that when they become Christians, they can take the authority. Spoilt children go through years, often, in the spiritual wilderness, finding it so different to knuckle under the fact that God means what He says. And no amount of talk about the grace and forgiveness of God can cover up that fact. Sooner of later we have to recognise it. It has been a long and painful thing for me to recognise it, I know. All of us still have much to learn. The Lord means what He says; and if we are to serve Him, then we have to learn to obey Him. Only those who learn to obey Him can then lead others.

Also, the Christian is not only a man under authority, but he is a man to whom the holy commandments have been committed (v. 21). Now this comes when Peter is talking about these men: "It would have been better for them never to have known the way of righteousness . . ." There it is: the way of righteousness, as well as the way of truth. Isn't that a lovely balance? Grace and knowledge; the way of truth and righteousness. "It would have been better for them never to have known the way of righteousness than, after knowing it, to turn back from the holy commandment delivered to them." What happens when I am converted? I think we need to say increasingly today that when I come to Christ He delivers to me not only forgiveness for the past, not only the power of the Holy Spirit in my life, but He delivers to me the holy commandment. And He delivers it to me to be kept.

When people say that love is the only thing that matters in the Christian life, they often forget that love in the Old Testament is *commanded*. And God commands love because He wants love not to be a matter of feelings, up and down, but a matter of every day. If you command love, it means that it is something which is largely seen in the actions we do: not in the temperature—emotional or spiritual—that we feel. So a Christian is marked out over against this, as a man under authority with the holy commandments delivered into his hands. That, then, is the first great question: Who are these men who cause such damage, and who will receive such condemnation? They are basically lawless men.

I think we need to bring this even closer. They are lawless men in that they sit under no authority—the authority of the local church; the authority of the elders; the authority of the Scriptures; the authority of Christian people, which can be very real—you see, they stand apart from all these things. They

124

give scant respect to these things. They lead people away from these things.

Now the next question is even more important: *What do they preach?* What do they offer? That is given to us in v. 19: "They promise them freedom . . ." That is almost breathtaking, isn't it? Can you believe it? These men, having dismissed the category of law, then turn around and say, "Now you can have liberty. The law was a shackle round your ankle: we have cut it off. Now you can go free." Now this is exactly what is said in society today, isn't it? Freedom is to be found by a rejection of the category of law.

But it is very frightening when we find this in the church of God. Freedom is to be found, people say, in the rejection of the holy commandments. These men are offering, you see, what one might call a higher Christian experience. They utter "loud boasts of folly" (v. 18). They utter loud and brash and foolish boasts, about what they can give to people, if only they will follow what they say. They say, "We can lead you above the experience that you have, to something higher, a life of complete liberty." This is their stock-in-trade. These false teachers are very often those who turn round to the Christians and say, "Look at them, and see how bound they are!" I think it would be better to say, "See how honest they are!"

The stable Christian knows very well that in this life there is no absolute, complete freedom; no absolute, complete freedom from sickness—and he is too honest to deny it. He knows that there is no absolute, complete freedom from sin—and he is too honest to deny it. He knows that there is no absolute, complete freedom from sadness, from battles, from pressure, from burdens: and he is too honest to deny it. But the mark of these men is not honesty: they promise something which they haven't got themselves. That is what v. 19 says: "They promise them freedom, but they themselves are slaves of corruption."

Now it is just because, while we are in this body, and while we are surrounded by the world, the flesh, and the devil, that we often as Christians long "to be with Christ, which is far better". We know that there is peace in our hearts, and we thank God for that; there is also a war on our hands. And we know that while we are in this life we cannot have that perfect freedom that belongs to the last day. Therefore we look very much with suspicion, surely, at those who come along promising perfect freedom. Such offers are always more or less dishonest: and that is what he says in v. 17, "They are waterless springs and mists driven by a storm."

Here is a man in a dry country, unlike this country: some of you who come from overseas come from a dry country, and maybe you are making a trek—a missionary trek. You are longing to boil your kettle, or fill up your water bottle. It has been very, very dry: and at last you see a notice that says, "Three miles to the spring". Well, you quicken your step, and you walk there looking forward to refreshment and some rest: and when you get there, there is the spring. It is all nicely newly painted: it has been there for a long time. And you let down your bucket—or whatever it may be—and you find that it is absolutely dry: there is nothing there. What a terrible disappointment: there is no disappointment worse than that which has been buoyed up by a signal which proves to be false; a promise that just isn't true. And you feel almost completely deflated, and wonder if you can go on. That is exactly what happens to the person who follows the false teacher, who buoys him up, offering him something which will not come to pass; and when it doesn't come to pass . . . Can I go on? How often I have seen that.

"They are like mists driven by a storm." That is to say, this is a country in drought, longing for the rain. The farmer is wondering when the mists will come, bringing the rain and the gentle dew with it. And here comes the mist: but it is driven over his head by a storm of wind, and it never comes down on his fields. What a disappointment! For days he has been expecting it: the weather prophet has told him that it is coming. He has been promised freedom from drought, and all will be well—and he goes back to his wife, and he sits down in his kitchen and takes up his cup of tea and says, "I'm going to give up farming!"

Notice the almost incredible truth that is given us in v. 19: "They promise them freedom, but they themselves are slaves of corruption." Those who make the biggest claims for a higher life are usually living a lower life themselves. This was true in Corinth. Never did a church make such claims; never was a church more sure that it was a church with everything. And yet if you read 1 Corinthians without rose-coloured spectacles, never do we find a church with lower standards. Why, we are told by Paul at the beginning of Corinthians that they behaved just like ordinary men. The contradiction that is given to us in such stark terms in 2 Peter 2:19 always leads in life to collapse and breakdown, either mental, physical, or spiritual. To promise or to preach something which is not true of my own life, in the end will tear me apart. It is not unknown in Christian circles, for men who have said great things, to end their lives very sadly. Let us be warned to live by the Word of God, and to promise nothing that God does not promise, and to say nothing which is not true: to be honest teachers.

It is not always so attractive: it does not always bring the crowds who are wanting something new. But in the end it pays dividends. The truth of the Bible and the truth of reality are closely intertwined. The world works, and the Christian life works, in the way God describes in the Bible. Therefore in the end, if you go by the Bible, you will find yourself able to understand the world and the Christian life. Yes, this is a sad chapter, and it comes very close to us. These are things that are not unknown among us.

Now read vv. 20–22, and we come to the end: and Peter gives us an astonishing climax. What does he have to say about these men who do so much damage? Incidentally, I always love v. 16, don't you? Often about these men —who seem to be so successful that nobody dares to oppose them, nobody dares to question what they say . . . Nobody dared to question Balaam: he had a reputation. So in the end God had to open the mouth of an ass! He often has to do that today! What does He do? Why, when some poor lady in the congregation feels she can bear it no longer: she says, "If nobody else will say it, I must say it. I'll feel an awful ass. I've never been trained. But I must go and say that's not what the Bible teaches!" Yes, if God cannot get us to come down to size through the ordinary ways, he opens the mouth of an ass.

Now look at v. 20. What he is telling us here is that their natures have never been changed; this is the explanation that he gives us for it all. "For if, after they have escaped the defilements of the world through the knowledge of our Lord and Saviour Jesus Christ . . ." It seems there, doesn't it, that they were real Christians? ". . . they are again entangled in them and overpowered,

126

the last state has become worse for them than the first." That is always the case. "It would have been better for them never to have known the way of righteousness than after knowing it to turn back from the holy commandment delivered to them."

But what is his verdict? Were these men truly regenerate people? Well, his verdict here is that they were not. "It has happened to them according to the true proverb, The dog turns back to his own vomit, and the sow is washed only to wallow in the mire" (v. 22). You can give a pig a birthday wash, but it will wander off very soon to get back to that comfortable mud. What he is saying is that in the end they go back to the world to which they belong. They return to the life-style which is no different from that of the unsaved. This sort of teacher has arisen before: they will arise again. But usually you find that they do not last very long. And usually you will find that in the end they return to the life from which they came, because their natures have never been changed. If their natures were changed they would listen to the Word of God; they would know their own hearts; they would humble themselves; and they would lead people as true under-shepherds of the flock.

I do not know whether this chapter makes you tremble, as it makes me tremble, as a pastor, a minister, in the church of God. To hew very carefully to the Word of God, and to live very carefully in the presence of God. That question, How should we live in the light of these tremendous truths and these great warnings? we must leave until tomorrow morning, when Peter shows us how—in the midst of all these things—we Christians may live a life that is worthy of Him.

Bringing the King Back

By the Very Rev. James Dunlop, M.A., D.D.

In 2 Samuel 19:10 we read, "Why speak ye not a word of bringing the king back?" The words were spoken of David some time after his spiritual restoration and his return to God; spoken by people who had rebelled against David in the revolt led by Absalom his son. That rebellion nearly succeeded. For a time all went well. Absalom was proclaimed the popular king with enthusiasm, while David was forced to go away into exile beyond the Jordan. But Absalom missed his chance. Instead of striking while the iron was hot, he listened to fatal advice from those who were really the friends of David; and while he hesitated and procrastinated, more and more men were gathering themselves to David beyond Jordan, resolute men, fearless men and loyal, until at last when the battle was joined with Absalom's forces, David's army was victorious all along the line. The young usurper was slain, and his forces were completely defeated. Then among the followers of Absalom an inevitable reaction set in—as is not unusual in times of defeat, they began to reflect bitterly on what had happened. They realised how foolish they had been. They remembered David, their own king; the man who had delivered them again and again in the past; the conqueror of the Philistines, and now rejected by them for a young rebel who, in the event, proved to be a poor, broken reed.

Disillusionment came to them: murmurings began among them; and presently someone whispered a word that passed from mouth to mouth, spreading like wildfire until it was being heard throughout all the ranks of Israel. And the word was this: "Why speak ye not a word of bringing the king back? We have been fools, fools ever to have rejected him. But it is not too late. Let us now make amends, and do the only wise thing. Why do we not speak a word of bringing the king back?" And on that word deeds followed, and ere long David had been restored to his rightful place as Israel's king.

Well, now, those are, I suggest, striking words in any setting; and they are words that come leaping out of the context, alive and meaningful, in the situation in which we find ourselves today. As we all know, we are living in times that are strange and critical and baffling. But there is a way to solve the problems that beset men and nations at this present hour. There is an answer to the deepest needs of mankind, and a solution for men's individual problems. It is to bring the King back, and give Him His place. For there is a King who, if He were allowed to rule, would meet every need, however baffling or stubborn. He is Jesus Christ, Son of God, Son of man, Saviour of the world, the only wise Leader and Counsellor for all people, the ever-lasting Lord and Helper of men: and He has been left out. "Why speak ye not a word of bringing the King back?"

Leaders of nations and leaders of the church would do well to heed that call. But, to be practical, what about our individual lives? We are not going to set the world right except by putting our own lives right where they have been wrong or mistaken. Do many of us not feel the cogency of this word, put in this way so long ago in this Old Testament story? For our personal lives, "Why speak *we* not a word of bringing the King back?"

Let me say three things, all brought out clearly in this old story. The first is this: *These words were spoken by the very people who had rejected David.* To some of us, I am sure, there seems to be something strange about this rebellion of Absalom's, in the enthusiasm with which it was taken up by the people of Israel. To turn so completely and apparently so unanimously against David their king, whom they had loved so well, now in his old age, is passing strange, until we remember what human nature is like. The fact is that the glamour of the young Absalom had carried them away, had captivated them. Put beside him, David seemed a bit old-fashioned and out of touch. And so they forsook the old, and went after the new. Do we not often see something like that today?

It seems to me that one of the rarest qualities is just that of constancy. There does not seem to be a lot of continuance, of stability, in the best of us

128

somehow, when we are put the test. Men are firm on swearing allegiance to some person or some loyalty, and then one day we find that they have drifted against their pledge; and that although often it is against their best interests. This can be seen in nearly every department of life; but it is most serious in the realm of personal religion, in the life of a Christian. Many of us may have been facing the miserable reality of this, as God has spoken to us of drifting, of broken vows, of compromise, of worldliness, that we have been discovering in our Christian lives; and which perhaps we never realised to be such until we heard His Word.

Do you remember in the first enthusiasm of your Christian life, thinking that every Christian, to be a Christian, must wholly follow and love and worship the Lord Jesus Christ? And then do you remember, perhaps, when you discovered that many who do not really do that, call themselves Christians? Do you recall a time when you really loved Christ and were enthusiastic for Him in a way that is not true of you today? Was there a time when you could not conceive yourself allowing in your life things which you commit now without very much thought, or doing anything else but obey and honour Jesus Christ? Indeed, I believe that not a few have been facing facts like these, and dealing with them by God's grace, as His challenge comes home to us.

But at what stage are we found now? Can it be that as the issue has been put—namely, that the outcome of a confession of sin and a turning to God for renewal in faith and repentance should be an absolute yielding of your whole life to the control and will and authority of Jesus Christ? Can it be that you still find this difficult, and you hesitate, finding it to be too far-reaching, or too all-embracing? And as a matter of fact you still reject Christ as your King in the true sense? It is a harsh word that, "reject". But does it draw a true picture? Your life is not yet as God intends it to be, for Christ's Lordship is still rejected by you, just as his subjects rejected King David.

We notice that these people were brought to their senses by an experience of defeat—a national defeat. It is very serious when God has to send some calamity into our lives to bring us back to our allegiance to Jesus Christ His Son; but sometimes that is His way. And that might be the explanation of what has happened in your life: bereavement, sickness, family anxiety, some disappointment or tragedy. The truth is, my friends, that God loves us far too much to allow us to go completely to the devil without trying hard to stop us. But sometimes—and more often—He rouses His people by just a consciousness of an unhappy, defeated, unsatisfied and unsatisfactory Christian life. And it is possible—I think it is probable—that that is how God may be speaking to us. Has He been showing you that you have been wrong and mistaken in some way; showing you that there is no true life away from the complete Lordship of Jesus Christ; that your heritage in Him is the abundance and the fulness of life, and that it is always a mistake to reject Him for any possible prize or alternative? Be honest, then, and be real enough to admit it.

Here is the essence of my word to you, which I believe is God's word: "Why speak ye not a word of bringing the King back—as King?" These words were spoken by the very people who had rejected their king; and they may be spoken by you if that is what you have been doing.

The second thing to notice is this: *David waited until he was invited back.* He waited *until* he was invited back. Absalom's forces were completely routed, and it would have been a very easy thing for David to go up and conquer Jerusalem with his victorious army. But that was not his way: and I think the reason was this. He was no foreign power or foreign enemy coming to smash and crush Jerusalem: he was their lawful king, and they were his people. And he waited—waited until these words were uttered by them, by the people, and they themselves invited him back.

Oh, how patient the Lord is with you and with me! But there is something more. The story tells us that while he was waiting David used his servants and his agents, getting them to speak and to persuade the rest of the nation. Again I think that is a picture of the Lord's way with you and with me. He knows we really belong to Him, no matter how far we may have gone astray from Him; and He waits for us to see and to acknowledge that. And He uses means, the means of the memory, the conscience, and preaching, and the words of friends, to persuade us to invite Him back. He wants the decision of your own mind in this, leading to action. He will not force: He never has done that. He did not make you a Christian in that way. That's not His way. But He does ask you to see the reasonableness and the necessity of this surrender to Him.

Why do you not speak this word? He is your rightful King, who has bought you, who owns you, and who is the only one to readjust your life. He knows enough to do that properly. He is the only one who can clear up the mess that we have made in life; He is the only one who can give fulness of life to you, under His grand control. And yet He waits—for you.

What will His kingship mean? We must, of course, be quite clear about this. Obviously what kingship means is complete control over every bit of our lives. To call Christ Lord is not to accept just so much of His will or of His doctrine as appeals to us, and leave out the rest. To call Christ Lord is to accept Him as King in every realm of life. If we do not receive Him and make Him Lord in that way, He is not our Lord at all. Surely that is obvious. We do not take Him simply in order to have some need met, or some problem solved, or to escape from consequences which only He can deal with— although we know that His Lordship means all that. To have Him as King is to have no interest into which He is not brought, no life in which He cannot share, no path that His will does not determine. It means to be content to have and to follow His wishes, to take His plans for every bit of our lives, instead of our own. So it is something that is essentially practical and all-embracing. If Christ is Lord, He will have the say regarding our leisure, our amusements, our habits, our work, our friendships. Christ will now have a person through whom He can live and work and do His will, and on whom He can depend. He or she will be at Christ's disposal, no longer governed by self, but by Him. The King will rule over everything: the use of money, pleasures, friendship, life-work, everything. He will have full control. That is what it means to have the King back as King.

And do we yet hesitate? Do we? Let us realise this, that the reward of crowning Christ King is infinite. For in this way do we come to know and experience the fulness of life for which He has redeemed us. And that life is worth any conceivable sacrifice, any cost that is involved in surrender. But, in considering this aspect of the issue, let us above all look steadily at the One who is standing there waiting, seeking and longing to be our King. He wears marks that distinguish Him as our King—the marks of nails, and He received them when He came to redeem us; and when He was tempted to turn back by the great adversary—because the cost was so great—He went on into Gethsemane and Calvary because He knew that this was the only way to redeem you and me. And He has redeemed us; and we know—trusting in Him now, perhaps for many years—that we received in Him the eternal blessings of life and salvation; received them from His hands. And all that we have and all that we hope for through all eternity, we owe to Him. And now He is saying to us, "Take my yoke upon *you*. Let me be your King. Take up the cross and follow me." And this is our King. Can we really do other than respond to Him?

> *Were the whole realm of nature mine,*
> *That were an offering far too small;*
> *Love so amazing, so divine,*
> *Demands my soul, my life, my all.*

Gladly, gladly would we swing open the doors that He may enter and reign. But will He then come in to reign? That seems an unnecessary question, in one way; but the third thing I have to point out is simply this: *David came when they made a move.* He waited until he was honestly invited back as king. But He came immediately they gave the invitation. He came when they made a move: he was utterly willing to come to his people as king—as Christ is to come to us. And with David, we may notice that there was no cheap standing on false dignity and pride. There was no holding up to them their folly and their rebellion. Quietly, gladly, he came to them as their friend and their king, accepting their repentance, forgiving them freely, and resuming his reign over them.

Jesus, in returning to us as King, to whom we must give full obedience, does not come as a conqueror, gloating over our surrender. He comes to reign, yes; but to do so in our hearts in love. He graciously puts away the past mistakes: He blots them out and makes things new. "Behold, thy King cometh unto thee meek and lowly, and having salvation." That is His way, just as it was when He came to Jerusalem for the last time in the days of His flesh. And, note it, He comes to make us like that. This is the humility of character that He will produce in us when He holds sway: we shall find rest unto our souls. Isn't that the whole thing? "Take my yoke upon you—honestly, fully—and learn of me; for I am meek and lowly in heart: and ye shall find rest unto your souls."

He will teach us to cease from self, to bring forth His fruit by falling like seed into the ground to die; and then reckoning ourselves alive only unto Him. This is, in fact, the essence and meaning of His Lordship in us, which can be experienced and manifested because He now lives His life in us, and produces His character in us by the Holy Spirit. He cannot do it until He is given control. We can only have Christ formed in us, in being possessed by Him through making Him King.

So it comes down to practical issues. Let us, then, in a definite and whole-hearted act, make Him King; bring Him back, and crown Him as such individually. Let us henceforth allow Him to reign over our claimed, restored life. Let us say now to Him in full sincerity:

131

Jesus, Lord and Master, love divine has conquered,
I will henceforth answer, Yes, to all Thy will.
Freed from Satan's bondage, I am Thine for ever,
Henceforth all thy purposes in me fulfil.

I remember the Rev. George Duncan telling this story of Dr. Graham Scroggie. Dr. Scroggie had been conducting a service, and afterwards he noticed a young woman remaining in one of the pews. Everyone else was slipping away, but she stayed there. He did not go to her immediately: he just watched her, and then he went alongside and said to her quietly, "Would you like me to speak to you?" "Yes," she said. And she told him she had been greatly challenged through his message, and that it had come to a very vital issue for her. She had to choose between making Christ her Lord in truth, or continuing to have as lord someone else, with whom her affections were greatly involved.

Dr. Scroggie did not speak very much to her, because she knew the issue: she knew what she had to do. He tried to help her, and he turned her to a passage in the book of the Acts, the story which tells of Peter on the rooftop of the house, when he saw the sheet let down from heaven, and in it all manner of four-footed beasts and creeping things. And the voice came to Peter and said, "Peter, arise, kill and eat." And Peter said, "Not so, Lord. I will not eat that which is not clean, that which is common." And Graham Scroggie pointed to the three little words, "Not so, Lord", and showed her that you cannot have both: one or the other. Either your decision, "No: not so", or your decision, "Yes, Lord".

He went away and left her, but he stayed; for she remained there in the pew. After a time he looked in: she was bowed in prayer, and her Bible was open on the seat beside her. And he slipped up the aisle, and before speaking to her he glanced at the Bible, and he noticed that with her pencil she had stroked out the words, "Not so", and had left "Lord" only.

What is the issue with you? May I repeat again the chorus—

Jesus, Lord and Master, love divine has conquered,
Henceforth I will answer, Yes, to all Thy will.
Freed from Satan's bondage, I am Thine for ever,
Henceforth all Thy purposes in me fulfil.

And He will come, and He will do it. Now then, speak the word, bringing the King back.

The Spirit-orientated Life

By the Rev. K. A. A. Weston, M.A.

May I turn you to John 6:63–64, the words of the Lord Jesus Christ: "It is the Spirit that gives life, the flesh is of no avail; the words that I have spoken to you are spirit and life. But there are some of you that do not believe." I wonder if it would cheer you up if I told you that Cambridge ever so nearly won the Varsity cricket match yesterday! Well, they did in fact ever so nearly win it. And I should have been very happy if they had won it, because, you see, I am a Cambridge man. But I had to come 275 miles from my home in order to tell you that, because if I were to say that in Oxford, I should be torn limb from limb! It all depends, you see, which side you are on. If I say to you, "Aren't you cheerful, that Cambridge nearly beat Oxford?" and you say "Yes," I am assuming that you are a Cambridge supporter. But if you shook your head and said very crossly that Oxford had won, I should assume that you are an Oxford supporter.

Now, mind you, my life was very much complicated by the fact that while I was at Cambridge, I had two brothers at Oxford. They used to take me to the rugger match, because in those days Oxford usually won. So I replied by taking them to the boat race, which Cambridge usually wins. But there was a tension in our family because, as you see, half of us were Cambridge supporters, half of us were Oxford. Now when I went to Oxford, we were all Cambridge supporters to a man! I am sorry to say that two of my children have defected to the other side.

Now, why this illustration at the beginning? Well, I want to try to bring home to you that the Christian has *two spheres of experience* in his life, and I think the Lord Jesus Christ is referring to these two spheres in this verse. May I turn to the verse again: "It is the Spirit that gives life, the flesh is of no avail." Here are those two spheres, being referred to, I believe, by the Lord Jesus Christ. And the lessons behind these words of the Master are very relevant to us as Christians today. The realm of the spirit, and the realm of the flesh: and your enthusiasm for the one or the other depends on whose side you basically are.

You see, the realm of the spirit is that over which God rules. I do not mind for the moment whether you spell "spirit" with a capital "s" for the Holy Spirit, or with a small "s" for that spiritual side of your life which owns its allegiance to God. You will be interested to see in this verse in the varied translations, whether the translators have referred the word "spirit" to the Holy Spirit, or to the spiritual side of man's nature. Personally, I prefer to think of this as a clear reference the to Holy Spirit, and so I would make it read, "The Spirit . . ." with a capital "s" ". . . gives life." And the realm over which the Spirit gives life is God's realm. Jesus goes on to say that "the flesh is of no avail"—"it profiteth nothing", as the Authorised Version says.

133

And that is the realm which owes its allegiance basically—because it has been usurped—to Satan. The realm of the flesh is that which answers to Satan in the unregenerate person; the realm of the Spirit is that which answers to God in the regenerate man. And God's purpose by His Holy Spirit is to bring to us life in its fullest sense, life which is spiritual life, eternal life, that which satisfies for life and eternity. And the realm of the flesh, says Jesus, profits nothing for that purpose; nothing by way of satisfaction, nothing by way of salvation, nothing by way of hope for eternity. Indeed, if we see the realm of the flesh in its true light, we find that it is opposed to God. And so St. Paul can say in Galatians 5:17, "The desires of the flesh are against the Spirit, and the desires of the Spirit are against the flesh; for these are opposed to each other." Two realms of experience: that which the Lord calls "the realm of the flesh", and that which He calls "the realm of the Spirit".

Now we can see this illustrated, I think, in the previous verses of this chapter. You remember that this chapter begins with the story of the feeding of the five thousand, the wonderful miracle that Jesus wrought, bringing food to those five thousand people on the hillside. But on the next day people gather again in the same place: it says, "Where they ate the bread after the Lord had given thanks" (v. 22 ff.). They gathered *in the same place*. "And when they found Jesus" (v. 25), Jesus says to them, "Truly, truly, I say to you, you seek me, not because you saw signs, but because you ate your fill of the loaves" (v. 26). Their motive in seeking the Lord Jesus was not that they might have the spiritual truths that He brought to them, but the fleshly satisfaction of being filled with bread.

Or again, look at v. 27: "Do not labour," says the Lord Jesus, "for the food which perishes, but for the food which endures to eternal life." Which way are you orientated, so to speak? Are you looking for that which will satisfy this life day by day, and make you happy here and now—the possessions, the money you can jingle in your pocket, and so forth? Or is your first thought, Jesus seems to be saying, for that which satisfies for eternity; that which will take you over the grave, and into that which lies beyond? Are you looking for food which will satisfy your spiritual needs? Which realm are you looking toward, the realm of the flesh, or the realm of the Spirit?

Or again, I think we see it referred to in v. 15. After the miracle, Jesus said that He perceived "that they were about to come and take Him by force to make Him king". And so He "withdrew again to the hills by Himself". They were about to take Him, and forcibly to make Him their king. And, oh, how the heart of Jesus must have sighed at this ignorant approach to what He had come to do; for He had not come to set up an earthly kingdom: He had come to set up a spiritual kingdom, to proclaim a kingdom, as He Himself said, which was "not of this world", the kingdom of heaven. And so their desire once again sprang from the fact that they were orientated toward the world and the realm of the flesh. They wanted their fleshly desires satisfied—someone they could set over them as an earthly leader against the Romans; whereas Jesus had come that He might satisfy their eternal needs, as a King for their life and eternity.

So behind these verses, I suggest to you, we see Satan—whom Scripture calls "the prince of this world"—plotting to draw men from the spiritual truths of which Jesus is speaking in this chapter, and that they might be blinded to the truth of the spiritual realm which was His prime concern. He

134

was the One, He said, who had "come down from heaven" (v. 50). He had invaded this world, so to speak, from the spiritual world of God's heaven. He had come down from heaven to earth, that He might, like the manna which descended, feed hungry souls. And all they were interested in was bread for their bodies.

Two realms of experience: that of the flesh, and that of the Spirit. May I try to point this out more effectively by referring you again to the words of the Lord Jesus, in the parable of the rich fool, in Luke 12. You will remember the story well enough. A most successful farmer—he was already rich—whose ground brought forth so much that he had to pull down his barns and build greater ones. Then at last he said, "Soul, you have ample goods laid up for many years; take your ease, eat, drink, and be merry." He had everything his body could want. The desires of his fleshly nature were completely satisfied—so he thought. He could take his ease, sit back and relax. Everything was now his. And that very night God said to him, "Thou fool, this night thy soul shall be required of thee: then whose shall those things be which thou hast provided? You are rich as far as the things of the fleshly realm are concerned; but you are terribly poor—in fact you are devastatingly poor—concerning the things of God's spiritual realm." The flesh profiteth nothing.

I know of a number of people who are like that, who humanly speaking have everything that this world can provide; but they are desperately sad, desperately lonely, desperately needy people. For they know perfectly well, deep down in their hearts, that if God called them out of this world, they would take nothing whatever with them, and they have nothing to look forward to.

But I also know Christians who get so involved in the attitude of the world, that one would think this world is all they are involved in. Their thirst for spiritual things seems largely to have been dissipated. In the parable of the rich man and Lazarus, in Luke 16, it is striking that the Lord did not say that the rich man was a particular sinner, in the way the world sometimes talks about sin. He was not immoral; he was not a thief; he was not a murderer; he was not dishonest. He was simply self-centred; flesh-centred, if you like. The god of his life was the god of the realm of the flesh. Therefore he "fared sumptuously every day", and he cared not a bit about the things of God and the things of eternity. He was unconcerned, in his comfort and in his richness.

Lazarus, on the other hand, lay at his gate full of sores: he had nothing whatever of this world's goods, but surely we must infer from what the Lord said about him that he was nonetheless rich toward God, for when he died he was carried by the angels into Abraham's bosom—a lovely, graphic picture of the wonder and peace of heaven. Now he did not go to heaven because he was poor; and the other man did not go to Hades because he was rich. Rich men sometimes find their way to heaven: Abraham was a rich man. Even though it is hard for a rich man to be saved, there are those to whom God gives riches who are truly saved: and praise God for them. But there are many poor people, too, who know nothing of the riches of heaven, and they go to hell. But you see the point of the parable. The rich man in the story had his whole life orientated to this world, the realm of the flesh, which profits nothing. The poor man, though Jesus did not exactly spell it out, must have had his heart and soul orientated toward the things of God and the Spirit, for when he came to the end of his life he was rich toward God.

Two realms of experience. Jesus said, "The Spirit gives life; the flesh profits nothing." Now did you notice that I said there are two realms of experience *for the Christian*? I believe that these two realms of experience are relevant to us who are Christians; for when you became a Christian God delivered you from the dominion of darkness, and translated you into the kingdom of His dear Son (Col. 1:13). He rescued you from the realm of the flesh, over which Satan presides, the realm of the world over which he is prince, and he translated you—transferred you—to the kingdom of God's dear Son. You no longer, therefore, belong to the realm of the flesh: you belong to the realm of the Spirit. Your life has been redeemed from the thraldom of Satan, and you now owe allegiance only to the Prince of Peace. The world, the flesh, and the devil have no claim whatever upon your life and upon your heart. You, by God's grace, are destined for heaven.

But, Christian believer, you are not yet in heaven. And that is one of the problems, because you are in this world still. Even though you are not *of* the world, you are in the world. And simply because the world is still all around you, it clamours for your attention. It argues its claims, so it thinks, upon your love and your allegiance. It titillates your desires. It presses its conviction on you that its motives are more convenient than God's motives for doing things; that its desires are more stimulating, that its attractions will really satisfy you more than spiritual things.

Christian believer, you know this, don't you? The pressure of the world, the flesh, and the devil is not something from which you are exempt. You know what it is to be tempted, perhaps sorely. The Christian lives under this constant pressure. He does not belong to the world, but the world seeks to squeeze him into its mould (see Romans 12), and all through his earthly pilgrimage he is led through this world, as in *Pilgrim's Progress* Christian and his friend had to pass through Vanity Fair; and they felt its pressures upon them.

Are you a Christian who faces opposition? Somebody here may be facing opposition in their home or in their work. I say to you, do not be surprised. Of course you face opposition, because you are not of this world; and you are not to be surprised, said Jesus, if this world hates you. Is there a Christian here who is facing terrible temptation, maybe? You find its pressures on your life day after day. I say to you, do not be surprised. You have been translated from the kingdom of this world into the kingdom of God's dear Son: but you have still got to walk through Vanity Fair. The pressures of this world sometimes come very heavily upon a Christian: of course they do. Do not be surprised.

In fact, I would go further and say it may well be that the fact that you undergo great pressurising from the world, the flesh, and the devil, may be one of the most real indications that you are a child of God. Because Satan does not bother so much about those who are on his side: he will leave them alone. But when a man or a woman turns from Satan to serve the living God, then Satan is angry, and will bring all the pressures he can to bear on that life, if possible to bring that life back into bondage to himself. So do not be surprised if you are pressurised by Satan; do not be discouraged if temptation becomes fierce. Do not be discouraged if your Christian life sometimes goes through a terribly dry, difficult passage. I say to you, of course it will, from time to time. Of course Satan is going to get at you. Of course you are going to feel the pressures of the world, the flesh, and the devil.

"Beloved," says Peter in 1 Peter 4:12, "do not be surprised at the fiery ordeal which comes upon you to prove you, as though something strange were happening to you." I wonder if I may press this home for someone here. When I was a young Christian I got very puzzled by the fact that I seemed to be tempted in all kinds of ways, much more than other people appeared to be. They talked of the victorious Christian life, and I did not quite understand that they had the same kind of temptations as I had. I remember being for very long times of quiet on my knees, trying to seek out from God why it was that I was undergoing such terrible pressures. And I learned ever so slowly that this was not a proof that I was a poor backslidden sinner, but that in fact I was one of the Lord's own children, and that Satan was interested in me simply for that reason. Therefore instead of getting overwhelmed in a situation of constant temptation, I was to lift my head up and look to the Almighty God who claimed me as his own, and thank Him for the trials and testings through which I was being brought.

Temptation is not sin. The Lord Jesus Christ was tempted in all points, just as we are, yet without sin. And, Christian brother or sister, if you are feeling in your life the appalling pressures of the world and the flesh and the devil upon you, then look up to God your Saviour, and thank Him. "Count it all joy when ye fall into divers testings", says the apostle James. They are a great proof of your relationship to God. Don't get discouraged. Do not be surprised. The realm of the world and the flesh and the devil will press upon the man, the woman, whose life is committed to God.

Now let us go on to a second point which I think will be helpful. Two realms of experience in the Christian life: but I believe also that Jesus indicates in these two verses *two basic principles* for the Christian in this situation. May I point to you the clues in this verse. I would label them, first, *A truth to believe*; and second, *A discipline to accept*. The truth to believe is contained in these glorious words: "The Spirit gives life." Surely a reference to the Holy Spirit, the Lord and Giver of life. He is the life-giving Spirit—lovely names that are applied to the Holy Spirit. It is the Lord the Spirit who gives life. He is the One who empowers and strengthens the frail Christian to live for God, and to stand and not be bowled over.

When you go back to your situation which you find difficult; when you go back to that world which you find hard and discouraging; when you go back to your place of work where you are the only Christian, and you are under severe opposition from others, maybe, or ostracism; when you go back to that home which is problematic and difficult—you go back as a Christian, not just as a frail, lonely person; you go back with the Lord who gives life indwelling your heart. That is the fact to believe, the truth to believe.

Our children at one stage enjoyed playing with puppets—the sort that you put on like a glove. Suppose, then, that I had in my hand one of these glove-puppets. It represents you. I put round this glove-puppet a string, and I put the glove-puppet down on the desk. Then I give the other end of the string to Canon Neech, and I say—may he forgive me—"Canon Neech, you are the world, the flesh and the devil. And the world, the flesh, and the devil have an exerting pressure on the Christian", I say. "They are pulling at the

Christian, trying to get him down." Now, imagine hard: if Canon Neech were to pull on that string, what would happen to the glove-puppet lying on the desk there? Why, it would get drawn to Canon Neech, wouldn't it? Nothing to stop it.

Did I say this is a picture of you? It is only a picture of you if you are not a Christian. That is why the worldly person gets drawn into the world's ways without ever realising what is happening. That is why people can apparently do things without any conscience. That is why so many people have no thought for God. They are full of the world's ways.

But listen! That is not a picture of you if you are a Christian. So imagine hard again. Here is the glove-puppet. I am putting my hand inside it. Now there is a new power inside the puppet, isn't there? It is the power of my hand. The pressure is still upon the glove-puppet: he is still in the world, even though he is not now like the world, dead in its trespasses and sins. There is a new power at work—and Canon Neech can pull at the string, but instead of finding the glove-puppet moving easily toward him, there is a pressure resisting him. And pull as he may, he is not going to get the glove-puppet, because inside there is my strong hand holding the puppet back. A very simple illustration, but don't you find that helpful?

Within you, Christians, there is the Lord, the life-giving Spirit. And you go back to a situation like that, not on your own, but with the power of Almighty God at work in your life. And no matter how Satan may pull, if you live a Spirit-orientated life, then Satan cannot overcome you. "Sin shall not have dominion over you." The pressures are still there; the attractions of the world are still there: but live your life Spirit-orientated, trusting and relying in the power of the Holy Spirit who possesses and fills your life, and "sin shall not have dominion over you". And may I say it?—the power of Almighty God makes the strongest power of Satan's attractive seducing look very trivial indeed.

So here then, I suggest to you, is a truth to believe: The Spirit gives life. "I will put my Spirit within you . . ." That is the promise of Ezekiel 36:27. ". . . and cause you—*cause* you—to walk in my statutes, and . . . keep my judgments."

May I then go on to the second basic principle: *A discipline to accept.* A truth to believe, and a discipline to accept. Discipline, you know, is an unpopular word these days; indeed, in certain student circles it is almost a dirty word. But it is a divine word, as Leith Samuel says, as well as a dirty word.

Discipline is part of our Christian life here below. It's got to be; and it is the discipline of orientating yourself day by day to the Spirit-realm of God's word. That is why Jesus goes on to say, "The words that I have spoken to you are spirit and life." The Christian, therefore, whose life is to be Spirit-orientated and Spirit-controlled, is the Christian who submits himself daily to the mastery of Christ's word in his life. "Why do ye call me Lord, Lord," said Jesus, "and do not the things that I say?" It is all very well to call Jesus "Lord" in the happy fellowship of a Convention meeting like this; but He wants you to call Him Lord and mean it in that difficult place to which you go. The world, the flesh and the devil continue to clamour for my attention, but my attention must be fixed upon the Word of God, and the beauty of His will.

This constitutes for me a daily, hourly, discipline, from which I shall never be freed until one day I see Him face to face, and all my attraction will be taken up with Him. To hear His word, to listen to it in a disciplined way, to seek by His Spirit to understand it, and by His grace to obey it—a daily, hourly, discipline for the Christian.

I find this illustrated for us in James 1, where you will remember St. James speaks about the problem of temptation, the constant pressures upon the Christian in the world—temptation and testing. James says we are to clear away "all filthiness and the rank growth of wickedness"; and secondly, we are to "receive with meekness the implanted word, which is able to save" our souls. Now, do you see the point? What awful growths of wickedness Christians sometimes allow to come up in their lives, to spoil their fellowship with God; to cloud their vision of God! Now, says St. James, by God's grace clear it all away: get rid of it from your life; and then let the implanted Word of God bring you daily experience of salvation. "The words which I have spoken to you," says Jesus, "they are Spirit and they are life. They will orientate your heart and soul toward Spirit-realm, toward my realm." And they will minister to you life for today, and life for the pressures of today, that you may be a Christian who stands upright, no matter what Satan may try to do to you, because you are drinking in what God says to you day by day, and you are obeying it day by day.

I wonder if I may be very pointed, and suggest to you that one of the reasons why you may be a defeated Christian is because you are not accepting this discipline in your life? How easy it is to let the television just remain on into the evening, when the discipline of a Spirit-orientated life will turn it off and open up the Scriptures at the time when you are due to meet with your God? How often it is that the morning comes round, or the time when you have your quiet time, and a strange sense of disinclination comes over you to read God's word and pray. That is when the discipline of a Spirit-orientated life will get a hold of you, and you will open God's word and read it, that your mind and heart and soul may be open to heaven and to God, before ever you go out into the new day.

How often it is that you are attracted by the things of the world, sometimes things which we know instinctively are wrong, and yet we are attracted to them. Or sometimes we get caught up in the affluent way of life, and we think that the all-important things in life are to have the sitting room painted, and have the next best thing that we can find, and so forth. And all the while God is seeking to draw us away from these things, and more to Himself. The discipline of a Spirit-orientated life will be always opening its heart and soul to God, and listening to His word.

A truth to believe: the Spirit is life. But a discipline to accept—to surrender day by day and moment by moment to His word, and to the will of the Master. "The words that I say to you are Spirit and life." What is your spiritual life like today? Which way are you facing as a Christian? Toward the world, toward these petty things that the world puts before us, toward those things which Satan is subtly dragging in front of you, cluttering up your life with all sorts of worthless things? "The flesh profits nothing." Or are you, by God's grace, seeking to orientate your life toward God, and the realm of His Spirit, to let His Spirit have full control of your mind and your heart and your will; and are you doing this by a daily, hourly, discipline of listening to the words that Jesus has spoken to you, which are spirit and life?

139

Nothing hurts a Christian's life more than basic indiscipline about the means of grace. Nothing robs a Christian more of his assurance, and of his effectiveness in service, than laziness, which causes him to become half-blind to the realm of God's Spirit, his mind attracted day by day and moment by moment by the things of the world. God wants you to be a Christian who is strong to resist the pressures of the world, and who is therefore effective in God's service.

How sad it is that v. 64 reads, "But there are some of you that do not believe. For Jesus knew . . ." And Jesus knows all about you. He looks into your heart. What does He see? Oh, may God grant that He sees a heart and mind and will which at last are submissive, surrendered to God, saying, "Away with all the world's things! Lord, give me grace to cut them out of my life, and grant to me the whole surrender of my heart and will to you, that the Spirit Himself may bring life, joy, peace, and effectiveness in my Christian life."

The Key to Fruitfulness

By the Rev. Alan Redpath, D.D.

I feel led to speak to you on the subject of the key to a fruitful life. I am sure that it is fruit that God wants from those whom He has forgiven and cleansed and redeemed and indwelt by His Spirit. He expects a high performance from those who are redeemed by His blood; and most of all I am sure that He looks for fruit. John 15:16 tells us: "Ye have not chosen me, but I have chosen you, and ordained you, that you should bring forth fruit, and that your fruit should remain."

What sort of fruit? Not the kind of fruit that the world would expect. Not even the kind of fruit that the average Christian expects. Not success, not numbers, not results, not masses of conversions. But if you want to know the kind of fruit, you read about it in Galatians 5:22, where we are told that the fruit of the Spirit is love, joy, peace—that is, my relationship to God; long-suffering, gentleness, goodness—that is, my relationship to myself; faith, meekness, temperance—that is, my relationship to other people. That is the kind of fruit that God is looking for; and it can be all summed up in one word, *character*—or, if you like, Jesus. This is Jesus reproduced in the life of a Christian by the power of the Holy Spirit. This is the fruit for which heaven looks. To many people God is sort of way up there somewhere, way

140

up in distant space. God the Father, way up there. Jesus Christ, well, something less, down here. The Holy Spirit is sort of second cousin, a distant relative, completely remote. This is far from the truth. This is a tragic idea, for the only one who can live the Christian life is the Spirit of God; and God in me, and in you, is the greatest revelation in the Bible, and the only secret of producing fruit.

Therefore, in order that I may bear fruit, there is—

A DYNAMIC THAT I NEED. "Ye shall receive power, after that the Holy Spirit is come upon you."

When I read through the Acts of the Apostles, I get so excited, and yet so disappointed. Most of us imagine that it is a sort of fairy tale. These things don't happen today. The church was always intended to embody the life of the Lord Jesus, and to be an incarnation of spiritual power. Everything that she did could only be explained on the basis of miracle. Her survival was a miracle. Everything she accomplished had only one explanation: God has done it. And she began to move out, and as she moved out, as long as she kept moving, she had power. But soon she began to dig in for safety, protection, and she lost her power. Now, as Christians, we have dug ourselves in up to the ears, to defend ourselves against society. We "do our thing", we play church—hymn, prayer, hymn, reading, notices, offering, solo, hymn, sermon, hymn, benediction, twice a week, fifty-two weeks in a year; and nobody stops to wonder where it is getting to. Preach to the saints in the morning and the sinners in the evening, as it was in the beginning, is now, ever shall be. Nothing changes in our church. It was good enough fifty years ago; it is good enough today.

Oh, I don't want to be scathing, but I want to discharge a burden; I want to unload my heart to you! Thank the Lord for the many churches which have seen the light, and to which this may not apply. Many who are, spiritually speaking, on the ball; they get out where the action is. They don't sit inside a church and wait for people to come. The church that does that is dying on its feet. The average church service today, believe me, is about as irrelevant to the state of the country and the need of the country today as would be a battalion or a regiment or an air force squadron sunbathing on the beach at Brighton during World War II. It was war in those days. My friend, it is war now. And our country is in far greater danger than she was in 1940, attacked by a far greater spiritual force and power. And the only answer to this power is the Spirit of God released through a Christian submitted to the Lordship of Christ. Only when the Holy Ghost can make contact and communicate to society through redeemed men and women abandoned to the will of God can we possibly see the tide beginning to turn.

Well, we need power. What is power? I would say that power, for one thing, is a spiritual force of sufficient energy that can transform a rebel into a saint. Not simply to make a decision for Christ. This emotionless act of accepting the Lord, to use an evangelical cliché, bears mighty little relation to the whirlwind conversions of the New Testament. We need the power that can turn a man who persecuted the church into a man who is beside himself with the love of Christ. A man who is absolutely transformed. Only the Holy Spirit can do that.

Power, a spiritual unction which makes our worship sweet and fragrant with the presence of Jesus; where showy sermons, streamlined personalities,

Christian entertainment are out, and the emphasis is on Jesus Himself in the midst. Power, a quality which makes the church a divine thing, something to be feared. Today there is little that you can't account for by psychology, and as my friend Dr. Tozer said, "If you can account for a Christian's experience by psychology, you've got a church member on your hands, but you haven't got a believer." The Christian has no explanation but miracle. You can explain him only by miracle. Once he was bitterly opposed; he was a rebel; once he was against God; once he was anti-Jesus; once he was blaspheming with the name of Christ: now he is on fire for God. He is absolutely transformed. Power. That is what I mean.

I read in Acts 5:13, that in New Testament days "Nobody dared join themselves to them". They saw fire, and they backed off. They were afraid of it. But Holy Spirit conviction was so tremendous that it overcame, and multitudes were added to the church. Afraid of fire. Nobody is afraid of ashes, nobody! Today they all slap us on the back, saying, "You're not bad sort of fellows after all." They get familiar with us, and they slap the bride of Christ on earth on the back, and say, "Jolly good solid chap you are. Come and have a drink with us. Share our entertainment. Share our fun. Just be as like us as you possibly can be." We need the dignity of the Holy Ghost, and the reverence of the man who walks with God, and the majesty of a man who is upright and filled with the Spirit; a man whose life is itself a question-mark—"Why does he react like that? Why does he behave like he does? Why doesn't he blow his top like everybody else does? Why does he keep his temper? Why does he keep calm? How does he get through suffering and trouble so peacefully and so calmly? What is the explanation of that man?" I have no right to expect that anybody should come anywhere to hear my sermons, but every right to expect they should watch my life seven days a week; and, boy, they do it! That means they are watching every time my reactions, my temper, my conversation in my home, my treatment of my family. The Christian is a man who has the dignity of the Lord about him. This is what makes the Christian fruitful.

Mark's Gospel, you will remember, tells us in the sixteenth chapter, "They went everywhere preaching the word, and the Lord confirmed the word with signs following." And the greatest moments in church history have been moments when that verse has been true. Everywhere gossiping the Gospel, preaching Christ. Oh, not because we are overworked: it is because we are under-motivated that it doesn't happen. The love of God is not shed abroad in our hearts by the Spirit. Power, unction, utterance, power, like that. Power is that which makes a man repent and believe. Not eloquence, not oratory, not argument, not even sermons beginning with three points and ending in a fitting conclusion. That doesn't do it, not itself. More convincing than all: "Thou shalt receive power when the Holy Spirit is come upon you." And you might as well fight with lightning as fight with the Holy Ghost, when He moves in. It is His promise, "the Holy Spirit shall come upon you". The rest is up to us. Power, that is what I need today in my life. That is what you need. That is what the church needs desperately: the power of God the Holy Spirit.

But why is this so lamentably lacking? Why is it that somehow we haven't got it? What is the matter with us? I have searched my heart about this, and I feel it is because of—

A Distinction that we Haven't Made. We have failed to distinguish between God's part in our salvation, and our own part. And so we are completely powerless. There are some things that only God can do. There are some things that I must do. I will try in vain to do what God's saving grace alone can do. But equally in vain do I ask Him to do what He has, in his sovereign authority, commanded me to do. Only God can redeem. Calvary, the blood of Jesus, makes atonement available for everyone. But it doesn't save anybody. Only God can regenerate. Only God can forgive. Only God can justify. But none of these are effective to us individually unless we do something. God cannot do my repenting for me. It is impossible for one to repent for another. He may incline me to repent, but repentance involves a moral revolution. When a man repents, he stops lying. He does it; God doesn't. He does it. He does it in the power that God gives him, in the indwelling Jesus in his heart, when he really means business. And when a man really repents, he turns to God, and he stops lying and he starts telling the truth.

We are told today that all has been done, and we have nothing to do. We are told that we are punished for what we are, not for what we do. And so we have a sort of spiritual hang-up between the first Adam and the second, the Lord Jesus. You know, Adam did all the sinning; Jesus did all the dying; so we have got nothing to do. But my friend, this takes all the moral fibre out of our Christian experience. I am not lost because of what happened long ago when a man became a rebel, and bequeathed to me a rebel nature. I am lost because I stay like that, when God has provided an answer to it in the death and resurrection of Jesus Christ, His Son. He has slain that rebel nature at Calvary, in His death. I must repent and climb on the cross with Him. I don't conquer my sin by doing anything. I conquer it by dying to it. I can poison myself if I want to die; I can drown myself, I can shoot myself, I can hang myself: but I can't crucify myself. But Jesus has done it for me. "I am crucified with Christ," says Paul, "and the life which I now live, I live by faith in the Son of God who loved me, and gave Himself for me." And if I repent genuinely, thoroughly, it means, "All right, Lord, I'll climb on that cross." And then He imparts His nature to me. I cannot delegate my repentance, and it is repentance which makes all this a reality.

Power. God can't repent for me. Have I repented? Have I died to my sin, myself? Have I gone to the cross about it? Have I accepted crucifixion? That is repentance.

Another thing. God can't believe for me. Faith is the gift of God, but whether I act on it or not is another matter. I acknowledge His trustworthiness, I trust His promises, I obey His commands. That is Bible faith. It is impossible to have saving faith without a real determination to do God's will. I listen to a sermon—or you do—and go out and wait for God to do what He tells me to do. To escape the error of salvation by works, we have the opposite error of salvation without obedience.

We love to quote Ephesians 2:8-9, "By grace you are saved . . . it is the gift of God; not of works, lest any man should boast." Wonderful. But what is the next verse? "We are his workmanship, created in Christ Jesus unto good works, which God hath before ordained that we should walk in them." Be mighty careful, dear friend, of confusing the good works which can save nobody, and the good works which are the only evidence of salvation.

The Bible recognises no faith that doesn't lead to obedience. It doesn't recognise any obedience that doesn't spring out of faith.

Romans 1:16, "The Gospel . . . is the power of God unto salvation to every one that believeth." Hebrews 5:9, "He is the author of eternal salvation unto all them that obey him."

The essence of sin is self. The essence of salvation is obedience. Long ago in 2 Samuel 3:17, Abner said, "You sought in times past to make David king over you. Now then *do it*!" And I would say to you, if you want power, "You sought in times past to make Jesus king over you. Now then *do it*." Repent; turn to God, and put Jesus on the throne. That is His rightful place. Now then, do it. Act. Don't wait for God to do what He has told you to do yourself.

The dynamic that I need. The distinguishing thing that I must observe. One more thought—

THE DELIVERANCE THAT I WILL EXPERIENCE. Acts 5:32, "He hath given the Holy Spirit to them that obey Him." That is the key to a fruitful life. May I read to you in sequence four verses from the Old Book. Listen to them:

Matthew 7:24, "Whosoever heareth these sayings of mine, and doeth them, I will liken him unto a wise man, which built his house upon a rock." If I hear, and if I do, I am on a rock; and that rock is Christ.

John 14:21. What a wonderful promise this verse is! "He that hath my commandments, and keepeth them, he it is that loveth me: and he that loveth me shall be loved of my Father, and I will love him, and will manifest myself to him." Yes, obedience, the key to building on the rock; obedience, the key to being loved by the Father, and having Jesus made known to you every day.

John 15:10, "If ye keep my commandments, ye shall abide in my love; even as I have kept my Father's commandments, and abide in his love." Abiding in the love of Jesus. The fruitful life; the key to it, obedience.

And Romans 6:17–18, "God be thanked, that ye were the servants of sin, but ye have obeyed from the heart that form of doctrine which was delivered you. Being then made free from sin, ye became the servants of righteousness." Free from sin, by the power of the Spirit of God controlling a life submitted to the Lordship of Jesus. My dear friend, God is ready to pour out His blessing if you are willing to obey His plain word. You don't need any new doctrine. You don't need any great preaching. It is as clear as a three-lane motorway, the path, the key to a fruitful life.

Listen. Repent from lying, repent from adultery, repent from gossiping, repent from impurity, repent from unchastity, repent from sin, dishonesty, and all of it. Stop playing Christianity. Stop playing church. Be finished with religion without a cross. Forgive those who have wronged you. You carry a grudge through your Christian life and you are powerless. Forgive them. Practise forgiveness. Forgive those who have wronged you. Get right with someone you have wronged. Go and apologise to them. Seek the will of God in the Word of God. Submit to the sovereignty of Jesus. End the regime where you have been the centre, and move over and put Jesus on the throne. Claim the power of the Holy Spirit, and go out to fight in His power and His strength, and to win.

I'll never forget the day when I was at Stoke-on-Trent. I went one Saturday night to speak to a Youth for Christ meeting, and a Salvation Army officer was giving his testimony. He was an enormous man, very fat, and he told of his conversion at a Salvation Army meeting. And he said, "The next day I went to the holiness meeting, came back home, and my wife said to me, 'What's the matter with you? You look miserable.' 'Oh,' I said, 'I am.' I said, 'Everybody else has a red jersey on but me.' 'Well,' she said, 'there's no trouble about that. I'll knit you one.'" So she knitted him a colossal red jersey like a tent, and he put this jersey on and went out the next week to the Army meeting; and he came back looking just as miserable. And she said to him. "What's the matter with you now?" "Oh," he said, "everybody else had white letters on the jersey. I hadn't any." "Oh," she said, "I don't know what to do about that." She couldn't write, couldn't read. The next day a man came and put a ladder up against a shop window, and he climbed up the ladder and began to paint a sign. So she said, "I know what I'll do. I'll copy all he writes on my husband's jersey." So she copied everything on that sign on to his jersey; the next Sunday he went down to the Salvation Army meeting, and came back beaming. He said, "You've done it, my dear, you've done it. Everybody said I have got the best jersey of anybody." Do you know what it had written on it? "This business is under entirely new management."

I don't mind you smiling at the story. But I want to tell you, if you mean business with God, if you want power, that is the price of it. If you want to live a fruitful life, that is the key to it. Submit to the Lordship of Jesus; and do it now.

The Lordship of Christ

By the Rev. George B. Duncan, M.A.

The verse that God has laid on my heart is found in 1 Peter 3:15. In the Authorised Version it reads: "Sanctify the Lord God in your hearts." In the Revised Standard Version, a little bit more vividly: "In your hearts reverence Christ as Lord."

On the last Sunday in May I found myself facing the task of giving the final message to our young people's group in St. George's Tron for the session that was ending that night. As I anticipated that prayerfully, I found myself asking this question, "Is there any subject more important than another in the life of a Christian?" Indeed, I might well have added, "Is there any one subject more urgently relevant to our situation in the church today? In the life of the average Christian today, is there any one subject more relevant than another?" And what gripped me then, and what has gripped me ever since, is the Lordship of Christ in the life of the believer.

At the opening meeting, when the meeting finished on Saturday, the Bishop of Carlisle turned to me and said, "I doubt if there is any single gathering in the whole of these islands of ours that holds more spiritual potential than this gathering here." But the reaction in my mind was, "I wonder if there is any gathering in the British Isles where that potential is so frequently lost!"

What is wrong? We are orthodox. So often that is just about all. We are not Christlike in our character. We are not reliable in our service. We are not sacrificial in our giving. We are not faithful in our praying. Where does the break come? I would submit it is an almost total failure to accept the Lordship of Christ in our lives.

The American political and social weekly paper, *Time*, usually doesn't have much space for religion; but toward the end of last month it devoted twelve pages, including four or five pages of photographs, to what they called "The Jesus Revolution". Pictures in colour illustrated the movement that is spreading almost like a prairie fire in the United States, outside the organised church, among young people. The first picture showed a girl with a red pullover on, and on the back were just four words: "Jesus is my Lord." We usually like to say, "Jesus is my Saviour," and I question if there are many folk here who can't say it. But can you honestly say, "Jesus is my Lord"?

I want to note three aspects of the Lordship of Christ, and to recall that the title "Lord" was one which Christ Himself applied to Himself: "Ye call me Master and Lord, and ye say well, for so I am." So He is Lord. We must make Him Lord.

If I am thinking of the Lordship of Christ, then I must think of—

THE RIGHTS ON WHICH HIS CLAIM IS BASED. His rights are twofold. First, as *Creator*. There is a tremendous verse in Revelation 4:11, "Thou art worthy, O Lord, to receive glory and honour and power: for Thou hast created all things, and for Thy pleasure they are and were created." We have been made by God, and we have been made for God. Again, from the Old Testament, Isaiah 43:7, "I have created him for my glory. I have formed him; yea, I have made him." And again: "Thus saith the Lord that created thee, He that formed thee, thou art mine."

All this is reflected in the first of both the ten and the two commandments: "Thou shalt have no other gods before me." "Thou shalt love the Lord thy God with all thy strength, with all thy heart and with all thy mind and with all thy soul." Paul, writing to the Colossians, says: "By Him were all things created, and they were created for Him." His claim to Lordship is based, then, on His rights as Creator.

Second, His right as *Redeemer*. "What? know ye not that your body is the temple of the Holy Ghost which is in you, which ye have of God, and ye are not your own? For ye are bought with a price; therefore glorify God in your body, and in your spirit, which are God's." By purchase—which includes in the mind of God possession and occupancy by the Spirit—we belong to Him. "Ye know that ye were not redeemed with corruptible things such as silver and gold . . . but with the precious blood of Christ."

"Ye are bought with a price": the Redeemer rights. When I purchase

146

something, it belongs to me. And the rights on which the Lordship of Christ, and His claim, is based, are Creator rights and Redeemer rights. Nothing that you have is yours, and nothing that I have is mine. What profound truth there is in that threadbare story for children, of the wee boy who lost the boat that he had made. How many versions of that have been produced, only eternity will reveal! The size of the boat, its length, the details of the manufacture, the price paid when he went to the shop and saw it, and all the rest of it. But there is a profound truth here. You remember he lost the boat he had made. He saw it later on in the window of a shop, but the owner made him buy it back. And of course, north of the border, it was a Scottish laddie who made the boat, and as he went away with his wee boatie, he was heard to say, "You are my own wee boatie twice ower: I wrought ye, and I bought ye." I made you and I bought you. The rights on which His claim is based; and these rights are undisputed. There is not a Christian here who would dispute Christ's claim to Lordship. Not one.

The Lordship of Christ, then, makes me think not only of the rights on which His claim is based, but of—

THE REIGN IN WHICH HIS WILL IS DONE. "In your hearts reverence Christ as Lord." We are all familiar with the fact that a change of government leads to a change of policy. And with the Christian, when the government is upon His shoulders, it is always a change for the better.

So I find myself thinking of—*The Difference I will see in my Life*, a profound and basic difference, when Christ takes control; and that difference will be tied up with—*The Person He is*, and *The Purposes He has*. He is the one who is both light and love, and He will have very different ideas from me. And His ideas will determine what I do with my time, with my money, with my home, with my ability, with my children, with my gifts. Some things may have to go out of my planning. A whole lot more may have to come in because of His planning; but the basic thing to grasp is that the decisions are no longer my own. They are His.

Before you and I became Christians our pattern of life—what we did, where we went, how we spent our time, our money—all this was shaped by one of two principles. Paul tells us about them in Ephesians 2. The first principle, I did what I wanted, or I didn't do what I didn't want. That is what the Bible calls "fulfilling the desires of the flesh and of the mind". That is to say, I do what I want. That was before I became a Christian. The other principle was, I did what others did, or I didn't do what others didn't do. My life took its standards from the society of ungodly people among whom I worked and among whom I lived. When I became a Christian, that ended too. The decisive principle of the heart of a Christian life is not that I do what I want, or I don't do what I don't want, nor that I do what others do, or don't do what they don't do. These principles are pushed to one side, to make room for *the* principle. And what is that? This is it.

Saul stumbled across it in the very moment of his conversion. Many Christians don't seem to find it for years to come. Do you remember his two questions when that light shone dazzlingly bright around him on the road to Damascus? He heard the voice, saw the light, and he asked his first question: "Who art Thou, Lord?" That is how it reads in his testimony when he was on trial. I wonder if it was a question the whole way through! I am not certain that it was. I think there was a question there, and a recognition. While

Saul of Tarsus was asking the very question, "Who art thou?" suddenly he realised: "Who art thou, *Lord*?" Back came the confirming word, "I am Jesus." Then came the second question: "Lord, what wilt Thou have me to do?" That was the principle. Saul of Tarsus hit it in the very first minutes of his conversion, and he lived on it all the way through, till he was able to say, "Lord, I was not disobedient."

The reign in which His will is done. I think empty churches are a scandal and a disgrace to the name of Jesus Christ if they could be filled with believers. How many of you folk could go to church twice a Sunday and don't? Do you think it is a witness that brings glory to God if a straggling line of folk straggle into the House of God for the Lord's day, and the watching world look and say, "That is a dying cause." When it comes within the striking time of the hour of worship, does the Lord tell you to stay at home? Does He? Sometimes He may, but ninety-nine times out of a hundred He does nothing of the kind. You decide to stay at home, while a discouraged, disheartened, but faithful pastor breaks his heart, and you lounge in front of your television set and watch a pretty mucky kind of a play. They seem to pick Sunday for that kind. A converted man, a converted woman. You are not living in the Lordship of Christ, are you? You are just pleasing yourself.

Yes, a difference would be made, it would indeed; and if there is a difference that I would see in my life, there is—*An Assurance I would have in my Heart.* Now that my life is under the Lordship of Christ, it is going to be controlled by perfect love, perfect wisdom, perfect power. That will shape the pattern and direct the programme and set out the objectives and mould the standards. There would be no mistakes now through my lack of wisdom. There would be no fear of weakness because of my lack of strength. There would be no lack of motivation because of my self-centredness.

A hymn that I love, one of John Newton's great hymns, begins like this:

> *Be still my heart, these anxious cares*
> *To thee are burdens, thorns, and snares;*
> *They cast dishonour on the Lord,*
> *And contradict His gracious word.*

But I love this verse:

> *When first before His mercy-seat*
> *Thou didst to Him thine all commit;*
> *He gave thee warrant from that hour*
> *To trust His wisdom, love, and power.*

The difference I will see in my life, if He is directing it; and the assurance I can have. I don't need to be afraid. "In your hearts reverence Christ as Lord." The rights on which His claim is based; the reign in which His will is done. And then—

THE ROOM IN WHICH HIS THRONE WILL STAND. "In your hearts reverence Christ as Lord." Not on your lips, nor even in your lives, but in your hearts. There is the throne room: in your hearts.

S. D. Gordon, who used to speak from this platform—what a lovely man he was. His books were all called "Quiet Talks", and he always spoke in a whisper. Those of you who may remember him, will remember that if he had any special point that he wanted to thrust home, his voice dropped even quieter, and you could hardly hear it as he whispered, "Are you listening?" I remember him saying, "In every heart there is a throne, and a cross. If self is on the throne, Christ is on the cross. If Christ is on the throne, self is on the cross."

We think of Him, and rightly so, as exalted in heaven; but the throne He occupies in heaven is surely symbolical of the throne he is to occupy on earth, in the hearts of men. We sing that great hymn, "At the name of Jesus every knee shall bow", but you will remember there is a verse that goes, "In your hearts enthrone Him. . ." That is the room in which His throne must stand. "In your hearts reverence Christ as Lord."

Just two thoughts as we come to a close. First, I see here—*An Unseen Action which Acclaims His Lordship*. In every reign there is a moment of coronation. In Romans 6:13 we read the words: "yield yourselves unto God . . ." That is implied as being an action taken decisively, once and for all. There has to come a time when, in one action, in one place, at one given moment, we crown Him Lord of all. Yield yourselves to God. Evan Hopkins used to say that yielding meant three things. It meant *ceasing to resist*: to resist the claims to resist the voice. Just as a girl can resist the approach of love, and then finally gives in and gives herself to the love of another in marriage, so you and I are to cease to resist. Have you been resisting the Lordship of Christ? In your hearts? You don't mind giving Him this in your life, you don't mind giving Him that in your life, a little bit here, a little bit there: but that inner throne room, no.

It means *ceasing to withhold*. How often we are willing for the will of God in various areas of our life, but in some areas we don't want His interference or control. We have a notice on that particular door, "No Admittance, Private". The Lordship of Christ means ceasing to withhold. This may not mean that some things even of which we are afraid are to go out. They may not have to go out; but they have to go out of our control, even if they don't go out of our lives. It means *ceasing to struggle*. Yielding means giving ourselves without reserve to Him, and to the riches of His love and grace. Action. An unseen action in your hearts proclaiming His Lordship, the moment when we place the crown upon His head.

In one of my parishes there was a lady who was a very close friend of the Royal Family, and at the service of the coronation of our Queen she sat fairly close to the Queen Mother. I remember her telling me how, during the coronation service, when it came to the moment when that stripling of a girl was crowned queen, this lady turned and looked at the face of the Queen Mother and saw the tears streaming down her cheeks. I don't think anybody could have watched that moment unmoved. Most of us watched it on television, and the crown was placed upon the one who has the right to wear it: the only one. There is only one person who has the right to the crown in your life and mine; only one, and that is Jesus Christ. Have you crowned Him, or is your life still a matter of just using Him when it is convenient? The unseen action which acclaims His lordship when I bring the whole of my life, every aspect of it—all I am, all I have, all I hope to be, the whole thing—and in my heart I place the crown upon His head. I recognise His claims, and His reign begins.

149

The unseen action which acclaims the Lordship of Christ has to be followed by—*The Unchanged Attitude which Accepts the Lordship of Christ*. The action of a moment becomes the attitude of a lifetime. Some of you may remember Bishop Taylor-Smith. "The Bishop", he was. There was only one Bishop, apparently, when he was alive! I remember him saying how every morning when he woke up, his first conscious act was to turn his bed into an altar, and his whole personality into a sacrifice. My whole life totally available. You see, it is my time that is no longer mine, but His. I didn't think I had time to become a choir member, but that is what I thought. It is not what He thought. It is my money that is no longer mine. It is His. I know money is tight, we say. Fantastic, isn't it, though, that so many families now have cars; so we must have more money—and it is nice that we have. I am not saying there is anything wrong in having enough money to have a car. Don't misunderstand me. All I am saying is, "What is the Lord getting out of our money?" The half-crown went a long time ago, didn't it? A lot of us used to put a half-crown in the collection. We have forgotten all about that half-crown, haven't we, and now it is just a ten-penny piece that goes in. That is less than what we used to give. And I am not talking to widows who are living on a widows' pension; I have found that they are often the folk who give more sacrificially than anybody else. Is the Lord really Lord of your money and mine?

What about your life? What about your plans, you young folk? Are you planning it all out yourself? The girl you are going to marry. The fellow you are going to marry. The job you want. Are you planning it all out yourself, selfishly, wanting a job with good money and short hours? Or did you ask the Lord what He wants to do with your life? You are in agriculture. Have you asked whether it is in England or Africa where your training is to be used? Every day, the action of the moment that crowns Him Lord is to be followed by the attitude which acknowledges Him. Not that that surrender achieves anything, but it does allow God to trust me with work, with power, with opportunity, responsibility.

> *O happy day that fixed my choice*
> *On Thee, my Saviour and my God!*
> *Well may this glowing heart rejoice,*
> *And tell its raptures all abroad.*

We sing that, don't we? Notice exactly what we sing:

> *O happy day that fixed my choice*
> *On Thee, my Saviour and my God!*

Then there is a verse that goes on—

> *High heaven, that heard that solemn vow,*
> *That vow renewed shall daily hear;*
> *Till in life's latest hour I bow,*
> *And bless in death a bond so dear.*

We all have hymns we love. I end by quoting another. I have the words of this pasted into the front of my Bible—

Only one life to offer Jesus, my Lord and King:
Only one tongue to praise Thee, and of Thy mercy sing;
Only one heart's devotion, Saviour; Oh, may it be
Consecrated alone to Thy matchless glory;
    yielded fully to Thee.

Only one life to offer: take it, dear Lord, I pray;
Nothing from Thee withholding, Thy will I now obey;
Thou who hast freely given Thine all in all for me,
Claim this life for Thine own, my Saviour,
    To be used every moment for Thee.

"In your hearts reverence Christ as Lord." The rights on which His claim is based; the reign in which His will is done; the room in which His throne must stand.

I want to ask you one simple question. Is Jesus Christ your Lord? Is He absolutely in control in your heart? Do you reverence Him as Lord? If He is not, would you put the crown where it belongs?

At Filey, every day ends with the singing of Molotti's setting to the Lord's Prayer. There are some moments in one's spiritual life that seem to be peculiarly wonderful. I don't know, somehow or other when we come to the end of that lovely setting to the Lord's Prayer sung by three thousand folk in the Late Night Extra at Filey, and we come to that tremendous climax—
Thine is the kingdom, and the power, and the glory, for ever . . .
I just say to myself, That's it; committed to the will of God, confident in the power of God, concerned for the glory of God.
Thine is the kingdom, and the power, and the glory, for ever . . .
Jesus is my Lord. Is He yours, in your hearts? In your hearts, the unseen action. Will that action take place tonight, leading to the unchanged attitude? Will you take the crown, and give it to the only one who has the right to wear it, and ask pardon and forgiveness that you have kept it so long?

"In your hearts reverence Christ as Lord." Would you dare to whisper to yourself those familiar words, that come at the end of the Lord's Prayer—"Thine is the kingdom, and the power, and the glory, for ever."

Thank Him that He is your Saviour. Tell Him He is your Lord now, and go out to live with this question constantly in your mind: "Lord, what wilt Thou have me to do?"

Ruanda Mission personalities at Keswick.
Above: Bishop and Mrs. E. Lawrence Barham (left) entering
the Missionary Reception.

Below: Dr. and Mrs. Algie Stanley-Smith, with the Misses
Langston, daughters of the late Rev. E. L. Langston,
one-time Chairman of the Convention Council.

Thursday July 15th

10 am Bible Reading

The Way to Christian Stability
(4) The Implications of the Knowledge of Christ
  (2 Peter 3:1–18)
Rev. R. C. Lucas

TAPE NO. 292a

11.50 am Forenoon meeting

Our Great High Priest
Rev. K. A. A. Weston

TAPE NO. 305

3 pm Afternoon meeting

The Church's Power
Rev. James Dunlop

TAPE NO. 305a

7.45 pm Evening meeting

The Holy Spirit—a Blessed Person
Rev. Dr. William Culbertson

TAPE NO. 302

Christ Glorified and Expressed
Archdeacon H. W. Cragg

TAPE NO. 302a

Call to Spirit-filling

The penultimate day of the Convention sees the culmination of certain aspects of the ministry of the week—the final Bible Reading; the last of the young people's meetings, and of the open-air witness. A note on the youth gatherings appears on page 200.

Although Wednesday evening's meeting had presented a climactic challenge to many, the messages of Thursday were by no means an anticlimax. Indeed, they were splendidly complementary, presenting the call to Spirit-filling, and to the manner of life which the fulness of the Spirit alone can impart. Once more the divine design in the programme was manifest: without prearrangement by the speakers, they complemented one another, and led on to the culminating challenge through Archdeacon Herbert Cragg.

By way of preparation for this, the Rev. Keith Weston turned our eyes in the morning to our great high priest, our ascended Lord, in the Majesty on high. In the afternoon, Dr. James Dunlop clearly indicated the secret of power—acknowledging the church's lack of it, and showing where and how it may be known and possessed.

The great tent was completely filled for the evening meeting, when Dr. William Culbertson, in his gracious, paternal manner, spoke from John 14:16-17 on the Person and work of the Holy Spirit—the promised Comforter, or Advocate, dwelling in us, as Jesus Himself is our Advocate at the right hand of God.

In bringing the final message and challenge, the Ven. H. W. Cragg asked, "How can I make sure that the experience of this week is more than a passing splendour?" The answer lies in a clear understanding of the ministry of the Holy Spirit. He has come to enable us to *know* Christ better, and to *show* Him better. Christ is the inexhaustible storehouse: for the fulness of the Godhead is in Him. And our fulness is in Christ. To be filled with the Spirit is to be filled up full with Jesus.

He is the author of a holy life. The power of the Holy Spirit brings us enabling grace to express Christ, by life and lip, and in our daily walk. In a direct application which was manifestly pressed home by the Spirit Himself, the Archdeacon stressed that this was the moment of opportunity and testimony. The Holy Spirit is available to all who obey Him. Christ may be expressed in our human weakness, as the Holy Spirit enables us to know Him better, and show Him better.

As the great congregation dispersed quietly, quite a number remained behind for counselling or personal prayer of response and committal to all the will and purpose of God in their lives.

The Way to Christian Stability

(4) THE IMPLICATIONS OF THE KNOWLEDGE OF CHRIST (2 Peter 3:1–18).

By the Rev. R. C. Lucas, M.A.

We turn now to 2 Peter 3. I shall begin by giving you some headings for it, so that we don't get in a muddle. The *reason for his writing* is restated in vv. 1–2. Peter, like John, has the delightful habit of telling us quite plainly in his letters why he is writing them. Verses 3–7, *The false teachers reassessed.* Verses 8–10, *The true believers reassured.* Verses 11–16—the real challenge of the whole letter, *The logical demands of our faith.* And then, vv. 17–18, *The final appeal and summary*—which we have already studied.

Now, vv. 1–2. Here he tells us the *raison d'être* of his letter. He is reminding us here, just as he did in 1:12–15, of what he has taught them, because his teaching, the apostolic testimony, is the authoritative foundation on which the church will be built. Therefore they are to remember his words as of unique worth. So he says, "This is the second letter I have written to you, my dear friends; and in both of them I've tried to arouse your minds to remember the prophetic word and the apostolic testimony. The Word of the Lord comes to you through the Old and the New Testaments." "The prophetic word", as we saw in chapter 1, is a phrase to cover the whole of the Old Testament, though here he thinks in particular of the predictions of the Old Testament prophets. So he says, "You are to remember the voice of God that comes to you through the prophetic word, and through our apostolic testimony."

So we might say that the *raison d'être* of this letter is that Christians are listening to the wrong voices. They are listening to the voices of these new teachers; and what they say will be disastrous ultimately, in the long term. So, over against those voices—which seem to be very loud and at the moment very successful—Peter urges the Christians to come back to the authentic voice of God in the apostles and prophets.

I wonder if some of you were here at Keswick for the Holiday Convention two years ago, when I took Colossians. It is very interesting to see that the fear and the desire that is in the mind of Peter here, is exactly the same in the mind of the apostle Paul. You see, the new teachers were not only noticed by Peter, but by the apostle Paul as well; and in his letters, especially in that to the Colossians, he does exactly the same as Peter does in his epistles. He calls people back to the authentic, original teaching, which brought the church into being, and which brought them into life: "As therefore you received Christ Jesus the Lord, so live in Him, rooted and built up in Him and established in the Faith . . ."—Faith with a capital F—"just as you were taught, abounding in thanksgiving" (Col. 2:6–7). The Gospel—the Faith,

155

the truth—that brought you to Christ in the first place, is the authentic Gospel, says Paul. Don't wander from it. Don't think that the developing Christian life means that you move away from those foundations. Come back to those foundations if you want to grow. Come back to those foundations if you want to be stable.

So the same message that Paul gives to the Colossian Christians, Peter gives to his brethren as he writes this letter. What he is really saying to them in vv. 1–2 is, "Tune in again to the authentic note", just as an orchestra tunes in. I have not a good enough ear, as a matter of fact, to understand what they are doing, when an orchestra starts scraping before each piece. You know, the violinists go in for a rather mournful business, and the pianist goes on pinging the note "a", and my ear is not sufficiently well tuned to know whether or not they are out of tune. The trouble is that many of us Christians have not got our ear sufficiently attuned to the authentic Gospel, to Bible teaching. Because our ear is not attuned to it, we move away from it. So what Peter is saying here is, "Get back into tune. And the way to get back into tune is to move back to the prophetic word, and to the apostolic testimony." The church must always be turning back to this.

So, individually, this is a call to Bible study. I want to urge that call upon the younger Christians in particular. I don't think that Bible study is done today in the way that it used to be done. I hope that does not sound rather a middle-aged sentiment. I am middle-aged; I can't help that: we just have to take life as we find it! But I think that Christians used to set aside more time for solid Bible study in their week. They would reckon to spend, for example, one evening in the week for two hours' solid Bible study. They would take some book like *Search the Scriptures*, or *Every man a Bible Student*, and they would work through Bible themes and Bible chapters and Bible letters. In this way they would tune in to the authentic Word of God; and this kind of work stands you in very good stead in your Christian life afterwards. Life gets busier and busier, surprisingly. If you don't do the work when you are young, it may never get done. So, individually, I think these first two verses are a call to private Bible study.

Corporately, they are a call for Bible training and Bible schools in an expanding church. I was so pleased to meet a number of people yesterday in the missionary reception, who are engaged not only in Bible translation but Bible teaching. One was telling me how in South America, where the church is expanding so fast, there is particular need for Bible training and Bible schools. It is certainly a work worth giving your life to, to see that as these churches expand and grow so fast, they don't develop beyond the authentic Word of God, simply because they are moving too fast; but that the young men are trained and tuned afresh to the authentic Word, that they may pass on that authentic Word to others.

Now if, in fact, these friends of Peter to whom he is writing had kept near to the authentic Word, they would not have wandered away from this central affirmation of his concerning the coming of Christ. Nor would they have needed to be told so often by the apostle in this letter, that false teaching would abound. Because the one thing that is quite certain about the New Testament is that it says both things repeatedly. You can hardly turn to a page of the New Testament without a mention of the coming of Christ in glory. And you can hardly turn to a letter in the New Testament without repeated warnings about the dangers of false teaching. So the very fact that Peter has to remind them of these things, shows that they were wandering away. And I want, if I may, to go off the main road just for a moment into a lay-by, to fill in the background concerning these two things. Otherwise we may come to this chapter unprepared and unready.

May I say a few words, then, about the coming of Christ? This is central, of course, to the Old Testament prophetic message. The Old Testament prophets looked forward to the coming of Christ. This was to be a great and powerful coming for the whole re-creation of the world. The power of God was to be manifested in His Messiah, in His Servant, to do just this. We know now that that coming the Old Testament prophets foretold, would in fact come in two stages—something they did not fully realise. At the second coming, Christ would come to destroy this world, marred by sin and unfit for divine habitation; and to inaugurate the new heavens and the new earth. But He would not do this at His first advent. At His first advent the Messiah would come to call out a people for His name: not to destroy the world, not to bring in the new heaven and the new earth, but to call out a people for His name, who would in time inhabit the new world that He would make. Now that is the Biblical order. He comes to call out His people first; and having found that great multitude which no man can number, He then comes again to prepare for them a habitation.

The mark of the first advent is weakness. The birth of Jesus Christ, at His first coming, is marked by weakness: born in a stable, unnoticed, of poor family. What a picture of helplessness! His death—again supremely a picture of weakness: given up to the hands of wicked men, resistless, just like a lamb going to the slaughter. What a weak picture that is—a man dying on a cross, bleeding, apparently finished! Does the resurrection contradict this? Well, of course, it does contradict it: but it didn't contradict it to the world at large, because the world at large never saw the risen Christ. He was only revealed to His disciples, and then He left them. So the world has not seen the power of God revealed in the transfiguration and the resurrection. All the world sees today is the church: and the mark of the church in this age is still weakness. That, of course, is perfectly plain in the beginning of the first letter to the Corinthians: you remember that at the end of the first chapter Paul reminds the Christians how weak the church will be: "Not many wise according to worldly standards, not many powerful . . . not many of noble birth: but God chose what is foolish in the world to shame the wise . . . the weak in the world to shame the strong . . . what is low and despised in the world . . . to bring to nothing things that are." There won't be many intellectuals in the church; there won't be very many able people; there won't be many people out of the top drawer. That is what he's saying, quite simply. They will be ordinary people in God's church.

Furthermore, not only is the membership weak, but the message is weak. "We preach Christ crucified, a stumbling-block to Jews and folly to Gentiles, but . . . the foolishness of God is wiser than men, and the weakness of God is stronger than men." The message is, as far as the world sees, weakness, folly, absurdity. That is what the university would say. That is what the school of philosophy would say.

Not only are the members and message weak, but the messengers are weak: "I was with you in weakness and in much fear and trembling." You remember how Paul frequently said that in his correspondence; and in the second letter to the Corinthians he says, "Yes, I know very well that my letters are weighty and powerful, but you think that my presence is rather weak. I don't make a very great impression when I come, as a person; I don't *seem* to be a very great man." Isn't that rather a surprise? The members of the church very ordinary; the message of the church always seeming to be rather weak to the intellectuals in the world; and the messengers often nervous, often conscious that they have no great presence, often conscious that they have no great gifts.

Don't misunderstand me, of course there is power in the church, as we were hearing last night. But that power is known to His church: it is not known primarily to the world. It is known to His church: we know the power of God to take us out of the world, to escape the passions of the world—as we saw in the first chapter. We know the power of God to regenerate us, and to make us new creatures in Christ. Indeed, Paul says that the power of God to make one man a new creature in Christ, is the same as the power of God extended to create the world. So we know the power of God. But although this power is known by His people, it is not largely and generally and universally known by the world. The mark of the first advent was, and is, weakness.

The mark of the second advent, on the contrary, is power. That is what we saw, isn't it, in 1:16, "We made known to you the power and coming of our Lord Jesus Christ." Then the world will be unable to deny the Lordship and sovereignty of Christ. The verdict, which has been announced already at the first advent, will be executed at the second advent of Christ. It will be supremely a day of revelation and power, when the old world—already marked by sin—will be destroyed; and the new world—to be indwelt by righteousness—will be created. Now this wonderful conception gives the Christian what otherwise he would lack, and that is a world view. The Christian faith is not simply God's plan for the individual: it is God's plan for the whole world. A world view means a true view of the sovereignty of Christ over everything and everybody.

To deny the coming of Christ in glory and power, therefore, is actually to hit at the root of revealed Christianity, because it is to deny both the power and the purposes of God. It is to deny that God can deal with the world; that He has the power to deal with it according to His own purposes. That is why this truth is so important. Destroy this, and the faith has gone: we are on the road to atheism.

Now just a word about the warnings. The false teachers work in two ways in history, and I think this is most important to see. They work by neglect of truths, and exaggeration of truths. In this letter, as we shall see, they work by the neglect and denying of certain truths; but the false teachers in the history of the church also work by the exaggeration of truths. In Matthew 24 Jesus tells us about certain false teachers who will exaggerate and take extreme lines about His coming: "If any one says, Lo, here is Christ, there He is; do not believe it." I hope you realise that the Bible tells you *not* to believe certain things, as well as to believe certain things. When these people come along with their extravagant teaching, their extreme teaching, don't believe it! You see, the devil would like us to ignore certain teaching. And if we won't ignore it, he raises up people who exaggerate it: they carry it to extremes. He is always doing that.

158

As I look back to my own youth as a Christian, I can't remember really that any of us as young men at college, and in the Christian Union, used to discuss the coming of Christ in glory. It was a doctrine that was left out. Why did we neglect it? Well, I think sometimes that it was because it had been exaggerated in extreme ways. People had used it wrongly, and therefore the result was neglect.

Now with these few words in our minds, let us turn to vv. 3–7 where *the false teachers are reassessed*. The method of the false teachers is neglect. "First of all you must understand this . . ." Now that phrase, you may remember, came in 1:20, where he says, "First of all we must understand that prophecy is the Word of God; it is the voice of God." So having said in chapter 1 that the important thing to realise is that God speaks through the prophets, and that God has spoken to His church, here he says that it is of importance to understand that false voices will come into the church. He is repeating himself. "It is of the first importance that you should realise that these scoffers will come, and not be surprised by it. Remember that these teachers are inside the church, not outside."

They are scoffers. That is to say, they are mockers. How hard we find that to bear, especially when we are young. We hate to be thought unlearned; we hate to be thought old-fashioned; we hate to be laughed at. One of the most devastating weapons in the devil's armoury is scoffing and laughing. He did it in the eighteenth century when he raised up scoffers to call those Christian people who were bringing new revival to our country, "methodists". It was a word of opprobrium in those days, not a word of honour. Today he raises up people with similar kinds of theological swear-words, like "fundamentalist" or whatever it may be. And there are some foolish Christians who squirm when these words are hurled at them. I shouldn't worry too much! You'll have far worse things said about you!

Now what is really wrong with these scoffers? Why do they engage in this particular trade? Well, it says they are "following their own passions". "Cynicism and self-indulgence regularly go together", says Michael Green: and that is true in experience. There is a close link between a man's life and his opinions. If a man wants to live a self-indulgent life, he will soon find that he moves away from apostolic Christianity. He will not teach it. It is inconsistent and inconvenient to do so. So the basic test that our Lord Jesus gives us concerning the false teachers is a very good one: "Don't listen to what he says; look at how he lives. By their fruits ye shall know them."

So here are the scoffers, following their own passions; they want to live their own way, and therefore they choose their own truths to live by. What do they say? Well, they make a dogmatic statement: "Where is the promise of His coming? For ever since the fathers fell asleep, all things have continued as they were from the beginning of creation." They make a sweeping statement, and sweeping statements are always impressive. It is said with great dogmatism and confidence, "Where is the promise of His coming? Why, since the fathers fell asleep all things have continued as they did from the beginning of the world."

This is the oldest weapon of propaganda. Just before I came to Keswick I read an article on *The Little Red Book* which has been in the news. *The Little Red Book* uses exactly the same method of propaganda. Let me give you just one example. It makes this statement when telling young people to go in for

159

free love: "Venereal disease can always be cured." A confident, sweeping, dogmatic statement. Now it so happens that the church where I work is largely made up of medical students and nurses; and only the week before, a couple of nurses, Christian girls, had been telling me that the only job they disliked was to work in the wards where there were venereal patients. One of them said to me, "It is a really terrible experience." Now that was a girl who actually loved her job. It is just not true to say that venereal disease can always be cured. It isn't medically true; it isn't factually true. But, you see, it is said by people of apparent authority with sweeping dogmatism.

You know the old saying about the preacher in Hyde Park who had in his notes in the margin, "Argument weak here: shout louder!" I don't know why that is applied to Christians; I believe we should apply it today to non-Christians. It is certainly true on television; it is certainly true on the radio; it is certainly true in the newspapers; it is certainly true in *The Little Red Book*: "The argument is weak here: shout louder." Say it again and again and again; and people will believe you. This is the modern method. If you've got a weak argument, go on repeating dogmatically what you want people to believe.

So, as I have often said to students, people in this mid-twentieth century have their minds full of second-hand doubts. In a previous generation it may have been a second-hand faith: not now. Today young people have second-hand doubts—doubts, that is, which they have picked up from round about them. They never examine those doubts: they have never doubted them! That's the trouble. They have picked them up because they have been said again and again and again, shouted again and again, louder and louder.

Now, what is Peter's answer to that? Well, it is quite quietly, but firmly, to say, "It is not so." Sometimes that is our duty: to refute it, to refuse to let these statements go by. "They deliberately ignore this *fact* . . ." Facts are not what they are concerned about. "They deliberately ignore this fact, that by the word of God heavens existed long ago, and an earth formed out of water and by means of water, through which the world that then existed was deluged with water and perished." They deliberately ignore the facts of history, recorded in the Scriptures. And the fact in Scripture is this, that the world God created, He will hold to an account and judge: and He has already shown us that He will do this by what He did in the days of Noah. He is still the same God: He will still ask for an account: He will still judge the world: He will still bring things to a climax when He will ask people to give an account of what they have done.

Now in alluding to the story of the flood, Peter knew very well that the flood had been long delayed. Nevertheless the judgment did come, although it was long delayed. I often think how hard it must have been for Noah to be patient, believing that God was right when He said that judgment would come: and yet judgment didn't come. It was a hundred and twenty years to wait; and I reckoned the other day that it wouldn't have taken more than twenty years to build the ark. So a hundred years to wait—by that time I imagine the coach tour operators were already bringing parties round to see the ark! "Interesting, isn't it? This we call Noah's Folly! He did this eighty years ago, you know. He believed that God was going to judge the world; but of course we don't believe that sort of thing now. It's old hat!" And so this kind of teaching has been "old hat".

160

I wonder if v. 7 is "old hat" in quite the same sense today, in this age in which we live. It has a rather uncomfortable ring of truth about it today that perhaps it did not have in previous generations. "By the same word the heavens and the earth have been stored up for fire, being kept until the day of judgment and destructions of ungodly men." Now, don't let us get this wrong, of course. It is not a nuclear explosion triggered off by some human dictator which is in his mind here: it is divine judgment, which starts by the Word of God.

So Peter makes, then, a brief reassessment of the false teachers. He has dealt with them in chapter 2; but he reassesses them again. He says, "Don't be surprised that these people are all around you and trouble you. Don't be surprised at this scoffing attitude. They are following their own passions; they want to live their own kind of life. It suits them, therefore, to live like this and to teach like this. It suits them to teach that we shall never have to give an account." That is what this really means: to live as though there were never any reckoning. But they ignore the fact that the Bible tells us about reckonings in the past, and reckonings in the future. The Bible tells us that this is a moral universe, and we live in the light of the knowledge of God: and God does not forget. So the false teachers are reassessed, and put in their place.

Now we turn to vv. 8–10, and we see *the true leaders reassured*. Peter argues here, first, from Scripture, in v. 8; secondly, from the character of God, in v. 9; and thirdly, from the teaching of Christ, in v. 10. First, he argues from Scripture: Psalm 90:4. But he has quoted it and re-shaped, as an apostle may. He re-shapes that quotation from Scripture, which would be familiar to them, in these words: "But do not ignore this one fact, beloved, that with the Lord one day is as a thousand years, and a thousand years as one day." Let us look at that in detail: "One day is as a thousand years", that is to say, time means much more to God than it does to us. There is an intensity in God's view of time, which we do not share. One day is as a thousand years—one day in your life can be as important in God's sight as a thousand years. It might have been yesterday, when you did business with God; when we heard that great appeal through His servants. That day might be a thousand years, because it has such incalculable results. God sees time with an intensity which we do not share. Similarly, one day of evil, one day of reckless disobedience, can also have incalculable results.

Then, "a thousand years are as one day". That means that time means much less to God than it does to us, in the sense that He sees it with a perspective that we do not share. Time means more to God, and less to God. He sees it with an intensity that we do not; He sees it with a perspective that we do not. In other words, when we come to think about God and time, human calculations are bound to be wrong. So it is stupid to criticise God about His time-keeping. Verse 9: he argues from the character of God—and this is a wonderfully powerful verse, loved by Christian people: "The Lord is not slow about His promise as some count slowness, but is forbearing toward you . . ." patient ". . . not wishing that any should perish, but that all should reach repentance." Why is there a delay in the second advent of our Lord Jesus Christ? It is not powerlessness in heaven, but patience. It is not impotence, but mercy. "God desireth not the death of a sinner, but rather that he should turn from his wickedness and live."

Therefore God waits, that, as Jesus says in Mark 13:10, the Gospel may be preached to all nations. God wants to reach everybody: the uttermost parts of the earth. He desires that all men should be saved, and come to a knowledge of the truth. The heart of the God, the character of God—something that we come to share by the Spirit of God.

Verse 10: he argues from the teaching of Christ. (This is very concentrated stuff, isn't it?) He does not have to tell us what his allusion is here, because this statement, of course, about the thief coming in the night, making his unexpected and unwelcome call, was a familiar saying in the early church. "But the day of the Lord *will* come like as a thief . . ."—he is alluding now to the teaching of his Master—". . . and then the heavens will pass away with a loud noise, and the elements will be dissolved with fire, and the earth and the works that are upon it will be burned up." So, he says, "Remember what Christ said. You can rely upon what He said. Don't forget what He said. Don't ignore what He said. His coming in glory will be sudden and unexpected —though not necessarily soon, if you remember what He said." How often in those parables Jesus would tell of a nobleman going into a far country, and—words that were easily forgotten—"after a long time", he returned.

Now the more I have looked at vv. 8–10, this very precious paragraph in this last chapter, the more sure I am that speculative teaching about the Lord's return is receiving, in these verses, some mighty damaging blows: I'd call them body blows. In v. 8 he is telling us that speculative teaching is absurd, because we haven't got the tools with which to do the job. In v. 9 he is telling us that speculative teaching is perverse, because the delay is not in order that we may get out our charts and do calculations; but in order that we may take off our coats and do missionary work and evangelism. And v. 10 refutes speculative teaching by telling us that it is not only absurd and perverse, but that it is foolish: because if you knew when the thief was coming, why, then you would be able to prevent it, in that particular story. But it is always unexpected; it is always when you don't know. It is foolish, perverse, and absurd. The purpose of the delay is that the church may preach, and men may repent. That's all we need to know. Once we know that, it is doing that matters.

Now vv. 11 to the end. We turn now to *the logical demands of our faith*. I love the logic of the New Testament; I love the way in which it builds up its arguments. I know that my heart is only deeply moved when my mind is deeply convinced. And the New Testament letters go out of their way to convince our minds; and then at the end, when our minds are convinced, to bring the mighty logic of these truths to our consciences and hearts and wills. And that is exactly what the apostle does here. He has a phrase that he repeats twice: "*Seeing* then that all these things shall be dissolved . . ." (v. 11), and "Seeing that ye look for such things . . ." I think I prefer the Revised Standard Version: "*Since* all these things are thus to be dissolved . . ." (v. 11); "*Since* you wait for these . . ." Now here is his logical climax. "*Since* this is so . . . *since* this is so . . . *therefore*, over to you!"

Now what is the meaning of those two sentences? Incidentally, it is natural, isn't it, to demand reasons for a course of action. Only yesterday somebody said to me, "Why should I behave like this? I want to have reasons for it." Well, the Bible takes knowledge of the fact that you need reasons. The Bible calls us, incidentally, to rational behaviour, reasonable behaviour; and it is blasphemy really, as well as being a complete misunderstanding,

162

to say that Christian behaviour is unreasonable. It is the course of life that the false teachers put before people that was unreasonable. We saw that in 2 : 12, "These, like irrational animals . . ." They were the irrational, unreasonable people; and it was because they were "ignorant". Irrational behaviour is based upon ignorance, and it is the mark of the animal. The false teacher tells you to behave like an animal: but Christianity calls you to behave like a man, made in the image of God.

Therefore the New Testament gives you truth, that you may be knowledgeable, that you may have reasons for your behaviour. Now here are two reasons: "Since all these things are thus to be dissolved" (v. 11). Here is the first tremendous fact: that this world in which we live is to be destroyed. The moment sin entered this world that God had made, where everything was good, that moment God marked it out as a sphere that ultimately must be given up to destruction. Just as the forester marks the tree: "This must come down!" so the moment sin enters the world, there must be destruction.

Then the second great truth: "Since you wait for these . . ." What is that? "According to His promise we wait for new heavens and a new earth in which righteousness dwells" (v. 13). The old world is to be destroyed, because it is the home of injustice; the new world is to be made, which is to be the home of righteousness. Isn't that a thrilling thought?

Back to this first one, v. 11. All these things are to disintegrate: sin will be destroyed. But this disintegration is already beginning to take place. Sin and disintegration always go together in God's universe. He has tied them together. So this is not just a warning about the future; it is a warning about here and now. Physically, mentally, and spiritually, life begins to disintegrate if I continue in sin. That is very practical teaching, you know. It would enable many of us to leave behind the visits to the psychiatrist, the visits endlessly to a pastor, with these problems. So many people are going the way of physical, mental, and spiritual wreck; and they are going that way because of sin. Sin is the pathway to disintegration of personality. Righteousness is the way to integration of personality. What we need today is to be integrated people, and we cannot do it and walk in sin: that is what Peter is telling us.

"So since all these things are thus to be dissolved," since all these things are disintegrating, "what sort of persons ought you to be in lives of holiness and godliness?" There is another tremendous truth here. He is telling us that *matter is not permanent, but people are*. Nothing will ultimately survive except the lives of holiness and godliness—in other words, Christian character. To live for this world is to live for materialism, for matter, for things that ultimately are going to disappear, that are not permanent. And that's "plain stoopid". The things of the world—materialism—are going to be destroyed. The only things which will not be destroyed are lives of holiness and godliness. What a tremendous incentive, therefore, to a life of holiness and godliness, the preparation of a Christian character, so that at that last day I may be preserved in judgment! So then destruction and disintegration is coming to all those who follow the way of sin. We therefore surely turn from this in horror, to follow the life of holiness and godliness, waiting for that great day when God will destroy everything and everybody that opposes His will.

But we wait for new heavens and new earth. "Therefore, my beloved brethren, since you wait for these, be zealous . . ." make every effort ". . . to be

163

found by Him without spot or blemish"—in other words, just like the Saviour, who was without spot or blemish—"and at peace." This world is very beautiful: we know that at Keswick. But nevertheless as we look down, perhaps from a mountain, on to some beautiful valley scene, and we are not sentimental about it, we know that living in the houses of that village that nestles so beautifully under the hill, there are people whose hearts are evil. You say to yourself, "I should love to live there; I should love to have a cottage there. It must be perfect peace!" But when you go to live there, you'll find that it isn't! So although it is a beautiful world, injustice lives in that world. The new heavens and the new earth will be even more beautiful, but they will be beautiful in a much more deep and comprehensive way. The people who live in them will be righteous people, and righteous people only.

It will be a world in which righteousness dwells—and I think that's one of the most wonderful phrases in Scripture. We can't get away from it: whatever we do, however hard we try, this world remains a world in which injustice dwells. Open your daily paper: think of our own country. Despite every effort of all men who sincerely try to make this a better world, injustice continues to reign. There will never be a world in which righteousness dwells, until God gives us His new heavens and new earth. This is the goal of the universe; and naturally, I am to prepare myself for it.

Somebody was talking to me about their teenage son, and said, "He doesn't know what to do." They were worried about it, because, until he knew what to do, he couldn't make any preparations. Until you know your future, you don't know what to do to prepare for it. But when you know that you're going to be a teacher, well, you prepare for teacher training college. When you know that you're going to be an architect, you go to training college to learn to draw, and all the other things. And when you know that this is God's purpose for the world, this is the goal of existence, why you start to prepare for it. That is the meaning of v. 14: it is just common sense. There's nothing difficult about it.

Professor William Barclay has given some wonderful examples from heathen tombs, of what happens when men reject the belief that creation has a goal and a climax. May I just quote three: "I was nothing: I am nothing. So thou who art still alive, eat, drink, and be merry." In other words, that philosophy leads to hedonism, pleasure-seeking. That's all there is to live for. Here's another tombstone inscription: "Once I had no existence: now I have none. I am not aware of it. It does not concern me." The philosophy of apathy. That is very much the philosophy of some people today. "I don't understand life. I don't know where it's going. It's no concern of mine. I'll drop out." Here is the third inscription, which leads to the philosophy of despair: "What is below?" Answer: "Deep darkness." "But what of the paths upwards?" Answer: "All a lie." Then we are lost. The philosophy of despair. And what is so extraordinary about these things—and they come from the ancient world—is that they could be written about our modern world.

The philosophy of hedonism, apathy, and despair, is the philosophy of many able writers of our world today. They have fallen for this apathy and despair because they have no goal. They do not know where the world is going. And why do they not know where the world is going? Well, because we have jettisoned our Christian faith: we have thrown it overboard. You never

164

know what it is you've lost, till long afterwards. And one of the great things the modern world has lost through throwing the Christian faith overboard, is a knowledge of where we came from and where we are going: the beginning and the end. And to lose those two makes nonsense of life here and now. That's why people can't make sense of life here and now.

I often use a rather silly illustration to students about this. I say, "I want you to imagine that the room in which we are is a magnificent railway carriage. It has been specially constructed to carry us at many hundreds of miles an hour, through time. We have made it as comfortable as we possibly can. There are bunks for sleeping and cafés for eating; places to play games and places to read—a library, and so on. This train is going through life at many hundreds of miles an hour, and we are in it all together. And after we have been travelling for two years, some of you come over to me and say, 'Excuse me, Mr. Lucas. Could you tell us where we got on?' 'Very sorry!' I say, 'I'm afraid I don't know where we got on.'"

So for another ten years we rush through these marvellous views, which continue. We try to make the very best of the life: it's a good thing we have those books, we have this food, and we have one another. We make the very best of the life we have together, though I think that after these years we shall be beginning to get a little tired of one another! (I hope that doesn't sound rude!) And somebody comes up to me after ten years, and says, "Excuse me, Mr. Lucas. I'm very much hoping you can give me an answer to this question: Where are we going to? Where are we getting off?" I look very embarrassed. I scratch my head, and I say, "I'm very sorry, I've no idea! I don't know where we're going. We're just going."

Silly illustration? Not so silly as you may think. That is the philosophy of many people in the modern world—yes, very clever men. They cannot tell you where we started; they cannot tell you where we are going. So what they say to the people today is, "Make the very best of what you have here and now. Make the very best of personal relationships with those around you. But don't ask for any answers, because there aren't any."

That's why the Bible is such a tremendously important book. It gives meaning to life. The purpose of God's creation, the purpose why God began everything, is the coming of Christ in glory. The creation, the beginning; the coming, the end—or rather the new beginning. The purpose of God's creation, let me repeat again, is the glory of His Son Jesus Christ. But, thank God, Christ does not will or wish to enjoy this glory on His own. And so He came to this world to bring many sons and daughters to share His glory with Him, and to enjoy the position which His Father gives Him. He comes to us, and He says, "Will you share all this with me?" That's what the evangelistic message is, is it not?

So at the last day He comes—v. 14, "Therefore, beloved, since you wait for these, be zealous to be found by Him . . ." He comes to find us, the people He has called by His Spirit, called by His church; He comes to find the people whom He believes have responded to Him. Are you ready now? How will He find us? Ready? Prepared? Waiting? Looking forward? Knowing that this is the whole purpose of our lives? Or taken aback, unready, unprepared, having forgotten all about the purpose of the life which we were given by God?

Well, we must come down to earth as we finish. We are not there yet, of course. These glimpses are not given to us so that we may lose our heads, but that we should find our feet. So we come to vv. 17–18. "Therefore, beloved," he says, bringing us right down to earth, "knowing this beforehand"—understanding the purpose of God in creation, understanding where the world is going, understanding what your life is for—"beware lest you be carried away with the error of lawless men, and lose your own stability . . ."—our theme from start to finish. Don't get carried away by them. "But . . ."—and how very simple these words are; uncomplicated, quiet, strong words, aren't they? Nothing complex here—". . . grow in the grace and knowledge of our Lord and Saviour Jesus Christ."

Grow in your Christian experience; grow in your Christian understanding. Deepen yourself in a life of holiness, and a life of study, a life of understanding, a life of grace. And then you will be ready for the purposes that God has for this world in the coming of Christ. That, quite simply, in quite simple words, is the right way.

Our Great High Priest

By the Rev. K. A. A. Weston, M.A.

I should like to turn you to Hebrews 4:14, "Since then we have a great high priest who has passed through the heavens, Jesus the Son of God, let us hold fast our confession." I wonder if you would agree that probably the greatest danger for us as Christians is of our profession growing cold through neglect and carelessness. In *Pilgrim's Progress*, John Bunyan's God-inspired classic, on the Delectable Mountains Christian was given a spy-glass, because from those mountains, he was told, he could see the gates of the Celestial City, to which he was pressing on in his pilgrimage. Christian took the spy-glass, and "thought he could espy the gates of the Celestial City". And then, says Bunyan, "scarcely could he make them out, for his hand shook so as he held the spy-glass, for fear lest he should never reach those gates". Now, you say, what's happened to John Bunyan's doctrine of Christian assurance? Nothing has happened to John Bunyan's Christian assurance, but he is pointing to the fact that our hands may well quiver on the spy-glass as we look toward that great day when the Lord Jesus is coming again, and we by grace shall pass through those gates of the Celestial City. But God's hand upon us grants us Christian assurance and Christian perseverance; and that

166

is why, when we come to a passage like this, we are taught to consider Him, rather than considering ourselves.

Here is a boy or girl converted in teenage. But it is a good question, "Where will they be, Christian-profession-wise, when they are thirty or forty?" For, make no mistake, many who make a bright confession of faith in their youth, do not go on to perfection. Here is a Christian man or woman, but as the years flow past, their Christian cutting edge gets blunted by neglect or laziness in Christian things. Prayer gradually ceases to be prayer; the habit of daily Bible-reading which once was there firmly in their lives, begins to drop out; the busy-ness and the complexity of life, especially with a young family being brought up—and these Christian disciplines get left behind. Here is a Christian man who knows success in business; and nothing is calculated more effectively to hurt his Christian profession, unless he is very alive to that danger, than success in business. Here is a Christian who runs into tragedy, or a situation which is overwhelming, or a situation of deep sorrow: and sometimes that Christian man or woman becomes hard or bitter because of that experience, and does not go on to perfection.

No doubt we should all tremble at the thought that it might be us. It is a good thing to ask, "What shall I be doing in five, ten, twenty years from now?" Now the challenge to go on with the Lord Jesus Christ is, I believe, the first purpose of the epistle to the Hebrews. The theme of the whole epistle is, "Christian man or woman, by God's grace consider *Him*, and go on to perfection." You see, that is how this verse reads: "Since then we have a great high priest . . . let us hold fast our confession." Your Christian perseverance does not stand in your strength or your ability to go on: he says here you have a great high priest: go on and hold fast your Christian profession.

All of it is in chapter 6. In v. 1 he says, "Let us leave the elementary doctrines of Christ and *go on* to maturity." Or v. 11, where he says, "We desire each one of you to show the same earnestness in realising—or making real in your experience—the full assurance of hope until the end, so that you may not be sluggish" in your Christian life and profession. Here is the theme of the epistle: "Go on," he says, "to perfection. Hold fast your confession." The writer is concerned to rouse slothful Christians, and to encourage others to get up and to go on with Christ. That is why this letter is interspersed, as you will probably know, with straight-from-the-shoulder rebukes and urgings to go on in the Christian life. You can find one, incidentally, in chapter 5. It is rather delightful how it comes in. The writer is talking of the Lord Jesus Christ as a great high priest, and wants to make the point that the Lord Jesus Christ is "a priest for ever after the order of Melchizedek" (v. 6). And he goes on, "Being designated by God a high priest after the order of Melchizedek" (v. 10).

And I see the writer of this epistle pausing, putting down his pen on the table, and thinking: "But what use is it, telling these people that the Lord Jesus Christ is a priest for ever after the order of Melchizedek? What on earth will they make of that? They are such poor Bible students. They haven't the least idea who Melchizedek was. I've got a superb point to make, and I've tried 'being a priest after the order of Melchizedek', and look at their blank faces as they read my letter! They haven't a clue as to what I'm talking about." And so he picks up his pen again. "About this, we have much to say which is hard to explain, since you have become dull of hearing. For though by this time you ought to be teachers, you need someone to teach you again the first principles of God's word. You need milk, not solid food . . . What's happened to your Christian profession? You're still a baby! And you ought to be mature. For every one who lives on milk is unskilled in the word of righteousness, for he is a child. But solid food—like saying Christ is a priest after the order of Melchizedek—is for the mature, for those who have their faculties trained by practice to distinguish good from evil. Therefore let us leave the elementary doctrines of Christ, and go on to perfection . . ."

Do you see how the thrust of this insertion in the epistle comes? He says, "You're babes in Christ. Thank God you started in Christ. But, oh, I wanted to tell you truth which belongs to mature Christians, and you can't take it." Then he goes on to give them the glorious truth which he felt they would be unable to take.

Now I wonder how often the Holy Spirit would teach you lessons which maybe are hard things to explain, deep things of the faith, the strong meat of which St. Paul speaks. But the Holy Spirit, if I may say it reverently, shakes His head, and says, "What use is it? This person will not go on. Oh, if only they'd let me teach them the deep things of their faith! If only they'd open their Bibles day by day, and read, mark, learn, and inwardly digest what's there! But, oh, how sad it is that this man made a profession of Christian faith—and it was a true one—ten, twenty, thirty years ago, and he's still a child in the things of God, when he ought to be mature. He still needs someone to take him by the hand and say, 'Look, let me spell it out for you', when he ought to be a teacher of others!"

I wonder how many come to the Keswick Convention year after year after year, and what really the Holy Spirit would say to them is, "Look, I want *you* to be a teacher of others: go on to maturity!" Because, be quite assured of this, that if we are idle about our Christian discipline of learning the basic facts of our faith, and building upon them day by day, and year after year, so that we are no longer children in the faith, but mature, strong men and women of God, then we are in grave peril of not going on to perfection in Jesus.

God will shake His head and say, "Oh, my poor child . . . when you ought to be a strong man of mine, you are still a toddler in the things of the faith." What parent would be pleased if their child never grew up? We sometimes, as parents, regret that days of babyhood go so quickly. I tell you, we should regret it far more if we had to say, "They're still in nappies!" A child of sixteen, and he has not grown up! May I say it? How often God has sadly to say of people like you and me, "Oh, you're still in spiritual nappies. *Grow up!* Become a *man* of God. In understanding be men, not children." That is the message of this epistle. Go on to perfection.

Now how does the writer of this epistle urge them on in their Christian faith? I tell you, not by making them introspective; not by turning them in on themselves and their own shortcomings; but by turning their gaze to Christ, their incomparable Saviour and Lord. "Consider Him" (12:3). Consider Him, so that you may not grow faint-hearted and weary.

The way to victory is not by a detailed examination of sin and self . . . May I put in brackets, "valuable though that may be on occasions", so much as by a detailed examination of our loving, incomparable God as revealed in the Lord Jesus Christ. Wasn't it McCheyne who said that for every one look at self, take ten looks at Christ? And if the Christian is gazing at Christ, and learning by the Holy Spirit's teaching what He has done, and what He is doing, then that man is going to "grow in grace, and in the knowledge and love of God". That is the thrilling theme of this epistle. It is all about Jesus.

For years I found this epistle very difficult. I am not a Jew, and I found it all about Jewish things. I remember going to Bible studies when I was a boy at school, and we tried to work out what was the difference between this type of offering and that type of offering. But I do not think we as children ever really came to any conclusions at all. But the main theme of this epistle was lost on me, because I got bogged down in things which I then did not understand. And then I read the epistle from cover to cover when I was a student at Cambridge, and the majesty of the truth began to come out of the pages. It is not just a Jewish epistle, based on Jewish ideas, which we who are not Jews may find difficult to understand. This is an epistle which says to me as a Christian, "Listen, Christian! You have a wonderful Saviour, the Lord Jesus Christ, whom he calls here your great high priest who passed through the heavens; and He is the One who is concerned about you, and who will by grace bring you home where He Himself is gone. Now go on with Christ. Let the Holy Spirit teach you more and more about what Christ, your incomparable Lord and Saviour, has done for you. Turn your eyes to Jesus over and over again, and then you won't be slothful about Christian things. You won't be a man who is prayerless. You won't be a person whose Bible gets covered with dust in your home. You'll be a person whose heart will be drawn irresistibly to Christ, through the working of the Holy Spirit. And you will be growing up as year succeeds to year; and you will become a mature man of God, woman of God." That is the theme of this epistle.

The vision of Christ lifts the sinner's eyes from the dust of his own failings: and that is the thing that the Holy Spirit seeks to apply to the believer's heart, as He possesses and fills that believer. "He," said Jesus, "shall glorify me." Are you allowing the Holy Spirit to glorify Him in your life? The heart that is possessed by the Holy Spirit of God is a heart where the beauty and grace of the Lord Jesus is being hourly displayed, weaning the believer from his attraction to worldly things, that he may be attracted to the glorious Jesus; quickening his love for his Saviour day after day.

I believe the fulness of the Spirit will be seen more in that way, than necessarily in terms of this or of that manifestation. More even than in terms of power, for which we long, and of which we speak often. Power, or strength, comes with maturity; and the Holy Spirit will lead us, if we will let Him, into a depth of love for Jesus, and a life of devoted sacrificial obedience to Jesus, as He glorifies Jesus in our hearts and lives. And the power will follow, and people will be turned to Christ by our testimony—the testimony of our lives, and the testimony of our lips—as we cease to become so much people who need to be taught, and become, more and more, people who in our own right, through the Holy Spirit's inworking, become teachers of others.

May I then turn your thinking to what this writer, I believe, would teach us about our great High Priest? Now look at v. 14: "Our great high priest . . . has passed through the heavens, Jesus, the Son of God." This is a title of the Lord Jesus which he has used already, two or three times, back in chapters 2 and 3. And I am struck by the fact that this is the only epistle in the New Testament which applies this title to the Lord Jesus Christ. I found myself asking myself, "Now why should the writer to the Hebrews call the Lord Jesus Christ a great high priest? Why is it that he chooses this particular title for the Lord Jesus? No one else does."

I believe the reason is, because he is addressing himself to Christians. He does not, you see, refer to Jesus Christ primarily as Saviour—though He is indeed our Saviour: praise God for that! He does not call upon us to consider Christ so much as Saviour, but as High Priest, whose responsibility is for those who are saved. As Saviour, Jesus presents Himself to the unsaved, and His whole ministry through the Holy Spirit is one of justification. But as great High Priest, Jesus presents Himself to the believer: His whole ministry that of glorification, of bringing the justified believer to glory, where He Himself has gone. "He has passed through the heavens", it says.

In the Old Testament the priest's ministry was different from that of the prophet's. The prophet represented God to man: his office was to speak the word of God to man. But the priest's office was different: his office was to represent man to God. That is what it says in 5:1, "Every high priest chosen from among men is appointed to act on behalf of men in relation to God." He approaches God on their behalf in a God-prescribed way, with gifts and sacrifices for sins. There is the Old Testament background.

Now, says the writer, Jesus, our great high priest, has passed through to the heavens, to the very glory of the Father's side, and He bears with Him the blood of the covenant (chapter 9). And what does He do this for? Why has He passed through the heavens to the glory? Why, that He might act on behalf of men, to minister in heaven on our behalf. Do you see what this means? What an encouragement, believer, this is for you. There stands at God's right hand One whose whole concern is for you, because His ministry there is on your behalf.

You remember that verse in 7:25, "He ever liveth to make intercession for us." Now the exact implications are very wonderful, and I am not sure that I understand all that is involved in them—how the Lord Jesus Christ in fact pursues His ministry of intercession, and in what particular way the Son intercedes with the Father. But I see the basic, wonderful truth here, that day by day the Lord Jesus Christ is ministering in heaven on my behalf, and yours. I should not dare stand up in my pulpit in Oxford if I did not believe that; and I should not dare minister to my children at the breakfast table with the Bible open, if I did not believe that their interests, their spiritual interests, are His whole concern in heaven, because that is the duty of a high priest. The whole concern of the high priest is for the congregation. And he acts on their behalf before God. And if that means anything at all, it means that while you sit there listening, while I stand here speaking, our great high priest is not idle or inactive, but He is busy on our behalf. Isn't that a thrilling thought?

May I put it very pointedly: all the aspects of your Christian life are His concern. Your great high priest is concerned about your prayer life: He knows all about it; I don't. He is concerned about it; and His loving concern is that your prayer life might be rich and full. He is concerned about your spiritual babyhood—if that is true of you. He is also lovingly concerned that you should go on to maturity. It is His whole concern in heaven: He is the great high priest who is concerned about the whole congregation, and His ministry is on their behalf. He is concerned about your particular problems.

Maybe you think nobody is concerned about your problem; it is too difficult to share with anybody. I say that the Lord Jesus Christ knows all about it, and He is concerned about it. He most lovingly wants that problem dealt with; and His whole ministry in heaven concerns you, in all the loneliness of your spiritual problem, which you think you can share with nobody. You have a great high priest who has passed through the heavens. Doesn't that encourage you? Tell Him about it. Open your heart to Him.

Your besetting temptation is the concern of your great high priest. He has you on his prayer list—may I say it? He knows. And you maybe did not realise that He has been making intercession for you on that specific thing, day after day, hour after hour. His whole concern is for you. Young man, young woman, your future is His concern: the great decisions of your life are His concern. He is your great high priest, too. You are worried about the decision as to whom you are going to marry. He is not worried: He knows, and He is concerned that you should find the one He has chosen for you. And I tell you from my own experience, there is nothing quite like that.

He is concerned about the career that is before you. You are worried about it? I live enough among students to know that many Christian students come to the end of their university career without a clue as to what they should do, and many of them are very worried about this, because the Bible says that God has prepared for us good works, that we should walk in them. Well, here is a Scripture that says He has prepared beforehand good works that you should walk in them: and I tell you, He is concerned that you should know what those good works are. So do not be perplexed and puzzled, and think that God has forgotten you. Long before ever you began to worry about your career, He was concerned in heaven. He is your great high priest, and He wants you to walk in the path of His will, trusting and obeying Him.

"Since we have a great high priest . . . let us hold fast our confession." Why, of course! Do you see the argument? If we have no great high priest, if we could not be assured that Someone (with a capital S) was concerned with us in heaven, why, there would be no reason for holding fast our confession. Let's drift! Let's be discouraged! Let's be disheartened! Let's give up! Let's remain spiritual babies! That does not nourish; it does not satisfy! Consider Him—and then go on. Don't be introspective about your problems. Let the Holy Spirit of God lift your eyes to see Jesus, and see what He is doing for you now; and get up and go on with a new confidence. We have a great high priest. Isn't that superb!

Our great high priest and His *unique ministry*: may I say, secondly, here is something about our great high priest and His *unique ability*. To match His ministry is His ability. That is what the writer goes on to talk about. "We have not a high priest who is unable to sympathise with our weaknesses, but One who in every respect has been tempted as we are, yet without sinning. Let us then with confidence draw near . . ." If I felt that my great high priest could not understand my particular problem, my particular difficulties, my particular weaknesses, then I might not be so keen to draw near with confidence.

Sometimes parishioners come to me with great difficulties, and, because I am not a particularly good parson, they say, "You just won't understand!" And I have learned to say, not "Oh, I think I should", but, "I think you are probably quite right. But there is One in heaven who will. Why not share it with Him? Why not talk with Him about it, because in heaven you have a great high priest with unique ability to understand." We have not a high priest who is unable to sympathise with our weaknesses, but One who is qualified, because in every respect He was tempted as we are, but without sinning. And I tell you, that means your particular problem was in His earthly life His particular problem. He knows about it from first-hand experience.

I wonder if you pray to God as the psalmist prayed? I wonder if you ever pour out your complaint to God? I think this is a mark of mature Christianity, when you can really share with God the things that are troubling you; when prayer does not become just recitation, but getting hold of God, and saying to Him, "Lord, this is my problem. Why aren't You doing anything about it?" I do not think, if that is Spirit-inspired, it is irreverent at all. It seems to me the way the psalmist prays. "Why have You gone to sleep?" "I haven't," He says. And in this way the psalmist and his Lord come very close together, and the Lord makes known to the psalmist some of the deep things about that relationship. And the psalmist gets off his knees having got his problem off his chest in the right way. As Mr. Lucas said in the previous session, we should not need psychiatrists if we learned to do this.

May I tell you a funny story, to loosen the thing up? I was going through a period of considerable stress and strain earlier this year, and I wanted to pray in that way, as the psalmist prayed. So I went to our church, and locked the church door, and I walked up and down the middle aisle, praying to God. Have you ever done that? Talking to yourself, some people would say. No, I don't think so: just getting it off your chest! I am sorry for you chaps who have not a church where you can go and lock the door: but find somewhere where you can guarantee you are alone; and then go and get it off your chest alone with God. "Oh, my God, why have You allowed this to happen? Lord, I'm absolutely devastated by what's happened. Lord, I'm worried: You can see it. Now, Lord, do something, please, for me." And to walk up and down like that in the church, I find a great release.

You say, "What's funny about that?" Well, my wife lent the spare key of the church to the builder, without knowing that I was there. He had come to look at the roof, which was leaking. And I turned round in my urgent prayer to God—aloud: nobody was there, I thought—to find four astonished builders standing at the back of the church. It was very embarrassing! I still do not know what they said!

I hope that the inadvertent stumbling upon a Christian really trying to get to grips with God, may have done some of those men's souls good. But I tell you, it is a great practice to have somewhere where you can really be alone with God, and tell Him your needs; because, says this passage, He is Somebody who understands. "We have not a high priest unable to sympathise with our weaknesses"—with our weaknesses. Do not pretend you are strong: tell Him about your weaknesses. "But One who in every respect has been tempted as we are, yet without sinning." This is His great qualification.

I wonder if I might share with you what I believe to be the meaning of this phrase, "yet without sinning". I find myself supported by most of the commentaries on the epistle to the Hebrews on my shelf. "Without sinning..." This was an illuminating thought for me, and I hope it is Scriptural: I hope

172

it is true. But I put it over in that way, so that you may test it thoroughly in your own thinking. "Without sinning"—it could mean either that He simply never gave in to sin: He was tempted in all points as we are, yet He never gave in to sin. That is certainly true. What I am not sure is, whether this is what the writer is actually saying, or whether in fact he is saying more than that. It seems to me more likely that what the Greek means is that He was tempted in every way as we are, yet His experience was uniquely outside of sinning: in other words, it was in a unique sense impossible for Him to sin. The totality of His self-giving to the will of the Father made it, I suggest to you, impossible for Him to sin; and therefore in this sense He was without sin.

"Now," you say, "this seems to detract from the force of what you were saying. If He never had the possibility of sinning, how can He understand my terrible propensity to sin?" I do not think it weakens the argument: I think it strengthens it. Did he have to enter into the experience of sin, in order to help my need? No, of course not: He couldn't. For that would have put Him in need of a Saviour Himself, and prevented Him from being my Saviour. The fact that He is outside of sin means that He can be my Saviour, to save me and lift me out of sin. But two things, I think, come from what I am trying to say. His being outside sin means, in effect, that the real suffering of temptation had to be endured by Him to the bitterest extreme. You see, in a sense, to succumb to a temptation is to end the temptation, isn't it? To succumb and give in, the temptation immediately loses its power: it has done its job. And you know from your Christian experience, that not to succumb to temptation, to resist temptation, is not to end the temptation; but sometimes it will hound you and hound you.

Now if the Lord Jesus Christ was tempted in all points as we are, yet without the possibility of succumbing to it, do you see what it means? It means that He endured temptation to the extent none of us have ever had to endure it; more than any have ever endured temptation, Jesus did, because it was impossible for Him to succumb to it. Therefore the temptation hounded Him, and hounded Him, and hounded Him. I believe this is what the writer is saying.

May I try to illustrate it? Suppose there was a person who was incapable of dying. Now suppose that person is exposed to the murderous assault of a killer. Suppose that person attacks that man incapable of dying with a knife; and he drives the knife home, but he cannot kill him. He drives the knife home again, again, again . . . until that poor man's body is absolutely peppered with knife-holes. But he cannot die. You see, if he had driven the knife home into the heart the first time, and he had died, it would have all been over, the agony gone. But the fact that he is without the capability of dying, means that he has to go on enduring, and enduring, and enduring . . . I believe that that is what the writer is here saying.

It was impossible for Christ to succumb to sin, and so Satan drove his temptation home and home and home; and it was impossible for Him to succumb. The Lord Jesus Christ was therefore tempted in every fullest way that the world has ever been tempted, yet without sin. You see what this means. We have not a high priest who is incapable of understanding our temptation. What are your little temptations compared with what He suffered? Your temptations are fierce and frightening, but I tell you they are nothing compared with what our great high priest suffered when He was tempted and

173

tempted and tempted, yet without the possibility of sinning. He was tempted to the bitterest end that Satan could take Him, yet still without sin.

Now, says this writer, He can deal with your temptations. He understands. "Nobody", you say, "has ever been tempted quite like me." Now if that were true of the whole population of the world, there would still be a wonderful truth for you to learn. Because this passage means that I can say to you, "Yes, there is. Even if your temptation, which you have suffered and continually suffer, was unique in this world's experience, I should say it is not unique, because Christ suffered it, even more so. He was tempted to the bitterest end. And therefore He can help you."

We have a great high priest, therefore, with a unique ability. Let us draw near, the writer says, with confidence. Not with a sort of feeling, "Well, I really don't think the Lord can help me. I've prayed, but nothing's happened. My Christian life seems to be beyond His touch. Oh, if only the heavens wouldn't be like brass!" Well, tell Him about it. Because, surely, there was an occasion when He prayed, and the heavens were like brass, too. "My God, my God!" He said, "Why hast Thou forsaken me?" He understands. He has been there. And there is no temptation you have ever suffered, no spiritual problem, no situation in your Christian life, that this great high priest, with this unique ability, cannot help you with.

Climb to the top of the hill, then, and tell Him about it. Get it all out of your system. Pour it out. He is ready. He wants it, because He is unique in His ability to help. And you have the ministry of a great high priest like that, for your need.

So then, says the writer, "Draw near to the throne of grace with confidence." He repeats it in 10:22, where he puts it slightly differently: "with a true heart, in full assurance of faith". Oh, what a joy it is, when you begin to see our Saviour as He really is; when you see His concern for you at the right hand of God in heaven. You can draw near with confidence, with a true heart—not a heart which tries to veil its need, even before God, but a heart which is speaking the truth to God: a true heart. And, "in full assurance of faith", because you come to a great high priest whose whole ministry in heaven concerns you, and His whole desire, His whole loving desire for you, is that He may bring you where He is; to bring you home to heaven.

Surely this illuminates the two uses of the word "advocate" in the New Testament. 1 John 2:1 says, "We have an advocate with the Father, Jesus Christ the righteous." An advocate is somebody who pleads your cause; and Jesus Christ is our advocate with the Father, pleading your cause. Oh, thank God for that. There's even hope for me.

But the Lord Jesus Christ Himself said in John 14:16, "He will give you another Comforter, another advocate." It is the same word. And He refers, of course, to the Holy Spirit of God. And while the Lord Jesus Christ is busy with His unique ministry, in His unique ability, pleading my cause in heaven, the Holy Spirit is pleading His cause in my heart. Because the advocate is within you; the Holy Spirit of God who ministers for Christ's sake in your heart assures you of the truth of these things, assures you that the Lord Jesus Christ loves you, assures you, and glorifies the Lord Jesus in your heart.

You have the Holy Spirit, if you are a believer. Will you not let Him possess that frail heart of yours, possess you for this particular ministry, to tell you

174

about the Lord Jesus, glorify Him in your heart and life, to lift your eyes to Jesus away from your failures and sins? To lift your eyes continually in His ministry, and to plead the cause of the Lord Jesus in your heart, and say to you, "Look at your high priest; and don't you dare be disquietened or discouraged. Don't you dare give up, since you have a great high priest who has passed through the heavens, Jesus, the Son of God. Hold fast your confession, and go on to maturity. Because He will see to it that He brings you home"?

The Church's Power

By the Very Rev. James Dunlop, M.A., D.D.

As we read the Acts of the Apostles we cannot fail to be impressed with this thought, that the one thing that characterised the early disciples of Christ was *power*: spiritual life and power. And with that thought we are inevitably reminded of a contrast, or rather two contrasts: first, the contrast between that early church and the church of today. The Christian church today as a whole fails to touch the world of men with that impetus of life and power that is everywhere evident in the Acts. The other contrast is between the early church and those same disciples who made up the early church, but before the resurrection of Christ from the dead, and the coming of the Holy Spirit at Pentecost. Before those great events, the disciples were a weak, fearful, dispirited lot. After those events they were strong, bold, victorious, fearless. In a word, they had power, spiritual power, flooding through them.

Now I expect we should agree that in the Acts the church is as Christ intended it to be, in this respect at any rate. It just means, for one thing, that in so far as we have got away from the secret of this power today, we are away from the purpose and intention of Christ for His church. The fact that I have just mentioned, spelling out impoverishment in the church's life, and the ineffectiveness of the church's work from a spiritual point of view, is pretty well recognised. And within the church—and indeed outside the church, if we could only hear and truly interpret the restlessness of multitudes of people—there is a longing for spiritual revival. Men want God in real, saving, vital power, in the church. And the church knows the answer, knows where the secret of it is really found. We in the church today need, as the church has always needed, what those early disciples had.

"Ye shall receive power in the Holy Ghost coming upon you, and ye shall be witnesses unto me both in Jerusalem and in all Judea, and in Samaria, and unto the uttermost part of the earth." Now let us try to see what exactly it was that the early disciples had: what elements contributed to their power. For there are, I believe, several things to be noted.

The first is this—*They had a message*, a message to make known, a message to declare. They had something of inestimable value and importance to tell the world; something that they were convinced the world needed to hear. They had something to give without which they believed the world would be irreparably the poorer; indeed, without which the world would be lost. And having that message and that conviction, they had power. We need that conviction to be reborn in us today in the church, that we are a people set in this world by God with a message He wants us to declare, which men everywhere must hear, for their saving.

The message was, in one word, Christ—Jesus Christ. Christ was a tremendous fact to those early disciples; and the implications of His coming and His person and His work were tremendous, and the world must hear about them. And so they preached Christ; and not only by preaching to crowds of people in the technical sense, but in their living and in their talking with people. They moved about, and they declared Christ; the Christ who had come from heaven, from God, had tabernacled among men, had died and risen and ascended—God's greatest and final word to men. They preached, not an anaemic Jesus, not the Christ of man's theories and imaginings; but the Christ of the Gospel, the full Christ of the Bible, the Christ set before us here in the New Testament.

For the people of whom we are speaking were the people who wrote this New Testament; and here is their message. Here is the Christ whom they declared: Son of God, Son of man, Saviour, Redeemer, Lord, King, Judge. For in Christ there was this great fact continually being borne home to them and always vivid before their minds, that God himself had become manifest in Christ, here in this world, to redeem man to Himself by the sacrifice of Himself. They had the two great recurring themes: Christ crucified—the cross; and Christ risen again—the resurrection. For through the death of Christ there was redemption and salvation for all men; and in His resurrection there was the proof and the power of it. That was their message; a tremendous message, and the only message in all time to save the world of men.

The church today must learn that the first secret in getting back the power is that her task and her message is to preach Jesus Christ to people in His fulness: Lord, God, Saviour, Redeemer. Well, that is the first obvious thing; and if they had not had that conviction, they would not have had power with men. And unless we have that conviction, so that it really moves us, we shall not have power.

But I notice, also, those early disciples had *an experience*. You would never think for one moment that their message was mere head knowledge. Oh, no; far from it. They believed that message with all their hearts, because it was made vital to them by the witness of experience. They preached Christ, and had experienced the Christ whom they preached. Some of them had an experience, in the past, of trusting Christ, knowing Him in the days of His flesh, hearing Him speak, seeing what He did, keeping company with Him; and never once, from the day in which He called them to rise up and follow Him, until the day in which He was taken up from them into heaven, never once had He betrayed their trust. They had that experience. But more important than that, they had an experience of Christ in the present; a living, growing trust in Him, now that He was no longer with them in the body, but more really in the Spirit. Christ was real to them every day.

And today our experience of Christ must back up our message of Christ, if we are to have power. There is no use preaching Christ—however well we do it, and however orthodox our presentation—unless we are experiencing the Christ whom we preach. That is the significance of this message, round this Person. And when I speak of an experience of Christ I do not simply mean an experience of conversion through Christ—which is all-important, of course—but the living, growing knowledge of that new life that came to us at our conversion to Christ; our experience of Christ must be up to date. We shall be powerless men unless it is. I think that is why Christ Himself called His disciples by the name "witnesses", just witnesses to Him, speaking what they knew; because that is what a witness does. We witness to Christ, in distinction from preaching about Christ, in proportion to the reality of our experience of Christ.

Christ wants us to be witnesses in our words and in our living, and in the fact that He is dwelling within us. And the ironic fact is this, that all through the history of Christianity there seem to have been more good lawyers than good witnesses; plenty who will talk and argue and discuss: not so to many who will just witness for Christ, so that the reality of Christ is seen in them. And the divorce of Christian preaching from the reality of experience, we all know, has brought discredit upon Christ's church again and again. Men want reality: they want that today, and they are still prepared to respect reality when they see it. And so we must, if we would have power, have a living, present experience of Christ; an experience, of course, which He is only too willing to give us, as we trust Him. This is the essence of the Christian experience from the personal point of view, that Christ Himself comes to live in us. And as we witness to Him, and the truth that He has made known, and the facts concerning Him, Christ Himself is seen through us and about us. That is the second thing: these early Christians had not only a message, they had a living experience.

What was the third thing? They had *the fulness of the Holy Spirit*. And whatever that phrase may immediately suggest to our minds, I think we must all agree on this: that here is what seemed really to change those disciples, making their message live, and vitalising their experience. This is what gave dynamic to them and to their witness. "Ye shall receive power, the power of the Holy Ghost coming upon you, and ye shall be witnesses unto me, both in Jerusalem, and in all Judea, and in Samaria, and unto the uttermost parts of the earth."

The experience of those early Christians reached the full greatness that Christ intended for His church, in this respect. The promise of Christ to them was fulfilled, that if He went away from them, they would be better off, because He would come back to them by the Spirit, no longer to live in a human body, or in a particular local place, but He would dwell in them, each of them, all the time, wherever they were: and they would be better off. And we know how at Pentecost this promise was realised, the Holy Spirit came, and the Holy Spirit transformed them. Now we have the Holy Spirit, if we are Christians: the Spirit has not been withdrawn from the church of Christ. "If any man have not the Spirit of Christ, he is none of His." Christ is in us only by the Holy Spirit. We have received the Holy Spirit. Why does He not transform us today, as He transformed them? The only honest and logical answer, I think, must be this: that we do not make room for Him as they did; that we do not respond to Him as they did.

These men were not afraid of the Holy Spirit: they opened their hearts fully to Him, and He took possession. There were no half-measures with them, and they pleased God. The fulness of the Holy Spirit. Now I well know that there are varying and divergent views as to the conditions of receiving His fulness, and as to what are His manifestations, and so on. But let us fasten on this basic fact, that God Himself has made this provision for the life and witness of His people; and that here and now One who is the Holy Spirit is working in us and with us, whose power is almighty. And we are meant to use our full power in Him. There is power only there—in the Holy Spirit and His provision; and it is the privilege and the duty of every member of the church of Christ, of every Christian, to be filled with this power, to be filled with Him, the Holy Spirit.

That requires, it seems to me, two vital steps; the fulfilling of two conditions on the Christian's part. First, there must be *repentance from sin*; a frank and full reckoning with sin. We must put away all that is displeasing to our Lord as He reveals it to us. Second, there must be *whole-hearted obedience to Christ*, an acceptance of His entire will for us in a daily surrender to Him. And, my dear people, when those conditions are fulfilled, there remains nothing else but to ask for His promised filling, and believe that He grants it, relying by faith on Him as we relied on Him by faith when we trusted Him for salvation. As we yield daily to Him in this sincere way, so He fills us. As we make room for Him, so He possesses. We may grieve Him again, we may sadly disobey Him; but the way of renewed filling is ever open to us on the same conditions. When the heart is cleansed, and there is the attitude of simple faith and loving obedience to the known will of our Master, we can thank Him for, and count upon, such an infilling of His Spirit as shall be sufficient to meet every demand that He lays upon us.

The result of being Spirit-filled is nothing spectacular necessarily, but simply that Christ is magnified in us, and Christ's power ministered through us as we live and work for Him. As I speak to people, so yielded to Christ, the Holy Spirit is doing His work. I may not understand this, but this is God's way. It is His power, remember, that is all-important. We may and should grow in grace and the knowledge of our Lord Jesus Christ; but however far we advance, there is no spiritual power in *us*, apart from the Holy Spirit—although He can and should fill us to the greater extent. And practically it comes down to this: day after day our honest renunciation of sin and disobedience, and our honest choice of Christ's obedience—whatever it means— if we renew that daily, we may depend upon His power and His infilling.

The whole figure here, incidentally, is not that of a vessel being filled in some passive way and then overflowing, but a living involvement of our whole being *with* Christ, *in* His Spirit. We are personalities: He is a personality. So that His life is made manifest in and through us, even unconsciously to ourselves, but in the fullest degree that He intended and made possible. On our part obedience, yieldedness, faith: but He sees to the power and the fulness, and that is His responsibility. All the glory therefore is His, and must be; for when the Holy Spirit has His way, Christ, and Christ alone, is glorified

178

—not the person who has this experience of being used in His service.

The Spirit's fulness means a holiness of life that reflects and reveals Jesus Christ. It means freedom to work in power not our own, in saving men and women. It means so living as to glorify Christ in everything. And this effectiveness of the early Christians depended on this very important element— the fulness of the Holy Spirit. Here is one great essential element in their effectiveness: and they would never have thought of attempting anything apart from this. And why should we? "Ye shall receive power, the power of the Holy Ghost coming upon you, and ye shall be witnesses unto me both in Jerusalem, and in Judea, and in Samaria, and unto the uttermost parts of the earth."

They had a message: Jesus Christ in His fulness. They had that full conviction about Him. They had the experience of Christ living in them in fellowship. They had the fulness of the Holy Spirit, God's provision for His church. What else? Yes, there is something else. They had *a world programme*. If they knew the importance of the message they were given to declare, they had linked to that an adequate idea of its scope, and an anxiety to spread it quickly, all though the world. And as we read the record, there seems to be an urgency about these people. They give the impression that there was no time to waste. There was no waiting, for example, for a hundred years to evangelise Jerusalem thoroughly.

I suggest they had a more adequate conception of their task, and of the power of the Spirit. Their task was to witness and proclaim the message everywhere by the power of the Spirit. Christ's words to them were, "in Jerusalem"—at home. "In all Judea"—in their immediate circle. "In Samaria" —farther afield, to their former enemies, if you like, over the border. And abroad—"to the uttermost ends of the earth". And they sought to obey every part of that commandment at the same time. It was not Jerusalem *or* the ends of the earth: it was Jerusalem *and* the ends of the earth. And as they had that world programme and sought to fulfil it, they had power. And as we read the record there is an unmistakable breath of fire and life in it all— this world vision; and it was so ridiculous in one way, when you think of that little band of men, unknown, and not amounting to very much in this world, hidden in an upper room in Jerusalem, claiming the whole world for Christ, and going out to claim that world for Christ. And they were right. That is what He told them to do.

Have we lost this vision and this conviction? We must not excuse ourselves if we have. The tragedy is that where there is no vision, the people perish. What a glorious thing it is to belong to the church of Christ—not just that body that He has made to hold fellowship together, and to grow in grace, and have happy communion with Him and with themselves until He takes them to glory: but to be His appointed instrument to propagate His saving faith to all mankind—including the people around us, in the next street. The church to have power must be missionary. The individual Christian to have power must be a missionary. This is a part of it: this is an essential element.

They had the message of Christ in his fulness; they had the experience of Christ day by day, a living reality; they had the fulness of the Holy Spirit on whom they depended, and He was working in them and with them; and they had this world programme. What else? The only thing I would add is

179

this: they had *a faith that dared*. With all this knowledge, with all this equipment, with all this provision, with all this commandment behind them, they dared to go out and put it to the test. In conventions—and I have had long experience of conventions—the great danger is that we see these things and agree with them with our heads, and we just don't go out and do anything about it. And that kills the whole purpose and the whole reality of what we hear, and say we believe.

Here were people who were willing to put everything to the test. They were willing to trust and obey their Lord in all things, although it might cost them: and of course it cost them dearly; and with that revolutionary message they had, it was bound to cost. And they were willing for it. In every emergency they put Him to the test, and He honoured their trust. They believed in Him, and they proved Him. Here were men and women who dared to stand scorn, and opposition, and wrath, and persecution, and death itself: and therefore they had power—spiritual power. They dared to be obedient to Christ at all cost. They dared to condemn sin wherever they found it, in high places or in low. They dared to pay the price of sacrifice.

Do you wonder why we haven't power? We often speak of Paul as the outstanding apostle, and so he was; the apostle raised up to be specially the minister of Christ to the Gentiles. And what a gift to the early church was Paul! We say, "He was unique. You can't expect us to be filled with the power, and to have the influence that Paul had." And that's true—except from one point of view. There is no mystery about the power that Paul had from this point of view: that he paid the price for it, and he was willing to do so. "I suffer the loss of all things for Christ, and the knowledge of Christ, and the will of Christ. For me to live is Christ." And whatever it cost him, he took it! And he had power.

Is this not one great difficulty today, just the unwillingness of Christian people to give their whole interest and energy and themselves to bringing in Christ's kingdom? We are not willing to dare, we are not willing to be wholly about our Master's business. The enemy is never on holiday. Christian people seem frequently to take a holiday. And yet in all places, at all times, in season and out of season, we are meant to be busy, buying up the opportunities for Jesus, seeking men for Him. And how far do we do it?

My dear people, we must be wholly given to Christ; we must be wholly His, as He gives Himself wholly to us, if we take this thing seriously. What is our response, then, to this, and in today's situation? That situation certainly challenges us as Christian people. World forces like Communism, with their aggression and virility, certainly challenge us. Many foes are ranging themselves openly and blatantly against Christ and His cause. And on the other hand, Christ has set His church—us, and all other Christians—in the midst of this age, and given His church all provision to meet this situation victoriously. Why are we defeated? What is our attitude and our decision as individual Christians, as part of the church of Christ?

Surely there can be only one response. May I use an illustration from my early days as a student. I went out one year to Princetown, in America, to study; and I learned a little bit of the American way of life at that time. It is many years ago now. But one evening the football team of the university was gathered into the big university hall, and set up on the platform; and the rest of the student body for one solid hour yelled their college yell at those boys of the football team, because they had not been doing well in their games; and they thought this was the way to pep them up for the game that was to come the next day. This was their idea of pepping them up!

But that is only by way of introduction. In Chicago University they had the custom, when they had a home game, of sending the football team one by one through a room, before they went on to the field to play. It was not a very large room, and there was not much furniture: but on the wall there was a notice with four words—"For Chicago, I will". And you would see these big football giants coming in—for you have to have a certain physique to play American football—you would see them there with their pads, and their guards on their bodies, and holding their crash helmets in their hands, squaring themselves, reading the motto "For Chicago, I will" and then making their resolve—you could almost see it—and out on to the field to do and to die for Chicago. Some of them nearly did die; it's a strenuous game!

Over in California, on the far coast, in the foothills of the Rocky Mountains, a camp was held, organised by a YMCA for Japanese Christian boys. There were a great many at that time living there. At the centre of this camp was a glade in among the trees, an open-air amphitheatre; and you went into this between two tall pine trees. This was where the camp meetings were held, and they had their prayers, and so on. And one of the officers in the camp, who knew about this thing in Chicago, worked the motto of the camp in twigs between those two trees, so that the boys would read this motto every time they went in, and every time they came out again. I suppose you have guessed what it was: "For Christ, I will". It became the motto of the camp; and through the influence of the camp, it became the motto of many of those boys' lives. "For Christ, I will".

May I suggest to you that is the only fitting answer to the question I am putting to you? Not "For the church . . ." even; not "For the cause . . ."; not for any person, but for the only One who has the right to ask me for everything, and who does ask me for everything. That is the essence of His word to us; and He says, "This is the only way in which I can accomplish my purpose through my people." "For Christ . . ." to whom I owe everything, and who asks everything, "For Christ, I am willing—For Christ, I will." Is that our response?

I know that we are all in different circumstances. Some of us may be in active Christian work; others are not—housewives—and we all have our place to live in and our work to do. But we all have a part in the total witness of the church. And we all need these secrets, these elements of the power, that we may do our part, whatever it is, in His will. Our measure must be fulfilled. Let us make this response to Him: "By God's grace, I believe in this message of Christ. And that I will declare to the people around me, by His grace, near and far. I thank God that Christ is in me, and I hold fellowship with Him; and I renew that experience of Him day by day. I depend upon the fulness of the Holy Spirit, who can do all things; and I adjust my life humbly, by His grace, to Him. It is His work. I depend on Him; I believe in Him. And I have this world programme, for I know that everybody needs the Saviour; and I want this vision to be more and more clarified. Then by His grace I am daring to go out and do what He tells me to do. For Christ, I will."

Will we make that our response? He is responsible for the results; and all the glory shall be His, and certainly not ours.

The Holy Spirit—
a Blessed Person

By Dr. William Culbertson

In the section of the Gospel of John that is often referred to as the discourse of our Lord in the Upper Room, there are four separate and specific references to the Holy Spirit. I want to lay hold of one of those, and I read from John 14:14,

"If ye shall ask anything in my name, that will I do,
And if you love me you will keep my commandments.
And I will pray the Father, and He shall give you another Comforter, that he may be with you for ever;
Even the Spirit of truth; whom the world cannot receive, for it beholdeth Him not, neither knoweth Him: but ye know Him; for he abideth with you, and shall be in you.
I will not leave you desolate: I come unto you."

This is the first of that series of four references to the Holy Spirit in this discourse of our Lord. You will find that in each of these four references the Holy Spirit is alluded to as the Comforter. Joining with the passage which I have read, and to set us on our course, I read in Ephesians 4:30–31 these words: "And grieve not the Holy Spirit of God, in whom ye were sealed into the day of redemption. Let all bitterness, and wrath, and anger, and clamour and railing be put away from you, with all malice: And be ye kind one to another, tenderhearted, forgiving one another, even as God also in Christ forgave you." May I simply observe, from this passage, that it seems to me in a very unusual way it sets before us the personality of the Holy Spirit, for as it has been pointed out again and again, you cannot grieve an influence. You do not grieve a *thing*; you grieve a person. "Grieve not the Holy Spirit of God." He is a blessed Person.

Now I recognise that in our versions there are occasions when the neuter pronoun is used of the Holy Spirit. I understand why that happens to be. You see, the word "Spirit", in the language in which the New Testament was, written, is neuter in gender, and it is a law of grammar that that which modifies the noun, or the pronoun which stands for the noun, should be of the same gender. But I am glad to tell you that the New Testament breaks the laws of Greek grammar, and you will find that the masculine pronoun is used of the Holy Spirit many times. I personally like to use the masculine pronoun, using who and whom, instead of which; and using He and Him, instead of it. For He is a blessed Person, the Holy Spirit of God. He is God.

"Thou has not lied unto men, but unto God" was the word to Ananias and Sapphira; and the context speaks of their lying to the Holy Spirit. He is God. He is a blessed Person, and Christians should know Him. "Ye know Him", says John 14:17. How wonderful He is!

182

I think the importance of this subject, the theme of the Person and the work of the Holy Spirit, is established in many ways; but surely significant is the fact that in our Lord's closing discourse to His disciples, He spoke of the Holy Spirit on these four occasions. That says to me, this was a tremendously important message which our Lord had on His mind and heart to give to his disciples ere he left them.

You will recall that buttressing these passages in John 14, 15 and 16 are the references in Luke 24, and in Acts 1. Let me read those passages. In Luke 24, this was the word of the Lord Jesus as recorded in v. 49: "Behold, I send forth the promise of my Father upon you; but tarry ye in the city of Jerusalem, until ye be clothed with power from on high." Surely no one of us has any question but that was a reference that had to do with the advent of the Holy Spirit. "Tarry ye in the city, until ye be clothed with power from on high." And in Acts 1:4, I read: "Being assembled together with them, the Lord Jesus charged them not to depart from Jerusalem, but to wait for the promise of the Father, which, saith He, ye have heard from me. John indeed baptised with water; but ye shall be baptised in the Holy Spirit not many days hence." So this blessed Person came in answer to the prophecy of our Lord, and in fulfilment of what He said He would do as He was leaving His own.

Now there are just two things that I would like to cull from John 14:16–17. First, *The Request of the Son*; and second, *The Gift of the Father*. Says v. 16: "I will pray the Father, and He shall give you another Comforter, that He may be with you for ever." If you have a marginal reference Bible, it may be that there is a marginal rendering of this word "pray"—I will pray the Father. For example, in the American Standard Version, which I am using, there is a marginal reference, and it says: "Greek: make request of." And so the Lord Jesus is saying to the disciples, as He is about to leave them, "I will make request of the Father." And it is an interesting word that is used here, for it is not the asking on the part of an inferior of someone who is superior, for a boon of some kind or another. The word actually is a word that is used between equals; and here is an incidental inference of the deity of our Lord. "I will make request. As the Son of God, I will make request of God the Father, my Father and your Father, that He will give you another Comforter. I will pray the Father."

And there isn't any question. He says: "He shall give you another Comforter." Now I am interested in this word, *another*—"another Comforter". The language in which the New Testament was written, as most of you know, was peculiarly full and pregnant with expressions that were meaningful, and made distinctions of one kind and another. And you will understand, I am sure, when I say the Lord Jesus was saying: "He will send you another Comforter like me." Not a different kind of Comforter, but the same kind of Comforter. Now that which is inferentially given here is fully supported and evidenced by the fact that the word translated "Comforter" is used of the Lord Jesus, in 1 John 2:1. "My little children, these things write I unto you, that ye may not sin. And if any man sin, we have an advocate . . ." That is precisely the same word that is used in John 14:16 of the Holy Spirit.

The Lord Jesus is our advocate. He is our Comforter too. Did you know that as a believer in the Lord Jesus, you have two Comforters; one of them is in heaven at the right hand of God, and the other is indwelling you down here on earth. That is pretty good support and protection, isn't it? How wonderful! "Another Comforter." That signifies there already is one, you see; and He was there with them at the time; "another Comforter He will send unto you".

So the Lord Jesus is our Comforter in heaven. He is in heaven as our mediator, and as our intercessor, and as our advocate. And if I understand the teaching of the Word of God correctly, He is our advocate, and that has to do with sin. If any man sin, he has an advocate with the Father, Jesus Christ the Righteous. Now I don't think for a moment that the Father needs reminding of what the Lord Jesus did on the cross for our sins: but the Lord Jesus is there as the full and final answer to all the accusations of the accuser of the brethren; He is our helper in heaven. If any man sin, we have an advocate with the Father.

Please do not think of me as teaching anything that would savour of that which would outrage the teaching of the Word of God, or would in any wise teach antinomianism. But did you notice what it actually says here? It doesn't say, "If any man confess his sin, we have an advocate." It says, "If any man sin, we have an advocate." Now I don't know what that does to you, but that humbles me. That brings me low before God. Before this cold, callous heart of William Culbertson senses the conviction of the Spirit of God, and bows in repentance when William Culbertson has sinned, there is a man in the glory already praying for me. Hallelujah! "If any man sin, we have an advocate with the Father." And He is our mediator. He is our go-between. He is our daysman. And that is what we need. Cried Job, "Oh, that I had a daysman." We have: the blessed Son of God.

I know sometimes that we say we come immediately into the presence of God in prayer, and I know what we mean; but would you pardon me if I said we really don't come immediately; we come mediately. We always come through Jesus Christ our Lord. He is the Mediator. Now, bless your heart, we come into the immediate presence of God. That is true, and there is nothing between. Hallelujah! When the blood is cleansed, and when our hearts are right, communion and fellowship is vibrant and vital and wonderful indeed with God the heavenly Father.

He is the Mediator; and He is the Intercessor. And if I understand that aright, it has to do with our infirmities, our weaknesses. Do you remember that glorious word to Peter: "Peter, fear not, I have prayed for thee." And if the Lord Jesus prayed for Peter, don't you think He prayed for you too? He knows all the trials ahead, and all the tests. He knows of all the potential failures, and He is praying for us.

That brings me to this word "comforter". Actually it means "one called beside". Greek, *paraclete*. And, of course, if He is called beside, He has come to help us. I like that word, "helper". I sense my need of help; and I have help in heaven in the Lord Jesus, and I have help on earth in the indwelling presence of the Spirit of God. That is the request of the Son: "I will pray the Father, and He shall send you another Comforter [another one just like me], that He may be with you for ever."

The second thing is, *the Gift of the Father*. Did you notice how verse 16 concludes: ". . . that He may be with you for ever"? Here is something that God has settled in His eternal purposes; and His purpose and His plan is for the presence of the Spirit of God with God's people for ever. How wonderful that is.

We sometimes in our hymnody speak of the Spirit of God being taken from us; and I understand that in our fellowship with the Lord, we can get to the place where we are upset and distraught and disturbed, and perhaps tempted to think that God has forsaken us. But He hasn't. He is with us— how long?—*for ever.*

But notice, further, it says in v. 17 that He is "the Spirit of truth; whom the world cannot receive, because it beholdeth Him not, neither knoweth Him: but ye know Him".

I have had the privilege, from early days, of being active in attempting to lead people to the Saviour. Whenever I have dealt with a soul about coming to the Saviour, I have always used the Word of God; I have seen individuals just look absolutely blank. And then the light began to dawn, and sometimes— blessed be God—the joyful reality of it all comes, and it is very wonderful. And when that comes, I often say, "Now don't you want to thank the Lord for what He has done? Don't you want in my presence to confess Him, and tell Him what you have done?" And normally the answer is "Yes".

Now sometimes some folk need prompting, and need help; and I don't decry that. But normally I won't pray for them, and tell them to follow me in prayer. I just put them on their own, because I am very interested in what they are going to say. And you know, ninety-nine times out of a hundred the first word that falls from their lips is, "Father." And you do know what it says in Galatians 4:6, "God sent forth the Spirit of His Son into our hearts, crying, Abba, Father." When I hear that, I say "Thank you, Lord." That is exactly what the Holy Spirit teaches the newborn babe, "Father". So you know Him.

Blessed Spirit of God, who inspired the sacred Scriptures, and who illuminates the pages for us, and who leads the children of God home. Blessed Person of the Godhead. He is our teacher.

Well, one thing more as I close. Would you look at what it says at the conclusion of v. 17: ". . . the world beholdeth Him not, neither knoweth Him: ye know Him; for He abideth with you, and shall be in you".

It would be difficult for me to select from the Word of God that portion, or the scene that has meant most to me in the matter of Christian living. But I suppose, if I were put to it, I would have to answer that truth No. 1 for William Culbertson is this: that my body is the temple of the Spirit of God. That is what it is talking about here, isn't it? Says v. 17: "He abideth with you, and shall be—where?—*in* you." In you, this Spirit of truth.

Would you look at 1 Corinthians 6:19. In a context that, in my judgment, allows for no alternative but that the word "body" is speaking of the physical body of the believer. Verse 18 is speaking of a sin that has to do with the human body; and growing out of that is this question: "Know ye not that your body is the temple—is the sanctuary—of the Holy Spirit who is in you, whom ye have from God, and ye are not your own?" There was a famous American preacher who had a great sermon entitled: "The Expulsive Power of a New Affection." May I adapt the title of that sermon, and say the sense of God's Holy Spirit living in me day by day by day has a great expulsive power so far as sin is concerned.

A friend of mine, greatly used of God as a Bible teacher in the States years ago, used to say that he tried to make his first waking thought to thank God that his body was the temple of the Spirit of God. Just before he died, I had the privilege of visiting him. I said to him, "I want to ask you a question." "Well, go ahead." I said, "I have heard you say in public meetings again and again that you try to make your first thought of each day to thank God that your body is the temple of the Holy Spirit." "Yes," he said. "That is true." I said, "Why do you do that?" I knew why he did it, but I wanted to hear it from him. He said, "There are two things. I want that truth to live vitally in me every day. I want to be aware of it. One of the ways I can become aware of it day by day is to begin the day thanking God." "Yes," I said, "and what else?" "I live differently when I recognise that truth, because I let Him live the life of Christ through me, and the fruit of the Spirit is borne." Blessed Holy Spirit. The Third Person of the adorable Holy Godhead has come to live in you and me. Do you believe that? God bless you.

Christ Glorified and Expressed

By the Ven. Herbert Cragg, M.A.

A few weeks ago I met a young man who had returned from a Christian Convention. "Did you have a good time?" I asked. "Yes, it was marvellous. I wouldn't have missed it for anything." For a few moments I shared his delight, and learnt a little of the blessing that he said had come to him. Then we parted; and as I walked away I found myself asking, "So what?" Not that I doubted anything that he had said to me: far from it. But I just wondered.

On Saturday most of us go down from Keswick. So what? God has been laying on my heart during the last few weeks, in preparation for tonight, this simple thought, "How can I make sure that the experience of this week is more than a passing splendour?" And the answer I bring you lies in a clear understanding of the ministry of the Holy Spirit, not in crying out for repeated baptisms of the Spirit, for if you will look up the references to the baptism of the Spirit in the New Testament, you will find that for the Christian it is a past experience. "By one Spirit were we all baptised into one body" (1 Cor. 12:13). Not in crying out for a succession of baptisms. Not in necessarily feeling that I must possess any or all of the gifts of the Spirit: they are distributed severally as God wills. They are not all for everybody, and therefore they may not all be for me. I must let God be God, and not cry out in my heart for that which He has not allotted to me in His sovereign pleasure.

The answer lies in a clear understanding of the ministry of the Holy Spirit; and I will beg you to note the distinction between baptism, gifts, and ministry. The teaching of the New Testament is quite clear and distinct on these three words; and the emphasis throughout is on the ministry of the Holy Spirit. Now if I were asked to summarise what the New Testament has to say about the ministry of the Holy Spirit, I would spell it out in two brief phrases.

First, the ministry of the Spirit is *to enable me to know Jesus better*, more clearly, more fully, more deeply. And secondly, the ministry of the Spirit is to *enable me to show Jesus better*, more clearly, more consistently, in a more widespread fashion, and in a greater variety of experiences and settings of life. To know Jesus better and to show Jesus better. A deeper knowledge, a clearer testimony. This is the objective of the Holy Spirit in all His ministry with the believer; and His instrument in this twofold ministry is Holy Scripture.

I want, if I may, in support of my two contentions, to turn to two passages of Scripture: John 16:12–14. Our Lord Himself is the speaker, and His disciples are gathered around Him listening to this final discourse, this mighty teaching from the lips of the greatest of all teachers, Christ Himself. "I have yet many things to say to you, but you cannot bear them now." Christ's teaching ministry was incomplete, simply because they would be unable to take any more for reasons that follow. "When the Spirit of truth comes, He will guide you into all the truth: for He will not speak on His own authority, but whatever He hears, He will speak: and He will declare to you the things that are to come. He will glorify me: for He will take what is mine, and declare it to you. All that the Father has is mine: therefore I said that He will take what is mine and declare it to you."

He will glorify me: the ministry of the Spirit in making the believer know more of Christ. Notice that our Lord said, "He will glorify me", not Himself. When I was a young Christian, I was at one point interested in a very zealous group; and then I left them, for the simple reason that they were constantly urging me to go further than Jesus, and although I didn't know very much, I felt I couldn't. Nor could I. Nor can I. Nor can you when you are under the ministry of the Holy Spirit. The Holy Spirit brings you to Jesus, and keeps you close to Jesus, and teaches you more of Jesus, and never takes you beyond Jesus. The theme of the Holy Spirit is Jesus. "He will glorify me", not Himself, not His teaching, not His gifts, not anything He brings: "He will glorify me."

And how will He do this? Verse 13: "He will guide you into all truth." We have had reference in our Bible Readings to our Lord's promise in John 14:26, where He said concerning the Comforter, "The Holy Spirit, whom the Father will send in my name, He will teach you all things, and bring to your remembrance all that I have said to you." The Holy Spirit would remind them of what Jesus had said. He would take up the truth that they had already heard, and keep it fresh in their minds, and begin to unravel something of its significance to their minds, and apply its importance to their hearts and to their lives.

But in John 16:13, Christ goes further: that when the Holy Spirit comes,

He will not only remind you of what I have said, but He will tell you the things I can't now say. "He will guide you into all truth . . . by declaring the things that are to come."

Now the literal phrase there reads: "He will declare to you the coming things", that is to say, the things that were just about to happen. They hadn't happened when Jesus had this discourse with His disciples, but they were about to happen. These disciples couldn't be expected to understand them before they had happened, however much Christ prepared them; but when they had happened, the Holy Spirit would interpret the events in terms of truth.

What were the things that were about to happen? The cross, the resurrection, the ascension, the church. These were the things that were about to happen. And our Lord said to His disciples, "The Holy Spirit will glorify me by keeping in your mind, and explaining to your hearts what you know already, because I have told you; and adding to that, what you don't know already, because I can't now tell you." And without pressing the case too far, I am perfectly certain that John 14:26 is the promise of the four Gospels; while John 16:13 is the promise of the New Testament letters. And so it was that both these promises were fulfilled to those to whom they were first made, and God gave to His church, through His apostles, the clear, unmistakable authority to teaching that was to flow from what He had done in His life, and what He was about to do in His death and resurrection. So that in v. 14 He goes on to say: "He will take what is mine, and show it to you." I like that word "take". One old commentator has suggested that it carries with it the idea of somebody going to a storehouse, and lifting out of the storehouse what the needy friend he would help most needs; and taking it from the storehouse to the needy one. And this is the ministry of the Holy Spirit: Christ is the storehouse inexhaustible, never to be emptied out, never to be fully taken, never to be entirely exhausted; constantly something fresh in and through the pages He inspired those first apostles to write to bring to us. And as He did this primarily and authoritatively with His first apostles, so through the reading of the Scriptures He inspired, He does it constantly, daily, hourly, momentarily with me and with you.

What a great storehouse there is in our Lord! Did you ever think for a single moment that you would ever exhaust Him? If you did, it is just because you don't know Him. The unsearchable riches of Christ, and the inexhaustible resources of the Saviour, are at the disposal of the Holy Spirit, who is the executor of the Godhead; and what the Father has, the Son has, and what the Father and the Son together equally share, the Holy Spirit takes, that the church may share as well.

In our brief Bible studies at Christ Church, Beckenham, during these summer weeks we have been having a look at what I would call, Words worth weighing in the New Testament. A week ago I was looking at the word "fulness" in the Epistles of St. Paul—chiefly the Ephesian and the Colossian letters. What they have to say about fulness is pretty well parallel in the two letters. I quote from Colossians 2:9, where we read about our Lord that "in Him the whole fulness of the Godhead dwells".

Paul is saying that everything that there is in God, is in Christ: the whole of the divine Godhead is in Jesus. But the next verse says: "And you have come to fulness of life in Him." So just as the fulness of God is in Christ, so your fulness and mine is found in Christ; and the very fulness of God manifest in Christ is available to the child of God. John, in his prologue, has that delightful sentence: "Out of that fulness have all we received, and grace for grace." As I made this little study afresh last week, I found myself asking was there any link between the fulness of the Godhead in Christ for the church, and the command of Ephesians 5:18, "Be filled with the Spirit," or as the New English Bible so delightfully translates: "Let the Holy Spirit fill you." It is the same word, only the verbal form. The fulness of the Godhead in Christ; the believer's fulness—the word means completion or completeness—is found in Christ; and God says through the pen of St. Paul, "Let the Holy Spirit fill you."

The one who brings me Christ is the Holy Spirit. So that in the language of these two Epistles at least, the fulness of the Spirit is the fulness of Christ. And to be filled with the Holy Spirit is to be filled up full with Jesus. The ministry of the Holy Spirit is to enable me to know Jesus better. Don't we sometimes sing:

> *More about Jesus let me learn,*
> *More of His holy will discern,*
> *Spirit of God, my teacher be. . .*

And the lesson?

> *Showing the things of Christ to me.*

And all this to enable me to know Christ better. Is this your longing? Is this your determination? Are you going to let the Holy Spirit have a very slow and unwilling pupil? Indeed, are you going to contract out of the class?

Do you remember the lovely story of my beloved predecessor at Beckenham, Guy King, about a boy who left school before he was really old enough? And when somebody said, "Why?" he said, "Well, they can't teach me any more." And have I not found sometimes, alas, to my shame, that having now been a Christian for some few years, I have sometimes almost thought that He couldn't teach me any more? Oh the shame of even the shade of the thought! The Holy Spirit is the author of the holy life, and His instrument is the holy Scripture.

But the ministry of the Holy Spirit is also to enable me to *show* Christ better. To know Christ better, and to show Christ better; for I am not the end of His ministry, however much I learn. I love to compare two well-known sentences in the Gospel of John. Do you remember how in that Gospel it is normal for us to think of references to the bread of life as being references to our Lord, and references to the water of life as being references to the Holy Spirit? And you will recall that, in John 4:14, Jesus Christ spoke so tenderly to the woman on the well, and promised that "Whoever drinks of the water that I shall give him . . . the water will become in him a well of water springing up into everlasting life." In him a well. But in John 7:38, on the last day of the great feast of Tabernacles, Jesus stood and cried: "If any man thirst, let him come unto me and drink. He that believeth in me, as the Scripture hath said, out of his heart shall flow rivers of living water." The well for me; the rivers for the world.

Turn now to Acts 1:6, "So when they had come together, they asked Him, Lord, will you at this time restore the kingdom to Israel? And He said unto them, It is not for you to know the times or the seasons, which the Father has fixed by His own authority. But you shall receive power when the Holy Spirit is come upon you; and you shall be witnesses to me."

Ye shall glorify me, and you will know it. You shall receive power, and you will show it. Christ glorified in a deeper knowledge of Jesus; Christ expressed in a clearer testimony to Jesus. And the Holy Spirit is the secret of them both.

Now I wonder in what sphere of your life it is that you most need to express Christ better? May I deal with this closing part of my message to you, in terms of the word that Christ Himself used about the Holy Spirit. He said: "You shall receive power"; and the power of the Holy Spirit is the enabling grace of the Holy Spirit to be witnesses to Christ—that is, to express Christ, not only by word of lip, or by life, but by both and by all. Is it in your daily walk you long to express Christ better?

Just outside St. John's Church, Keswick, a young lady was hobbling along, with her shoe half hanging off, and an awkward bit of pebble inside it. A Convention speaker was walking up behind, and he said, "It looks to me as if something is impeding your walk." Is something impeding your walk? The apostle Paul is so fond of this phrase about your walk. In Colossians 1 he had this to say: We are to lead a life worthy of the Lord; and in order that we may do so, you may be strengthened with all power in the inner man. This is the power of the Holy Spirit indwelling the child of God, to enable him to walk straight, to walk worthy of Christ, and to show Christ in the daily life and character, which is produced by the indwelling Spirit. Do you long to walk to please God?

Do you remember the woman of Shunem, who turned to her husband as the prophet passed day by day, and she said to her husband, "I perceive that this is a holy man of God who passes by us continually." Oh, I know that it had something to do with his dress, but I think that she wouldn't have said that if it was only dress. It is possible to be dressed like a man of God, and not to give the impression of being one. The holy man of God. Is that the way you would love to show Christ more? I would.

Or perhaps it is that in some stiff and hard-slogging spiritual battle, you have wished you could show Christ more. May I give you a word for that very situation? In 1 Corinthians 10:13 we read about our Christian warfare: "God is faithful, who will not suffer you to be tempted above that ye are able; but will with the temptation also make a way to escape, that you may be empowered [literally] to endure it." You may be made strong to carry through with it; not to escape by running back, but to escape by pressing through. You long to express Christ better, to show Christ more in those hours of struggle and temptation, when Satan would drag you down. God is faithful, and you will find in the Holy Spirit power to endure it.

The building that houses the congregation I serve was blitzed during the war. The last bomb to fall on Beckenham fell a few yards to the side of our church, killing twelve people and blowing the church in from the side. But there was one part of the structure which remained unaffected, apart from chippings and scratchings. It was the spire. Why did not the spire fall? It had been internally strengthened in anticipation of trouble. Internally strengthened in anticipation of trouble, that you may be empowered to endure it. Do you long to express Christ better in the hour of battle? We wrestle not against flesh and blood, but against principalities and powers, against the rulers of the darkness of this world, against spiritual wickedness in high places. Don't you long to show Jesus then?

Or perhaps on a simpler note, it is just that you long to express it with your lips. And the promise is, "You shall be witnesses to me." I wonder if your experience is anything like mine, when you sometimes long to get those lips open just for a very simple word, and somehow or other it didn't come, and it ought to have come. And afterwards you said, "Why didn't it come?" Oh my dear Christian friend, as we go down from Keswick on Saturday, there will need to be some lips open somewhere, surely. "Have you had a good time up there?" "Fine." Is that all?

In Carlisle Castle you may go up to the keep and look out through the barred slits away to the north across the border toward the hills of Scotland; and if you look very carefully you will find that the red sandstone of the keep is grooved by the slits through which you look out. The story is told—I can't vouch for it; I just wasn't there—that when the prisoners from across the border during the border skirmishes were imprisoned in Carlisle Castle, they looked out, and they tried to get out; and the marks on the stone sills are marks of fingers that have grooved their way, clamouring to get out. Jesus has got in. Does He find it hard to get out?

Do you long to show Christ better in that moment of opportunity and testimony? This is the ministry of the Holy Spirit; and He is available to all who will obey Him. He has no favourites. He has no restrictions. He has no days off. There are no moments when He will not do His ministry fully and completely, if we will but open ourselves to His sovereign sway and allow Him to make Jesus King.

Or perhaps it is just that you want to show Christ better in human weakness. The apostle Paul, writing about the treasure that we have, the glory of God in the face of Jesus Christ, goes on to say in 2 Corinthians 4, "But we have this treasure in earthen vessels." Vessels of common clay, like the one that stands here, and the one that sits there. That is all we are; vessels of common clay. But in these vessels we have the wonderful treasure of the glory of God in the face of Jesus Christ. Why in vessels of common clay? Surely the Gospel of the glory of the grace of God deserves splendid vessels? But no, vessels of common clay. Why? That the excellency of the power—as Weymouth translates it—may be seen to come from God, and not from us. Christ indwelling human weakness by the Holy Spirit, that we might show Him better, as well as know Him better.

It was Saturday morning, and my sermons were not ready. The week had been very full. I was tired, as so often, just like you. I knelt to pray, I rose to study, I knelt to pray. I had no word from the Lord. And then, to nourish my own soul, I walked over to a corner of my study and picked up an old tattered copy of *Keswick Week*, 1911. It wasn't the addresses—I had no time to read them; but as I flicked the pages, looking for a nugget of truth that would set me right and get me going afresh, my eye fell on two short verses of poetry. I have forgotten the author—it doesn't matter. This is how they read:

I cannot do it alone. The waves draw fast and nigh;
The stars go out in the sky, and the storm beats loud and high:
But I know that we two shall win in the end,
*   Jesus and I.*

191

Coward and wayward and weak, I change with the changing sky,
Today so eager, so bright; tomorrow too weak to try;
But He never gives in, and we two shall win,
  Jesus and I.

Christ expressed in human weakness.

So you are going down from Keswick on Saturday. So am I. So what? Surrounded every moment by the gracious ministry of the Holy Spirit who, provided I will bend over the sacred page in loyal discipline and submission to truth, will enable me to know Jesus better; and when I lift my head from the page to go out to the task, to show Jesus better.

Will you pledge yourself to co-operate with the Holy Spirit to this double end: to know Jesus better, and to show Jesus better?

Archdeacon and Mrs. Cragg

Friday July 16th

10 am Missionary Meetings

General Missionary Meeting
Skiddaw Street Tent

TAPE NO. 306

Young People's Missionary Meeting
Eskin Street Tent

TAPE NO. 306a

8 pm Communion Service

The Day is Far Spent . . .
Archdeacon H. W. Cragg

Call to Service

Friday began joyously with testimonies to blessing received, at the general prayer meeting, in the Eskin Street tent, at 7 a.m. With an attendance of over five hundred—the largest of the week—the note of praise prevailed as some thirty or more told succinctly how the Lord had met with them in blessing through the ministry of the week: and more would have followed, had time permitted. Canon T. F. C. Bewes, who presided—as for several years past—guided the proceedings graciously, and gave the last of his series of brief addresses on "A Word from the Lord"—to Nathanael, Philip, Peter, Matthew, James, and Paul.

At the same early hour, from Monday to Thursday, missionary prayer meetings in the Methodist church were led once more by the Convention's "elder statesman", Canon A. T. Houghton. These, as ever, were characterised by informed, deeply concerned praying, with many missionaries and nationals from overseas taking part.

Friday morning was devoted as usual to the call to dedication and service in response to our Lord's Great Commission; but with a departure from the usual pattern, in that *two* missionary meetings were held, as described on the following page.

A question-and-answer session in the afternoon drew quite a large attendance to the small tent, when members of the team of speakers, under the chairmanship of the Rev. John Caiger, gave pertinent answers to questions which had been submitted concerning statements made and teaching given during the week.

The Convention closed with the customary but ever-moving Communion Service, conducted by the Ven. H. W. Cragg. It was a beautiful eventide—fitting finale to a glorious week—as the five thousand people assembled for the last time. "Sing we the King" was the appropriate first hymn; then Archdeacon Cragg spoke on the invitation of the two Emmaus road travellers to the unrecognised risen Lord, "Abide with us, for it is toward evening, and the day is far spent. And He went in to tarry with them . . ." In the hush of His recognised presence, the emblems of bread and wine were distributed and partaken, and the reality of oneness in Christ encompassed the great congregation in a fellowship of adoring worship.

A final hymn, "Jesus, Thou joy of loving hearts", closed the service, and the Convention.

Two Missionary Meetings

An innovation was made on Friday morning, in that two missionary meetings were held simultaneously, at 10 a.m. It had been felt that a more informal type of gathering might appeal to the young people, many of whom had seemed in recent years to avoid the main meeting: and so the experiment was tried, of a missionary meeting for them, in the small tent.

This naturally affected the attendance in the large tent: but a splendid crowd of around three thousand heard effective, factual and challenging addresses from four representative missionary speakers. Canon Alan Neech, general secretary of BCMS, and a member of the Convention Council, made a powerful plea for better support for missions, by prayer and interest and giving; and the meeting closed with the hymn "Jesus shall reign . . ."

A more free-and-easy manner prevailed in the small tent, where some 1,500 "under-thirty-year-olds" entered heartily into a by no means "traditional" missionary programme. Songs from *Youth Praise* were sung, and the Rev. Michael Baughen introduced a team of five younger missionaries who each spoke briefly and pertinently, in answer to questions raised by young people concerning missionary work—such as, How does a "call" come, What is it really like to be a missionary, What problems did you face on reaching the field, What support do you desire from home? All these were answered in very practical, down-to-earth terms.

Then, after a hymn, Canon F. T. C. Bewes, from his long and wide experience as a missionary and member of headquarters staff, indicated ten "points" for would-be missionaries. Questions from the floor, captured by a roving microphone, were answered by the team. Members of the Glass family, from Brazil, sang two Portuguese folk songs; and the Rev. Peter Coombs presented the challenge to full-time service, from the text, "Son, go work today in my vineyard"—which he emphasised word by word. There was a heartening response: and well over a hundred remained for some practical suggestions regarding next steps in putting their dedication into effect.

195

The Day is Far Spent

By the Ven. H. W. Cragg, M.A.

Abide with us, for it is toward evening—Luke 24:29.

It had been a long day. The first flush of early dawn had revealed two women hurrying to the sepulchre. All through the day the truth of the resurrection had been gaining ground: it was by now the talk of many in and around Jerusalem. The late afternoon was giving way to the chill of early evening as the two men in this record (Luke 24:13–31) set out for Emmaus, a Sunday-evening walk. "The day is far spent," they said to Jesus, and they constrained Him to abide with them.

This day is far spent. The last day of this Convention week, so crowned with blessing and grace from our heavenly Father's bounteous hand—a week we shall not quickly forget. And ere it close, just one more opportunity for every willing heart in this vast concourse of people to say to Christ afresh, "Abide with us, for it is toward evening, and day is far spent."

For some of us gathered here the day of life may be far spent. We know not what a day may bring forth. Not all of us are young, and the ticking of the clock beats out the day. We, too, shall want to say especially, "Abide with us, for it is toward evening." Then there are some who feel, and not without good reason, that the clock of human history is moving on toward midnight. We do not know when our Lord will come, but we do know He is coming.

> *It may be at midday, it may be at twilight,*
> *It may be, perchance, that the blackness of midnight*
> *Will burst into light in the blaze of His glory,*
> *When Jesus receives His own.*

But it is difficult not to feel that the day is far spent, though we don't know. "Abide with us, for it is toward evening"—the evening that closes the day; the evening that closes life's day; the evening that will close the day of grace. "Abide with us, it is toward evening."

Perhaps we shall be helped to pray such a prayer if we look again very briefly at the record before us in this chapter, and notice quite simply two ministries of Christ to these two men. You remember that first there was what I am going to call—*The Ministry of the Opened Word*. You remember the perplexity in their minds and the sorrow in their hearts, as slowly and steadily they set out on that brief walk to Emmaus. The perplexity in their minds revolved around the twin facts that, as far as they knew, their Saviour was crucified and buried. This was the only sure thing in their memories. "The chief priests and our rulers condemned Him to death and crucified Him: but strange to say, some women have been to the tomb and failed to find the body. They said they found some angels who said that He was alive. Where does the truth lie?"

And if they were perplexed in their minds, they were sorrowful in their hearts. "We trusted that He would have redeemed Israel; and beside all this, today is the third day since these things were done." Our Lord asked why they were so sad as they walked. Then you remember how delightfully St. Luke tells us: "He expounded unto them in all the Scriptures the things concerning Himself." How I should love to have been eavesdropping in that exposition! Wouldn't you? To hear from the lips of the Saviour Himself the long, detailed exposition of how the whole of their Old Testament Scriptures had pointed forward to the hours and days that now perplexed them. "He opened the Scriptures to them", in the ministry of the opened Word. And their hearts began to burn, and their minds began to understand.

That ministry has been with us this week in very rich measure, and with very deep and lasting and far-reaching blessing and impact. The Christ we worship tonight is the Christ of the opened Word; and He who has expounded to us through His servants the Scriptures, will continue by His Holy Spirit to expound to every willing learner the truths of the open Book. And if there is one thing that stands out above all others from the ministry of this week, it is that we are to get back to the Book, to the exposition of Scripture in our churches, to the studying of Scripture in our homes, and to the learning of Scripture day by day. The ministry of the opened Word.

"Did not our heart burn within us, while He talked with us by the way and while He opened to us the Scriptures?"—chasing darkness from their minds and sorrow from their hearts. "Abide with us." Do it again, Lord. Take the Book and make it plain. Chase the darkness from our minds, and the sorrow from our hearts. It is toward evening. Abide with us!

And you remember that in accepting their invitation to stay, He brought His own appointed confirmation of the Word: what I would call—*The Ministry of the Broken Bread*. The Lord's Supper is the greatest visual aid. Visual aids are not new. Christ gave two to His church, namely Baptism, and the Supper of the Lord—and the Supper of the Lord is the greatest visual aid that ever was or will be, on how the soul is sustained after birth, as it feeds on Christ. It is a dramatic presentation of the Gospel, the God-appointed confirmation of the Word.

Was it the way He gave thanks that they seemed to recall? Was it the way He broke the bread when He had turned aside with the two whose minds He had begun to open to the Word? Did they think back to the Upper Room, and the previous Thursday evening; or did they glimpse the nail-prints? St. Luke does not say. But Jesus dispelled all doubts, and they knew Him. And if in this vast concourse of people tonight there should be a heart that doubts the abiding love of Christ, for this very moment and for the moments that stretch ahead of us as we go down from Keswick tomorrow, there can be no more dramatic, convincing visual aid than that which is spread before us. "This do in remembrance of me." The ministry of the Word is the ministry of the broken bread.

Those of you who come from Scotland will be familiar with the life story of Robert Murray McCheyne. If I recall it aright, he was converted at the age of eighteen, having been a nominal church-attender, but never having attended the sacrament meal. He was not a believer: his mind was full of doubts, and his life was full of sin. When a brother of his persuaded him at long last to turn up at the Scottish kirk for the parish communion, he went. And that night he met his Lord.

Wounded for me, wounded for me,
There on the cross He was wounded for me:
Gone my transgressions, and now I am free,
All because Jesus was wounded for me.

And here, spread before us, are the tokens, the symbols, the confirming signs of that amazing sacrifice, so that we need not only hear it, but see it; and seeing it, be at last persuaded of it by His grace.

And so God has given to His church the ministry of Word and sacrament. Not sacrament without the Word, of course; and not the Word without sacrament: but the two together—and in that order. The ministry of the Word and sacrament—the Word to my mind, the sacrament to my sight; and both to my heart. "They constrained Him, saying, Abide with us, for it is toward evening." And He went in to tarry with them; and they knew Him; and He vanished out of their sight.

No longer did they need His bodily presence: they had welcomed the One who said, "I am always with you, even to the end of the age." Could it be— I doubt it—could it be that someone here has never said to the Lord Jesus Christ, "Abide with me"? My friend, it is "toward evening", the day is far spent—this day, perhaps your day, perhaps even the day of grace. And to every heart that knows the sweetness of His presence there is a call afresh tonight to say to Him whom we love, and will love to the end, "Abide with us, for it is toward evening."

It was toward evening when Francis Henry Lyte, a clergyman of the Church of England, planned to leave for the South of France in search of the health which eluded him. He sat down and penned the words of the hymn "Abide with me"; and having written, his day was spent before he reached the end of his journey. "They constrained Him, saying, Abide with us, for it is toward evening." The abiding presence of the unseen Christ.

Young People's Meetings

Impressions

Rev. Peter Coombs

Holiday Convention Week

Impressions

Young People's Meetings

Impressions

It was a great pity that some of the "God is dead" brigade were not able to eavesdrop on the Eskin Street Tent for the five youth meetings of the 1971 Convention. They would have found that He is very much "in business" in the lives of the hundreds of enthusiastic 15–30-year-olds who crowded the serried rows of forms each morning.

"Down-to-earth, Biblical logic" is how one newspaper reporter described the ministry of the Revs. Michael Baughen and Peter Coombs, who shared the leadership of the meetings this year. If this was a fair description of the ministry offered, then it shows that the young people of our churches are eager and ready to profit from an authoritative word from God provided it is conveyed in the language and thought-forms of the seventies. From the vantage point of the platform, it was a cheering and humbling sight to see so much of the future leadership of the Christian church willing to submit their thinking and living to what the Bible says.

Not that all the talking was "one way". A roving microphone saw to that. If the expertise of its handler fell somewhat short of BBC standards, it nevertheless provided an invaluable tool in allowing "audience participation". Shrewd, probing questions from the floor put the speakers on their mettle. Indeed, some of the highlights of the week came during answers to questions put to Major Batt, Dr. Alan Redpath, Prebendary Maurice Wood and Dr. Helen Roseveare. Part of an answer by Dr. Roseveare to a question on suffering will live long in the memory. Referring to her experiences during the Simba rebellion in the Congo, she said: "They took away our possessions, our money, our homes, our freedom, our purity. But when they had taken all these away, we found we were left with Jesus. And He was quite enough for all our needs."

A new venture this year was the young people's missionary meeting. Recruits and young missionaries spoke briefly on how God had guided and sustained them in their work; Canon Bewes provided a veteran's viewpoint and following a closing challenge well over one hundred stood to signify their willingness to take the next step on the way to serving their Master in the place of His choice. These, and others, stayed behind for an "after-meeting" at which representatives of missionary societies were present.

The main talks at the meetings this year took the form of a basic exposition of the middle chapters of the Epistle to the Romans, and the supporting talks focused on four of the Ten Commandments—those dealing with "Sabbath", "Sonship", "Sex" and "Speech". But these were only the hard core of a fast-moving hour packed with singing conducted in his inimitable way by Tim Buckley of the London Bible College, and accompanied by pianists Kenneth Coates, Jim Seddon and Douglas Thornton. Plenty of vocal and musical talent was forthcoming from the young people themselves, and it was especially good to welcome three talented members of the singing Glass family from Brazil.

A fortnight after the Convention the writer returned to Keswick for a few hours. Instead of a vibrant tent full of enthusiastic young Christians, just an ugly slab of concrete. A depressing sight? Not really. For those young Christians were now out in the brass tacks of daily life. The place God would have them be. The only place they can put into practice the lessons learned during that memorable week in July.

P.B.C.

Rev. & Mrs. David Glass and their family from Brazil, who sang and played Portuguese folk songs at several meetings

Holiday Convention Week

Impressions

Keswick takes on, in mid-July every year, a quite distinctive character in Convention week. Indeed, the little Lakeland holiday centre is virtually "taken over" by Convention visitors. Ordinary holiday-makers must wonder where they have come, when they see the two enormous tents, the bookstalls and mission stalls lining the streets, the house-party banners, and thronging crowds of Bible-carrying Christians.

The Holiday Convention Week also has its own "personality" distinctive from that of the "parent" Convention. It must be difficult for those who attended the main Convention to visualise what Keswick was like the following week; while those attending the Holiday Convention have little idea what the full-scale "Keswick" is like!

The town undergoes a transformation on the Saturday, at the end of one Convention, and the beginning of another. Five thousand or more Convention folk depart in the morning: and about half that number arrive later in the day. Half the Council members go, and the complete team of speakers—and another arrives; half the bookstalls close; and there are few house-parties. But the Holiday Convention is *not* "Keswick muted" but a distinctive, different Convention with its own character and "feel".

On the Sunday, for instance, the tents were deserted, except for a children's meeting in the afternoon, until 8.15 p.m., when an after-church service was held. The large tent took on a "new look" during Saturday, most of the forms being removed and seats being set out comfortably to accommodate the smaller attendances in a compact congregation in the centre.

It was a beautiful, sunny evening as some 1,700 people gathered for the opening meeting, led by the Rev. John A. Caiger. "With harps and with vials" was the somewhat unusual opening hymn; then Canon A. T. Houghton led in prayer. Welcome to all was warmly expressed by the chairman, and Mr. Leith Samuel read Psalm 85 before his message based upon v. 8, "I will hear what God the Lord will speak . . ." Against the sombre background of the spiritual and moral state of our country today, he declared that there is a famine of hearing the Word of the Lord. If we will listen, He will speak His word of peace. "*But* . . ." and that "But" is God's ". . . let them not return to folly . . ." to lowered standards, the neglected Word and family altar. Mr. Samuel ended on that warning note: and the meeting closed with the hymn "I thank Thee, Lord . . ."

SUNDAY

All the churches of Keswick were filled to overflowing for their Sunday services; and in all, Convention speakers were the preachers. Another gloriously sunny day was drawing toward its close as the congregation assembled

202

in the tent for the after-church service. The hymn "Lord Jesus Christ, we seek Thy face", set the keynote; and it was echoed by the Rev. Stuart Briscoe in prayer. Then, after reading John 12:20–26, the Rev. Philip Hacking spoke on the request of the Greeks, "Sir, we would see Jesus."

The story, he said, presents three snapshots. First, of *the world and its pilgrimage*. These Greeks were desperate to find spiritual satisfaction. They wanted to find reality, love, and truth. So do many today. Secondly, *our Lord's picture of Himself*, expressed in terms of harvest. There is the *certainty* of harvest here; the anticipation of much fruit to come. Also, the *cost* of harvest: there is no fruit until the grain of wheat falls into the ground and dies. Thirdly, *the principle of Christian life*: that life springs out of the cross— for Jesus, and for us. We must be willing to lose our life, that we might gain it. The world needs to see this message of the cross worked out in experience, Mr. Hacking affirmed: only so will it see Jesus. In personal application of his message—very similar to that of Archdeacon Cragg in the final message at the main Convention—he asked, Have we so seen Jesus that we can reflect Him? Thus Sunday closed with the same challenge as had characterised the previous week, and re-echoed on the Holiday Convention.

MONDAY

Monday dawned cloudy and cool—a contrast to the glorious sunshine of the previous days. The first of the Bible Readings from the book of Ezekiel, given by the Rev. John Taylor, however, was well attended by approximately two thousand people. The Bible Readings are reported in full in following pages.

During the day the clouds cleared, and the sun broke through, giving the holiday-makers an opportunity to see more of the beauty of God's handiwork. We gathered again in the evening under the chairmanship of the Rev. John Caiger. After the opening hymn, "Eternal Light", the Rev. Philip Hacking based his message on Galatians 6:7–10. He spoke of the three harvests; that of the Spirit, sanctification, and service. In all three, we reap what we sow.

Continuing the theme of the sin of the church, the Rev. D. N. Carr directed our thoughts to John 21:15. Three times our Lord put the same question to Peter, "Lovest thou me?" We must put God first in our lives, and demonstrate our love to Him in sacrificial, spontaneous, and steadfast love.

TUESDAY

The overnight rain had cleared by morning, giving another bright and sunny day, by the time that visitors gathered for the second of the Rev. John Taylor's Bible Readings. At the evening meeting the speakers were the Rev. D. Stuart Briscoe and Mr. Leith Samuel. After the singing of "Full salvation", Mr. Briscoe said that this was a great hymn to sing, but an even greater experience was to enjoy full salvation. In Romans 5, we see that man is totally devoid of strength to live the Christian life, but the answer is given in v. 10, and we realise that we are saved from powerlessness and lovelessness by the dynamic life of Christ within us.

Mr. Leith Samuel brought before us the challenge of keeping the temple of God clean. He referred us to 2 Corinthians 6:16, linked with 7:1. Christian separation is not a cold bundle of negatives, but a glorious bundle of warm, positive, overriding priorities. Not only was there to be the initial cleansing, but a daily cleansing in the Word is essential.

WEDNESDAY

Once again rain came during the night, and the clouds hung low over the mountain peaks. It was still raining heavily as we gathered for the third Bible Reading. Canon A. T. Houghton, who presided, welcomed us to "normal Keswick weather", and told us that being an optimist he believed we should have a sunny afternoon. He proved to be a good weather prophet, for during the day the sun came out; and after another fine day we gathered in the tent to hear messages from Mr. Leith Samuel and the Rev. John Taylor.

Mr. Samuel read 1 Corinthians 9:24—10:13, particularly stressing the words, "so run that ye may obtain". There is an incorruptible prize to be won; and just as the Greek athletes trained hard to win their prize, so the Christian must train and go "flat out" for the prize. Daily dogged discipline was the key.

Mr. Taylor reminded us that the Spirit of God guides the speaker in his choice of message. Mr. Samuel had just given us the picture of the Christian athlete; now we were going to look at the Christian slave. Whereas the athlete demonstrated determination, the slave rendered submission and devotion to his master. We are the slaves of Christ, bought with a price, precious to Him; and He expects our devoted and willing service. Mr. Taylor pictured for us three Bible slaves: the runaway slave (Philemon), the indolent slave (Luke 19); the devoted slave (Exodus 21).

THURSDAY

In introducing the final Bible Reading, Canon Houghton voiced the general feeling that Mr. Taylor had dealt with the profound symbolism of the book of Ezekiel in a way which was simple and clear to us all. We also felt a warmth and informality in the meetings, and Mr. Taylor's sense of humour was appreciated by all.

A fine drizzle was falling as we made our way to the final evening Convention meeting, but this could not dampen the working of the Holy Spirit. The messages given by the Rev. John Caiger and the Rev. Philip Hacking spoke of Him and His ministry.

Mr. Caiger showed us from the Scriptures that, as people who are "peculiar" to God, we are precious to Him, because He purchased us in order to possess us. Mr. Caiger quoted Oswald Chambers, who said that people possessed by the Spirit of God are "incandescent" with God.

In the closing message, Mr. Hacking took us to Acts 4:23-31, where a prayer meeting was taking place. The apostles were in trouble with the authorities, but they committed their problem to a sovereign Lord, expecting Him to work; and then they in turn went out filled with the Holy Spirit who gives the enabling. Mr. Hacking said that the fulness of the Spirit is an empty phrase unless we really *want* to live and speak boldly for the Lord. He linked up the last verse of the Bible Readings in Ezekiel, by reminding us that if we allowed the Holy Spirit to use us to turn the world upside down, then once again *Jehovah Shammah* would be written across our nation, the church, and our own lives.

FRIDAY

The Keswick message includes not only the "taking in" but the "giving out", and so we met on the final morning to hear of the work of God in other parts of the world. Three missionaries spoke of the work in Pakistan, in Japan, and in Ruanda.

From Romans 1:14–16, the Rev. Stuart Briscoe reminded us that we do not need to be apologetic about the Gospel, for it is like a stick of dynamite, when used in the right way. The Gospel must go to every stratum of society, for we are debtors to all. St. Paul was still eager, and even straining at the leash, to get to Rome to preach, even though it meant danger.

Mr. Briscoe closed the meeting with a challenge, and over one hundred people of all ages stood to signify their willingness for service wherever God should call.

The climax of the week was the Communion Service, when between 1,500 and 1,600 people attended. The presence of the Lord was very real, and it was a blessed time of fellowship and a fitting conclusion to a memorable week.

In speaking to various people at random towards the end of the week, the general impression gained was one of gratefulness to God for the direct challenge received from the messages, and the stimulation of thought from the studies in Ezekiel, and there was a quiet note of determination that from now on things must be different.

Youth meetings

An average of 220 children gathered each morning at their own meeting, and were encouraged in the things of God by a Scripture Union team led by Mr. Peter Lee, assisted by members of the Girls' Brigade.

Local young people as well as those from camps run by various Christian youth organisations faced the challenge of salvation, and also a deeper experience with the Lord, as they attended the special meetings held each night after the Convention meeting. These meetings were ably led by the Rev. Philip Hacking, assisted by the Rev. Stuart Briscoe. On the final evening over nine hundred gathered in the Eskin Street Tent. I was given to understand that the popularity of these meetings with the local young people was due to the fact that some who had been in early in the week had passed around the news that the men in the tent spoke in a language which they understood.

STANLEY A. COLEMAN

The Living God

Four Studies in the Book of Ezekiel
By the Rev. John B. Taylor, M.A.

(1) BY THE WATERS OF BABYLON (1:1—3:27)

Someone said to me, "Why ever did you choose Ezekiel to speak on at Keswick? You can't find a Keswick message in the book of Ezekiel!" What nonsense! You can find a Keswick message anywhere between Genesis and Revelation, because the message is the Word of God. And in Ezekiel you find this. Here is a particularly difficult book, yet one that is, when you look at it and break it up, incredibly clear and easy to understand. I hope that, at the end of these four days, you will go away and say, "Well, I didn't know Ezekiel was so easy. I did not know it was such a clear message. And I didn't know it was such a clear message for today."

Let me give you three good reasons why I choose Ezekiel for a Keswick Convention in the 1970's. First, because the book of Ezekiel *was addressed to a demoralised church.* The year is 593, five years after the armies of King Nebuchadnezzar of Babylon had come on a punitive expedition against Jerusalem, because King Jehoiakim had decided he would not pay tribute any more. As they drew near, the people of the city became fearful; and when eventually the armies arrived, the king had died and his young son had taken over. And he, very uncertain of himself, had submitted and surrendered to the enemy forces.

The expedition did not last long: and the punishment was that the cream of Jerusalem society should be deported. So the king and the royal family went, and the nobility went, and the priesthood went; and the top men in industry and commerce were all taken away, leaving just the ragtag and bobtail of society to live on in Jerusalem. And so the best people went into exile into Babylon, with Ezekiel among them—though he was only an ordinary person; he was no important character; he was quite a young man—and with the rest he had been interned for five years in prisoner-of-war camps in the Babylonian desert. Ezekiel was stunned by this blow as anybody else there.

This is why they were a demoralised church. Because there were not many devout ones among them, like Ezekiel; but there were some. And the devout ones felt that God had failed them; and they had good reason for thinking so, because after all, they had been brought up with the idea that they were God's people, and that God had promised to stand by them and protect them under all circumstances. Not only were they His people: Jerusalem was God's dwelling place. His temple was there; and He had said many a time that He would never abandon His house.

Why, only a hundred years before—and this was a prophecy that stuck in their memory—the great prophet Isaiah had asserted that God would never abandon Jerusalem. In Isaiah 31:5 he says, "Like birds hovering, so the Lord of hosts will protect Jerusalem; He will protect and deliver it, He will spare and rescue it." So they said, "All right. Jerusalem is safe, and as long as we stay there we shall be safe as well." And they proved this, not only by the Word of God, but by the miracle of God. Because in Isaiah's day an army had come against Jerusalem, and had surrounded it—the army of the Assyrians, under Sennacherib: and when they had prayed and trusted God and believed God's Word, they went out one morning and found that the army of Sennacherib had disappeared, and left a whole crowd of dead corpses outside, because a plague had smitten the army. The angel of the Lord had come down, and the army had gone, and they were delivered.

So they knew that they could trust God as far as Jerusalem was concerned; but now God had let them down, or so it seemed, and their faith was shattered. They said, "Where do we turn? It's not our fault: it's God's fault." They never thought of asking if their sin had built up so much that God was now justified in withdrawing His promise. They never thought of that, because whenever things go wrong the natural man always says to himself, "Whose fault is it?" and very often he will blame God.

Some people did not blame God: they blamed the older generation. It is a popular thing to blame the older generation, isn't it? They said, "It's their fault: they've sinned, and we're suffering for it." And in 18:2 you get that famous proverb, "The fathers have eaten sour grapes, and the children's teeth are set on edge." "They did the wrong deeds, and we are suffering the penalty of it. It's our fathers' fault." They never said, "Perhaps it's our fault." Odd, isn't it? This is the "It's not my fault" theology that has been popular with human beings ever since the garden of Eden, when Adam said it was Eve, and Eve said it was the serpent, and "Lord, just remember it was You gave the serpent, so ultimately it's Your fault as well." And today people are good at blaming others. Christian people may fulminate against the permissive society, and sometimes they blame young people for it; or else they feel sorry for the young people and blame the humanists for it. And the young people blame the generation gap, and everybody joins together on blaming the Victorian era that started it all off.

How often have you heard someone say, "I wonder if it is partly my fault"? When Jesus in the Upper Room, at the Last Supper, said to His disciples, "One of you is going to betray me," each turned to the other and said, "Is it I?" What an example! I think if we had been there we should have said, "Is it him?" And in church life, too, we blame other people. If our congregations are dwindling, it's never our fault: it's the new pastor's—"He's not like the old one." Or, "Most of our good people have moved away, and we've got new people coming in, and they're not the same sort as the old ones." It is never our fault. Listen. If we are going to study the book of Ezekiel, the first thing that we have to get straight is that we are willing to say to God, "Lord, where have I gone wrong? Show me, please." That is one reason why they were a demoralised church, because they were blaming everything and everybody for their troubles.

But also they were troubled because *their leaders spoke with different voices.* You see, back in Jerusalem, and also in Babylon, some of their leaders —prophets of the Lord, they claimed to be—were saying, "Don't worry. It won't last for long. Two or three years, and you'll be back home in Jerusalem." Other prophets, like Jeremiah, were saying, "Don't believe these false prophets who say it's going to be two or three years before you're back. It is going to be a steady seventy years." "Well," they said. "Who do you believe? Two years, or seventy years?"

Just like today: they are saying, "Why can't our leaders speak with a clear and a single voice?" Answer: They never will. The only way you can get a clear and a single voice is if you have only one leader. Because as long as there are different leaders in Christian society, you will find some of them speaking the truth, and some of them speaking falsehood. Therefore we have to learn from Ezekiel that leaders will speak with different voices, but we have to use discernment, which is the true voice of God, and which is not the true voice.

There will be all kinds of voices raised to explain the present situation. Chapter 13 tells you how to recognise a true prophet of the Lord. The unbelievers gloried in the church's disarray: another sign of a demoralised church life. In chapter 12:22 some of them were saying about the prophecies of the men of God: "The days grow long, and every vision comes to naught." What did that mean? It meant, "Look, time's going on, and all the things that you are saying and prophesying, are not happening. So I'm not going to bother to listen to you people any longer. The church is ineffective. None of its words really count. God is not interested in us: God has given up. God's dead"—and we've had that said often enough! Now are not all these symptoms of the church's demoralisation noticeable today? Everybody blaming everybody else for the failure of the church. No clear leadership being given; the much vaunted "death-of-God" theology, and the contempt of unbelievers for the established church.

This is one good reason why Ezekiel has a message for the 1970's. And here is another good reason: because the book of Ezekiel *begins with a new vision of a great and holy God*. And I believe that is what we need today. We do not need a new theology. We do not need gimmicks, and television sets in every pulpit. We do not *just* need brighter and more modern services in our churches. What we need as the people of God is a new vision of God. And isn't that what you've come to Keswick for? I hope it is. If you have come to hear bigger and better sermons, then you may very well be disappointed. Because bigger and better sermons can impress you; and if you are a preacher you may take down notes and use them again later on, and say, "Well, that was a useful one for my collection." But it will not touch you unless you have met with God, and got a real vision of God the way Ezekiel did. That is what I believe we need together.

The third reason why I have chosen this book is because in this book *God's answers to the problems of the day were to be met through one man*. He was a young man, only thirty when God called him. He was a "young married"; we don't know much about his wife, except the sadness of her death. We don't know if he had any children; but he was a young married, and God spoke to him at a critical moment in his life, when he was thirty.

Why thirty? Because Ezekiel had been trained to be a priest. His father was a priest, and he was going to inherit the duties of priesthood. And at thirty the priest came of age, and began his duties to which all his previous training had been simply the build-up. But five years before he was due to begin he was taken away from the area of his priesthood, the temple, and dumped in the deserts of Babylon. And as years passed he wondered, "Shall I ever get back there? Shall I ever be able to fulfil my calling?" And as he got to his twenty-eighth birthday he wondered, "Will it be yet?" Twenty-nine, thirty . . . and still he couldn't, and still all the build-up of the expectation of his life's work was ahead of him, but it was out of his reach.

And then, when he was thirty. God came and said to him, "You don't have to come to the temple to be a priest. I'm coming here to you; and I'm giving you a new job, not as a priest, but as a prophet." And it may well be that if you have a vision of God like Ezekiel, one of the things He will ask you to do is to change your job. He won't waste the training He has given you already, but He will use it in a different way. He will send you out in a way that only He can choose, because it is only you He is concerned with. He chooses one man, to minister to His people. And if God is going to do anything of real value this week, it is going to be to the individual. I chose this book and this passage, because my prayer is that as you sit by the river Derwent, the hand of the Lord may be upon you, and you may see God's glory; that you may hear His call, and may receive His message, and may have a new sense of responsibility to your fellow men.

Now let us turn to Ezekiel 1. I have divided what I want to say under four headings. The first deals mainly with chapter 1—THE GLORY OF THE LORD WHICH EZEKIEL SAW. In this magnificent passage we have Ezekiel's priestliness coming out. Because he was a priest, symbolism was his natural method of speaking. He lived symbolism. Every priest did: Symbolism and ritual were the way in which he worked; they were his vocabulary. And here is a passage shot through with it.

It is a passage that defies complete understanding, because it is a description of God, and you can't understand God. If this was absolutely crystal clear, we could pigeon-hole this vision of God and say, "Now I understand it, now I've got it all clear." You wouldn't have understood the God of Ezekiel. No, He is incomparable; He is indescribable. But it is a passage that sets the reader tingling with awe and wonder, in the same way that God does.

There are a number of different elements in this vision. He is describing the appearance of God as He comes out of the north. There is, first of all, God, who is seated on His throne. And the throne rests upon a platform or a firmament: and the firmament is resting on the four living creatures who are the bearers, the supporters of the Deity. The point of contact between the four living creatures and the earth are the wheels. And so you have the wheels, the creatures, the platform, the throne, and the Lord. Ezekiel begins from the outside and works inwards, because gradually we are focusing on the central feature of this vision. He begins with the things he can look at and can study—the wheels alongside the living creatures.

Verses 15–21 describe those. They move in all four directions without turning as they go. Let's get this "wheels within wheels" out of the way before we go any further, because I am sure you are dying to know what I think it means. Probably, of course, you know the answer. Basically I think a wheel within a wheel was like two solid circular discs fixed at right angles to each other, so that the wheel could go in any one of four directions without needing to be turned. It is about the nearest thing that the ancient Near East could get to those spherical casters that you fit on your settees: and they are so mobile that when you sit down with a slump on the settee, it moves about a yard further away from where you started! And this is the idea, that this is what God runs on, if you like; that God is not anchored to any fixed point; that God is infinitely mobile, and He can dart and move here, there and everywhere. This was a new idea for the people, because to them God was anchored in Jerusalem: He was in the holy of holies. But God said, "No, I can move anywhere. I can go anywhere. I can move like lightning, fast, quick. I can come out here to enemy-occupied territory in Babylon, and there I am." And so the infinite mobility of God is expressed by this wheel symbolism.

Then beside the wheels, the four living creatures. Human body, except they had four faces. And facing forwards of each one of these was the face of a man; and then there was the face of an eagle, a lion, an ox. Here you have the four pinnacles of God's creation: man—the greatest and the highest achievement of God. "Let us make man in our image"; there's man. The lion and the ox—the greatest of the wild beasts and the domestic animals, the cattle of the earth. The eagle—the greatest of the birds of the air. And here the greatest of all God's creation, called on to support His throne. What God has created is now upholding Him in honour and in adoration, and is serving Him.

Then you notice the symmetry and the orderliness with which everything is described: the faces looking in different directions, so that whichever way you look at this, you will find that there is one face of each creature looking toward you. And so you can work out the careful way in which Ezekiel has described this magnificent vision of God. And resting on their wing-tips, the platform, the firmament, which is simply the resting place for God's throne. And the throne—and now the description gets much more indefinite; the throne of dazzling blue, and on the throne, God. Except that it does not really say what God looks like, in v. 26. "Above the firmament over their heads there was the likeness of a throne, in appearance like a sapphire; and seated above the likeness of a throne was a likeness as it were of a human form. And upward from what had the appearance of his loins I saw as it were gleaming bronze, like the appearance of fire enclosed round about; and downward from what had the appearance of his loins as it were the appearance of fire, and there was brightness round about him. Like the appearance of the bow that is in the cloud on the day of rain, so was the appearance of the brightness round about."

Notice the eight times in which the word "appearance" occurs in these few verses. Ezekiel hardly dare say exactly what God looks like. It is just "the appearance of the likeness of the form of a man". Why a human form? Well, you could not describe God in any other way, could you? But not so clear that you can analyse and study Him closely. Yes, He is a man; but much greater than man. The words that are used to describe God are "dazzling brightness" and "fire", and each of those has its own symbolism and its own message.

"Dazzling brightness"—you can look at it, but you dare not stare at it, like the sun. Don't ever look at the sun, or your eyes will suffer. And you can't look too closely at God. He is too magnificent. We daren't and we can't look at God, except in the face of Jesus Christ, who has revealed as much of God as human beings can understand and take. And "fire"—God is like fire. You can get close to fire, but you daren't get too close. That is Ezekiel's

God, a God of dazzling brightness and of burning fire. You know, that is not the God of Evangelicals today. This kind of a God is a God you have to respect, and you have to keep your distance from, and you have to bow down before, and prostrate yourself before, and worship. But we have got infected today with a chumminess with God that is certainly not reflected in the Bible. Sometimes the way in which we pray—I'm glad we pray "You", instead of "Thou", very often to God: though I instinctively prefer to use the Thou form for myself; but for my children's sake, and for an unbelieving generation's sake, I think the You is often helpful. But I am never very struck when we "chat up" God. "Hi, God, how are You doing this morning? Are you running with me, God?" If you talk like that naturally, then you can be natural with God. But do not try to cheapen prayer by treating God in this chummy, chatty way, as if we can slap Him on the back: "We're all pals together."

His is dazzling brightness, and burning fire; and the church of God today needs to be reminded of God's holiness. And they need to fall flat on their faces before Him—the only place from which you can view the wonder of the Lord. Because you say, "I've no right to be here, Lord." Like Isaiah you say, "Woe is me! for I am undone." Like Simon Peter you say, "Depart from me, for I am a sinful man, O Lord." Like the writer of the book of Revelation, you say, "I fell at His feet as one dead." Does God ever touch you like that? This is the glory of the Lord which Ezekiel saw.

Then we move on to—THE VOICE OF THE LORD WHICH EZEKIEL HEARD (2:1–7; 3:4–11). Ezekiel was prostrate before the Lord. He was speechless before this magnificent vision which he had of the majesty and holiness of God. And when you are prostrate, and when you are speechless, you cannot help listening. And whenever God appears to people, He always appears to them with a message. I cannot think of anywhere in the Bible where God appeared just so that people would see Him. Every revelation is audible, as well as visible.

When God comes to us He comes with a message, and we must be silent if we are to hear Him.

Because God wants to speak, and so often we do not listen. And He says to Ezekiel, "This is my message to you. Son of man, I send you to the people of Israel" (2:3). It is a missionary call He has got for you. But it is not an overseas missionary call: "You are not sent to people of a foreign speech and a hard language" (3:5). "You won't have to go to a language school for the mission field that I'm calling you to. It is a home missionary society. It is a society which speaks to your own people, the children of Israel. There is no language barrier, and that is a help to you, Ezekiel. But there is a tremendous will-barrier that you'll have to overcome. Because these people are impudent and stubborn. They are a nation of rebels who have rebelled against me, and they've got a blockage and a barrier of the will; and that is harder than any language barrier or any culture-barrier that any man has to face."

The Jewish people have still got this barrier to the Word of God. Ezekiel was called to his own people, the Jewish people. And sometimes, because that barrier is so hard to break, Christian people turn away and say, "We won't bother with those. They are too difficult to evangelise." Yet I believe that every Christian has three areas of missionary responsibility. One, to his own people. Two, to the nations of the world. And, three, to God's people, Israel. I spent a year studying in Jerusalem, and I know the Jewish people pretty well. I have a very great regard for them, but I also have a great longing that they will come to know the God of Ezekiel revealed in Jesus Christ. And I believe that every truly born again Christian will share that desire and that longing. Do we pray for the conversion of the Jews the way we should? Do we give regularly to the conversion of the Jews the way we should? Do we have any sense of missionary call to the people of Israel?

There is a great will-barrier. But God says, "You go, Ezekiel; and I'll supply the equipment. I'll supply your need." Just what you'll be needing for that. Not a silver tongue to speak fluently. Not a disarming personality to get behind their barriers. Not enthusiasm or infectious optimism. But resilience, toughness. "Behold, I have made your face hard against their faces, and your forehead hard against their foreheads. Like adamant harder than flint have I made your forehead; fear them not . . . for they are a rebellious house" (3:8–9). This is the gift of the Spirit you need for this kind of missionary work: real Christian toughness.

In all conscience Ezekiel needed that, because he was a desperately sensitive man. It hurt him when people rejected him. It hurt him when people criticised him. It hurt him when people spoke about him behind his back, the way it hurts you and me. And God said, "I'm sending you: but I'll give you the resilience to be able to cope. And if I call you to it, then I'm not going to change my mind, and I don't expect you to change yours either." "The gifts and calling of God are without repentance." There is no turning back. They are irrevocable. Has God called you to a very tough area? Then He wants you to stay; and He wants you to have His gift to be able to keep going on. The voice of the Lord which Ezekiel heard.

Thirdly—THE MESSAGE OF THE LORD WHICH EZEKIEL RECEIVED (2:8—3:3). "Ezekiel, here's your message: lamentation and mourning and woe!" (2:10). And Ezekiel scratched his head and said, "Well, I'm not called to be a popular preacher. They're never going to say of me, 'Oh, I *loved* your message last night.' They're never going to say of me, 'Oh, what a lovely man!' " "Lamentation and mourning and woe"—and it is written on a great big scroll, and the writing is on both sides of the scroll, the front and the back. That is unusual: normally you use only one side of the scroll. Why was it? It may have been that he was intended to deliver double-length sermons, fifty minutes every Sunday! But I don't think so. I think it was because God's message to him so filled up the book that there was no room for any of Ezekiel's private additions. God has given to us a full book, and there is no room for any additions to it. It is all there, from beginning to end. "And you preach it!" He says to anyone He has called, "and don't you try adding your own theories to this Book, because it is all there that you will need, and your people need. And take my Book and open it to people: and you've got enough there for a lifetime of ministry. I know there are some bad things you've got to say: but then, my people need bad things said to them, because they are a sinful people."

Ezekiel took the scroll, and said, "That will be useful for my theological library!" No, he didn't! He did not fold it up and put in his hip pocket, so that he could carry it around with him. He did not open it up and begin to give it a critical and analytical study. No. God said to him, "Ezekiel, open your mouth!" "What, Lord?" "Open your mouth—and in it goes! This is the Word of God, Ezekiel. It's my people's sustenance. It's their daily bread. You eat it. Chew it over. Fill your stomach with it (3:3). Fill your soul with it. Make this Scripture yours. Read, mark, learn, and inwardly digest it. Because one day I shall want to use your knowledge of that scroll, that Word of God. And you'll have to have it so much a part of you, that you can come out with it and make it appetising and digestible for the people that I send you to."

May I say a word of advice to those of you who are under twenty-one? If you belong to Jesus Christ, He wants to use you very, very greatly. He wants to make Christian heroes out of you. He wants every one of you to be an outstanding worker for Him in years to come; and you can be that, and you will be that if only you will train. And you train by keeping your body fit, because you never know what demands God will make of your physique. Be ready for anything. You will get there if you train, by getting to know this Book, the Word of God, and making it your own, and saying, "I'm going to get to grips with this Word; and I'm going to develop a taste for it; and I'm going to have that Bible so much in my heart, that the Bible grips me, and I can speak it to other people." That is the man of God.

Ezekiel ate it, and even though its contents were sad and rather unhappy, it tasted sweeter than honey as he ate. Why? Because it was God's Word, and he loved it. You will never get a taste for the Word of God unless you begin to eat it; and as you eat it, that taste will grow better, and be sweeter and more delightful, more like honey as the days go by.

Ezekiel took the Word of God into himself, and even though it was sweetness to his mouth, he came away from this experience with a bitterness in his soul. "The Spirit lifted me up and took me away, and I went in bitterness in the heat of my spirit, the hand of the Lord being strong upon me; and I came to the exiles at Tel-abib, who dwelt by the river Chebar. And I sat there overwhelmed among them seven days" (3:14). This was an intense period of mental prostration: there was bitterness because he was saying to himself, "Why have I been called to a people who are never going to listen to me, and never going to appreciate me?" And then at the same time he said, "But this is God's call, and this is God's Word; and I must." He was rather like Saul of Tarsus after he had his conversion experience; there were days when he did not want any food, did not want any drink. He was trying to readjust to this tremendous experience that had come his way.

But God had yet another commission for him to fulfil. And so, lastly— THE FEAR OF THE LORD THAT HE WAS REMINDED OF. "Son of man, I have made you a watchman." The watchman has the fearsome responsibility of being the only man between a sleeping city and disaster. He is trusted implicitly by those he is set to guard; and if he fails them, he is responsible. The watchman's job, Ezekiel's job, was to warn the people when danger was coming. He was to warn the wicked that if they did not turn from their iniquity, then they would die in their iniquity. And he was to warn the righteous as well: "If you warn the righteous man not to sin, and he does not sin, he shall surely live, because he took warning; and you will have saved your life" (3:21). I do not suppose there are many wicked people at Keswick who need warning—not in the tent, anyway. But there are plenty of righteous people who need warning: they need warning that sin is just as dangerous now as ever it has been. Yes, in you, the believer, the old nature is on a spring,

213

and the slightest relaxation of pressure keeping that spring down will trigger it off; and it will be welling up inside you in a way that you did not believe possible. We, God's people, need constantly to be reminded by the watchmen of God of the potential of sin within us, and so to keep close to Christ; and to hold tight to the cross; and to maintain a disciplined life, dominated by the Spirit of God, lest sin comes, and begins to get the dominion over us that it wants constantly to have.

You Christians with pastoral responsibilities, you have to go out and warn the church of God's judgment still on sin. There is a hell, as well as a heaven. God judges, as well as forgives. You are a watchman, because without your words, Christian people can make shipwreck of their Christian faith; and without God's word of warning to you, you can do the same. What a responsibility you have for your fellow-men. God says, "Ezekiel, you are a watchman."

The Living God

(2) THE FAILURE OF GOD'S PEOPLE (8:1—11:25)

We begin with a date (Ezek. 8:1). Ezekiel is very tidy, and dates all his oracles as he goes along: and the date given in 8:1 is a full year—fourteen months, exactly—from the time of his call that we were considering yesterday. During that time Ezekiel has already begun to do things for the Lord, and to speak things in the Lord's name. Already he has developed quite a reputation among the exiles in their prisoner-of-war camp, and they have got used to coming round every day, no doubt to see what Ezekiel is up to this morning! Some of you may remember what it was like being in a prisoner-of-war camp during the war. If so, you will remember that everybody knew what was going on in the camp, even though there were five thousand people there. Yet because you had nothing to do, the regular routine was just to walk around seeing what everyone was doing: how this person was getting on with the model that he was building, how this group were getting on with what they were working at. So things moved very quickly around a camp, even though there were thousands of people there. I am quite convinced that Ezekiel began, immediately after his call, to do things in response to words from God. He did not preach: he did not have an open-air meeting, and stand up on a soap box and say, "Come here! I've got a word from the Lord for you!"

The Lord said to him, "Ezekiel, get a tile, and draw on it the silhouette of Jerusalem. It won't be difficult, that." If you had to draw the silhouette of London, you'd only need to put in the House of Commons, and Big Ben, and the Tower of London, and one or two other things, and people would immediately know what you were talking about. "And draw it there." Then He describes how Ezekiel should do it, in 4:1,—"Portray upon it a city, even

214

Jerusalem . . . and put it down on the sand, and build sand castles round it. Put siegeworks against it, and build a siege wall against it, and cast up a mound against it; set camps also against it, and plant battering rams."

Well, you wouldn't be doing that for very long without people coming round to watch! The word would go round, "Ezekiel's doing odd things round his house. Let's go and have a look." And they would come along and watch him; and then they would come again, and would watch him building up the pattern even more. They would say, "What does that mean? That's Jerusalem. I know—I recognise that: They're the walls of Jerusalem, and that's the temple. Jerusalem is going to come under siege: that's what he's trying to say. Ezekiel, what's it all about?" But not a word from Ezekiel. He just acts it out, and then when he has done his visual aid, he comes out with the word from the Lord which graphically turns the visual activity into a spoken word. And they get the message.

It must have been the daily camp routine to see what Ezekiel had from the Lord: and he did some strange things. He lay on his side every day for I don't know how many days—as described in chapter 4—signifying the siege, and signifying the punishment, first of all of the northern kingdom, and then of Judah in the south. I don't suppose he lay there all day every day; but during his half-hour or hour of early-morning visual-aid ritual, he would do these things. And people would stand around and say, "What's it about?" and they would be involved in this, and would discuss it, talking among themselves, and working out the solution to the visual word from God. That is good teaching technique. They were watching it intently, and it was a discussion point in the camp.

When he got a sharp sword and began to cut off all his hair, that was a day to watch Ezekiel! He threw it up in the air, and he divided it into three bits, and he got his sword and he slashed it . . . Read about it in chapter 5.

He was doing these actions, and the people were watching and learning, and Ezekiel was developing the reputation of a prophet. And all these oracles and messages were not about the exiles and what they were to do: it was about Jerusalem and the folk at home. That is all you ever think about in a prisoner-of-war camp: the folk back home, and how they are getting on, and when you are going to be back there. Every one of Ezekiel's words was about Jerusalem and the land of Judah. How did Ezekiel know what was going on? Why, occasionally news would percolate through: it took quite a few months to get news from Jerusalem to Babylon, but apparently it did come. We read in Jeremiah 29 that they were able to send letters occasionally to and fro, and a letter came from the exiles to Jeremiah in Jerusalem, and he sent a reply back. And Ezekiel used to latch on to the news, and incorporate it into his daily bulletins, his daily actions.

So when the story opens in chapter 8, the elders have come to consult him. He is not outside this time; he is inside—and he is holding a session with them. They have come to consult him: we do not know what they have asked him, but they are sitting with him there, and Ezekiel is sitting silently. When they came to ask him questions, he did not immediately have the answer: he was not one of these quick-off-the-cuff speakers, because he was speaking the Word of the Lord. He said, "Wait. I've got to listen, and it may take a long time before the Word of the Lord comes to me."

That is one of the signs of a true prophet of the Lord. The chaps who can come out with a quick sentence straight away, be suspicious of those, says the Old Testament. But those who really listen and wait, and then the word comes, then you know that that has come the right way. And as the elders were sitting with him, and he was waiting on the Lord, then suddenly the great thing happened: "The hand of the Lord God fell there upon me." He went into a trance, in the same way that he had done in the first chapter. With the elders still sitting there, he suddenly was taken out of himself: "Then I beheld, and it seemed as if the Lord God were standing in front of me." That is the only way I can understand this language: "A form that had the appearance of a man"—very much like that vision in chapter 1.

In all this language, we have what we call reverential vagueness, not wanting to describe God too much: the One who had the appearance of dazzling bronze. "He came, and He put out His hand and He touched my forelock, and the Spirit lifted me up between earth and heaven, and transported me to Jerusalem." Of course, not literally—in imagination. I don't know how long Ezekiel's body was sitting there in the house, with the elders around him, while his spirit was taken away, and he imagined he was being taken to Jerusalem. And the Lord said, "Ezekiel, I'm going to show you the abominations that are going on in my house."

How did he know what was going on there? I think some of the things that he spoke about, he knew factually to have taken place. He mentions a man's name in the middle of it: Jaazaniah the son of Shaphan (8:11); and he mentions him as being involved with the seventy men of the elders, who were going in for these vile abominations. But most of these things seem to be typical of what was going on, rather than actual events taking place. Because here he describes four abominations, and each one is peculiar to a certain group of people. Verses 5–6 deal with the image of jealousy; and this is the great sin of all the people, and particularly of the king, as they come to worship. Verses 7–13 deal with the elders of the people of Israel. Verses 14–15 deal with the women of Israel. And verses 16–18, with the priests and the Levites of Israel.

Here, he says, are four areas of unholy living. These are the—FOUR CARDINAL SINS OF THE CHURCH. I think the reason that the Lord gave Ezekiel this vision was because the question of the elders was related to it. The elders, I suspect—though I do not know this—were saying to Ezekiel, "Don't you think God has punished us enough? Don't you think the end will soon come, and we'll be able to go back to Jerusalem and enjoy life again? Ezekiel, haven't you got a word of encouragement for the people here, to lift their spirits, so that they'll be able to say, 'Won't be long now. We'll soon be back home. Cheer up, everybody.' And morale will boost, and they'll be able to say, 'We'll soon be home in Jerusalem, worshipping the Lord there'?"

But the Lord says, "Ezekiel, you don't know half the story, and these people don't know half the story, of what is really going on in their innermost shrine, in the sanctuary of their hearts, in the sanctuary of their nation, in the life of their church. I'll tell you!"

First, there is *blatant idolatry* (vv. 4–6). He set Ezekiel down by the entrance of the gateway of the inner court that faces north. The temple area consisted of an outer court—it was all-square, of course—and an inner court. On the west side of the inner court was the temple, looking eastward; and so

216

there were three gateways into that inner court, a north, an east, and a south gate. Via the north gate was the way in which the king entered. He was not allowed to go into the temple, because the inner court was reserved for priests and Levites, and nobody else. That is where the altar of atonement was. But the king was allowed to come to the entrance of the north gate, and that was his particular royal box when he came to watch what was going on inside.

Ezekiel is put down just by the royal box, and the Lord says, "Look, Ezekiel, there is an idol put there." Now the people knew that idols often stood there. If you turn back to 2 Kings 21:7, you will remember that Manasseh, who was one of the very evil kings of the previous century, had set up an image of the Asherah. The Authorised Version calls it a grove: never was a worse mistranslation, because it does not mean that at all. It is the name of a Canaanite goddess, Asherah. She was a sex-symbol of the Canaanite religion; she was the consort of Baal, the great king and lord of vegetation, of fertility, of war. Manasseh was rather gone on Asherah, and what she stood for. So when he went to worship the Lord he liked to have a reminder, just by the entrance, of his particular foible. So he set up this sex-symbol just by the entrance to the inner court, near the altar of atonement. With splendid irony Ezekiel says in 8:4, "And behold, the glory of the God of Israel was there."

How incredible! There was the Asherah and the glory of the Lord, side by side. Right where the Lord was, there stood the idol, put there deliberately by a wicked and lascivious king. Even though Manasseh later did repent, it got back there before very long, because when Josiah came to the throne the first thing he had to do was to remove another one that had been put there. Apparently that one had come back by Ezekiel's time; and it was a standing indictment of the people of Israel that their king was inclined to put his own private idols right where the Lord should be.

God says to Ezekiel, "Ezekiel, can you see this abomination?" And He says to us today, "Look into your heart, Christian; can you see the idol that is there?" It is the first question that we need to answer, if we seek God's rich blessing. It is the first question that we shall be asked if we want the fulness of the Spirit.

Blatant idolatry: then, He said, "I've got something else to show you, Ezekiel. Come with me." "He brought me to the door of the court; and . . . behold, there was a hole in the wall" (8:7). Here we have another sin of the church, and this is the sin of *evil imaginations*. Probably this is not an identifiable part of the temple, but it is certainly something that is hole-and-corner; the people who are doing it are ashamed of what they are doing, and they don't want the rest of the world to know. They think that God does not know they are doing it. They said, "The Lord does not see us; the Lord has forsaken the land" (8:12). "We're not worried about that." But they still do it secretly.

There are plenty of people who say, "God doesn't exist!" but they know very well God does exist. When they are by themselves they conceal what they do, because they are afraid and ashamed before God. He goes in there and sees the vile abominations that they are committing, "And portrayed upon the wall and round about, were all kinds of creeping things, and loathsome beasts, and all the idols of the house of Israel" (v. 10). Was it a kind of animal worship—for many of the peoples round about worshipped animals? In Egypt there was snake worship, serpent worship; and other different Near East religions had animal figures, that represented deities. Was it this? I don't know.

The important thing is, in v. 12, "This that you see, Ezekiel, that is happening in some unknown, mysterious cavern or dungeon or cell, this is typical of what the elders of the house of Israel are doing in the dark, every man in his own room of pictures." Did it mean literally that every man in his private house had a secret shrine where he did these things? Possibly; but I don't think so. This is Ezekiel speaking in his typical, symbolic way, saying that every person has within the house of his own personality a private, darkened room. What goes on there secretly and furtively is nobody's business. The evil imaginations in every man's room full of pictures; and it is loathsome. But God can see it, and He can even show Ezekiel it. He wants Ezekiel to tell the whole world that He knows, and you cannot hide a *thing* from God.

These men were elders. They were the leaders of the community; and even though we may be leaders in the Christian church, this does not give us any immunity from evil imaginations. We have this room full of pictures, whether we like it or not. The danger of an uncontrolled imagination lies in the fact that what today is in the imagination, may tomorrow be in the act. Yet imagination is one of the greatest gifts that God has given to his people. Out of the imagination comes all the artist's creativity, all our delightful day-dreams and our hopes and aspirations. It can be a clean and beautiful and sweet room; or it can be a dark and secretive and loathsome room. Because we are fallen creatures, our imaginations, God-given, can often be polluted; and they can be disorderly and crude and bizarre and frightening.

Now this is all part of our natural man, and we should never need to be frightened and worried by the fact that those thoughts do come crowding into our minds, because we are what we are. But we do not keep the door closed, and we don't enjoy the darkness, and we don't hide this room away from the Lord. We open it up: we let God look right inside, and say, "Here's the room of my imagination, Lord. Keep it pure and clean and wholesome and lovely today." This is the battle that the Christian has—the battle for the mind. Paul said that the only way to win this battle for the mind is by working positively at it, and whatsoever things are pure, and whatsoever things are healthy and wholesome and good and righteous, think on those things, and fill your mind with them. Because, in heaven's name, there is enough filth to fill your mind with, and it attacks you from every side. But we have got to be in the battle; and if the television set fills our mind with impurity, then we've got to switch it off. If the book we read makes it more difficult for us, then we've got to close the book and say, "I'm not reading that book." We need to watch what we see. Have you never had the awful experience of seeing a hideous picture, and then finding that that picture comes up on the screen of your mind again and again and again?

Not long ago I went to a meeting of Christian people, where they were discussing the menace of pornography, and the speaker—though I am sure he did it rightly—gave us some illustrations: and it nauseated me. It was weeks before I got the horrible taste out of my mouth and out of my imagination. I was an unwilling watcher, but my eyes saw it; and again and again it came back. Plenty of people today, whether they like it or not—good honest Christian people—will get pornographic photographs sent to them through the post; and you may have seen the first one before you have the presence of mind to tear up the rest and burn them. For God's sake do! Don't let your eyes stay there, because what begins in the imagination, and what may be cherished in the imagination, may well finish up in the act. Evil imaginations—oh, this God-given gift of the mind, ask for the light of His Spirit to flood in, and keep it pure.

Then, "There is a third abomination, Ezekiel, that you have got to look at." This is very briefly told in vv. 14–15, and it looks rather inconsequential; but it is much more far-reaching than it appears. "He brought me to the north gate of the house of the Lord; and behold, there sat women weeping for Tammuz." And that's all! Who was Tammuz? This was a mourning ritual over the vegetation deity, Tammuz. Tammuz is the same deity you find in the Greek as Adonis. He was very popular in the Greek world. His worship appealed particularly to the womenfolk. He was a sort of pin-up boy for Greek female society. He was represented as a figure of handsome virility. His consort was Aphrodite, the goddess of love and fertility. The mourning for Tammuz, and the worship of Tammuz, gave vent to everyone's extravagant romanticism and sentiment. Here is the sin of empty sentiment. There is nothing necessarily licentious or corrupt about it, but simply people love to wallow in their emotions. It is not just the sin of womenfolk; though here it is particularly attached to them. Though if you look at any bookstall at the women's papers and magazines that are offered and inflicted upon the gentler sex, then, really, really . . . Romanticism gone mad, isn't it?

Here it speaks not to the realm of the imagination, but to the realm of the emotion, and *uncontrolled emotion*—whether it is the romanticism of boy-meets-girl; or whether it is strongly erotic (and this is a deification of sex, so I do not think it is this specifically); or whether it is the longing for an emotionalism in our religious life, they are all equally dangerous. There is a cult among Christians today that we must have an emotional religion at all costs: and unless it grabs me emotionally, then it's no good. Unless I can experience everything, and have heightened emotions about it, then I've not been to a good meeting, or a good service.

This was one of the problems in the Corinthian church, of course. They did not feel they had had a good service of worship unless they had really hollered; unless they had really had a good sing and a good shout and a good pray and a good cry as well, no doubt. They wallowed in their emotions. Paul had to say, "Listen, your emotions are God-given. Let there be plenty of emotion in your Christianity. After all, love is an emotion, fear is an emotion, joy is an emotion, peace is an emotion, enthusiasm is an emotion. But emotions must always be under control, the control of the mind. So when I sing, I will sing with the spirit, but I will sing with the understanding also. That will control it, so it doesn't get out of hand. And I will pray with the spirit, and I will pray with the understanding also; and I will worship with the spirit, but with the understanding." So we must beware of uncontrolled emotionalism in our religious life. God has given to us our emotions, but He has given us our minds to guide and direct them. Empty sentiment!

219

Fourthly, he turns us to *downright disobedience*. "He brought me into the inner court of the house of the Lord; and behold, at the door of the temple of the Lord, between the porch and the altar . . ." this is the place where only the priests and Levites could go ". . . were about twenty-five men, with their backs to the temple of the Lord" (v. 16). When you pray, you pray toward "Thy holy temple", you don't turn your back on God. Yet here were the priests who had turned around. They were consecrated men; they were in the ministry; they had been used by God; they had doubtless been soul-winners in their time—if you could do such things in those days. But now they have turned their backs on God.

This is to me both a puzzle and a warning. It puzzles me that people who have been used by God could ever come to the position where they actually turn their backs on Him. But I know it happens, and I have seen it happen. I was looking at a famous church missionary board not very long ago, and one of the church members was describing the various folk who had gone out to this part of the world and that. When he came to one name he said, "He went out to Nigeria. But," he said, "he has renounced the faith now." And I thought, a man called by God to be a missionary has now turned his back on the Lord. It would be different if he had changed his churchmanship or modified his outlook. But he had turned his back on the Lord, and now he is an anti-Christian. It is a puzzle, but it is also a warning, because when I look into my own heart, I know only too well that in five or ten years' time they could be saying that of me.

"Yes, he was a priest in the house of the Lord. Yes, he used to lead the people in worship. Yes, he used to take the sacrificial animals and sacrifice, and the people were glad of his services. But now he has turned his back on the Lord. He has been attracted by that brighter sound, or so it seemed to him. He got rather tired of the dull routine of the worship of the Lord; he lost sight of the glamour of that Saviour who died for him. And he has seen the sun, bright and shining in the sky, and he has been attracted away." Christian workers, deacons, elders, ministers, fellow-servants, let him that thinketh he standeth, take heed lest he fall. How could it have happened to him? I don't know how, but it did: and it could be me, as well.

So the Lord says, "Ezekiel, have you seen enough? Blatant idolatry, evil imaginations, empty sentiment, downright disobedience—have you seen enough? Doesn't it nauseate you, the way it nauseates me? Lo, they put the branch to their nose" (v. 17). That is a crudity in Hebrew, so crude that in actual fact the scribes altered the word, because really in the original Hebrew it is, "They put the branch to my nose"—God speaking. But the scribes said, "We could never say that of God," so they deliberately changed it to "their nose", and they left a sign in the margin indicating that they had changed it for this reason. The word for "branch" probably does not mean that: it probably means a stench. "They stink in my nostrils. They do. And that is the way they are treating me, Ezekiel. Go and tell those elders all about it; and tell them that—THE JUDGMENT IS GOING TO FALL."

For then the Lord "cried in my ears with a loud voice, saying, Draw near, you executioners of the city, each with his destroying weapon in his hand. And lo, six men came from the direction of the upper gate, which faces north, every man with his weapon for slaughter in his hand, and with them was a man clothed in linen, with a writing case at his side . . ." (9:1-2), the proto-

220

type of the recording angel. But it is not going to be all destruction. It is not going to be all judgment. Listen to these wonderful words that lift our hearts, in v. 4. The Lord says to the recording angel, "Go through the city, through Jerusalem, and put a mark upon the foreheads of the men who sigh and groan over all the abominations that are committed in it." There is a chance of salvation for some, even though there is going to be judgment for the majority. "Put a mark . . ." because there are some people in the city still, who are touched with grief over the sin of the people, who are weeping over the people's sins, and not weeping over Tammuz, or anybody else like that. These are the silent minority, who are cut to the heart over all that has been going on. And for those there is going to be salvation. "Put a mark on their forehead."

The idea is reminiscent of what happened at the time of the passover in Exodus 12:21, where the Lord told the people, through Moses, that they were to sacrifice the passover lamb, and they were to get a bunch of hyssop, and dip the hyssop in the blood of the lamb; and over the doorposts of their houses and their lintels they were to smear the blood. "Then when the destroying angel comes, he will see the blood, and he will pass over the house." What a perfect illustration, we say, of us as Christian people being covered by the blood of Christ; because there is the blood-mark over the door of our hearts, and God will never destroy, never judge, and never punish, because the judgment fell on the Christ in whom we trust.

The strange thing about this Hebrew Bible that we are reading together is that the word for a mark is the Hebrew word *tau*, and it is the word for a cross. How incredible is God's inspiration! He said, "Put the cross on the foreheads of those who sigh and groan over the abominations of the people." Christian friends, thank God with all your hearts that, when the day of judgment comes, you are trusting in the blood of Christ for salvation, and you will be saved. Yes, even though some of us may be "saved so as by fire", because our lives have been such poor replicas of Christ's, we shall be saved through the blood of Christ. But, just supposing salvation were not dependent upon faith, but were dependent upon whether we sigh and groan over the sins of our people. Do we? Or have we got so used to it that we have lost any sense of shock? If that recording angel were coming round the tent today, should we have the mark on our forehead?

So judgment falls, and it is described in 9:4–6. But with the word, "Touch no one upon whom is the mark," He commands, "begin at my sanctuary". It is at God's house that they begin; and so the elders who were before the house received the judgment first. And it went from them right throughout the city, and right among the people. It was by slaughter; and it was horrifying, it was ghastly. God did not enjoy doing it any more than we enjoy reading about it. Then in chapter 10 it is by fire; and from the midst of the cherubim, God says to the man clothed in linen, "Go in among the whirling wheels underneath the cherubim, and fill your hands with burning coals from between the cherubim, and scatter them over the city"—for this city of Jerusalem is going to get the full Sodom and Gomorrah treatment: that's what He says. The blazing coals of God's wrath! These are the coals of fire that are always within the personality of God; the coals of God's judgment on sin. It is going to come down, and it will not come down the way it came down to Isaiah. The coal of fire used in the Isaiah vision was a coal that was taken off the altar, and it touched his lips, and it was judgment that was also cleansing. This is just unadulterated judgment. God's judgment will fall—as, indeed, it fell on Jesus Christ. He bore the coals of fire in His own body on the tree. All that devastating judgment that should be ours, He carried. No wonder He cried, "My God, my God, why hast Thou forsaken me?"

Then, the crowning tragedy of all—THE GLORY OF THE LORD DEPARTS. "Then the cherubim lifted up their wings, with the wheels beside them; and the glory of the Lord God of Israel was over them. And the glory of the Lord went up from the midst of the city, and stood upon the mountain [the Mount of Olives] on the east side of the city" (11:22–23). He left the place where He had lived ever since the day that Solomon built it. Hundreds of years this had been the Lord's sanctuary, but now it was ended: and the glory of the Lord departed.

This is a word, I say, not to the individual, but to the church. The Lord will never depart from His believing child: He will never abandon you and desert you if you trust in Him. You have committed your life to Him; He has committed Himself to you: and you are indissolubly linked together. You are safe: God will never take His Holy Spirit from you. But He does sometimes withdraw His presence from a church. In the Book of Revelation we hear of God taking away a candlestick, and saying, "This church has gone too far. I am going to withdraw my presence, and stand aside on the Mount of Olives, and wait and see what will happen."

What God can do to a church in Asia Minor, in the first century AD, He can do to our churches, He can do to the church in this land. He can withdraw His glory because the people have got so obsessed with their blatant idolatries; they have let their imaginations get constantly darkened; they have wallowed in the sentiment of an empty religion; they have gone clean against the revealed will of God. And God has said, "Enough is enough, I'm going." Perhaps this was the only way they could learn.

Have you got the message, Ezekiel? Wake up now! The elders are in front of you. Tell them. A word to the church.

The Living God

(3) ALL THINGS MADE NEW (36:22—37:28).

A long time has elapsed since the events we considered yesterday: several years in fact (37:1–14). During those years the most devastating culmination of all Ezekiel's prophecies had at last taken place. Between the year when Ezekiel was called to be a prophet, the year 593, and six years later, 587—when again the armies of Nebuchadnezzar, King of Babylon, came against Jerusalem, and this time besieged it (a siege that lasted eighteen months, and was devastating in its power)—Ezekiel's message had been this: "Israel, your time has come. Your sins have been such that there must be an end. God's mercy has run out on you. You have so persistently rejected God's word that at last Jerusalem is going to fall, and the glory of the Lord is going to depart." That vision that we looked at yesterday of the glory departing was a prefiguring of what was going to happen. God was going to depart, because the people merited it.

Yet the people took a long time convincing that this was the truth. In chapters 12–24, the people are constantly raising objections to Ezekiel's doctrine of judgment. They are saying, "Ezekiel, it's not our fault! It's our fathers' fault! It's not our fault! It's God's fault," or, "You can't talk like that. We're God's covenant people, and God's not going to break His word, and abandon us, is He? We're in the covenant. We know our theology as well as you do, Ezekiel." And Ezekiel had to tell them, "God made the covenant, and God is entitled to break the covenant. And He will."

Every argument they put up, he knocked down. They said, "Oh, but we've got some great saints among us. And maybe just the presence of those saints will save the city." Ezekiel had to say, "If great men like Noah, Daniel, and Job are in this city, they will only save themselves by their righteousness. You can't shelter under their great faith and their great Christianity." No one can shelter under anybody else's umbrella. One man, one umbrella. One man, one faith. "And as far as God's judgment is concerned, it is you, you, you, the individual, that counts. And so many of you have turned against Him that the end is coming."

They still would not believe him; and the very last word that Ezekiel spoke was not a word: it was another action, in Ezekiel 24. It was the most tragic action of the whole lot. At the halfway mark in Ezekiel, after twenty-four chapters, you have this word: "The Word of the Lord came to me: Son of man, behold, I am about to take the delight of your eyes away from you at a stroke; yet you shall not mourn or weep nor shall your tears run down. Sigh, but not aloud; make no mourning for the dead. Bind on your turban, and put your shoes on your feet; do not cover your lips, nor eat the bread of mourners. And it is going to happen today, Ezekiel."

"And," says Ezekiel, "I delivered my message to the people in the morning; and that very night my wife died. And on the next morning I did as I was commanded. I deliberately did not mourn. But my heart was torn from within me."

For God had said, "Ezekiel, this is going to happen. I know it is going to happen. You don't know: but it is. And when it comes you are not to shed a tear—at least, not so that they can see you."

What an appalling thing. Was Ezekiel hard-hearted? No, he was not. God had given him a forehead that was harder than flint: but his heart was a heart that loved and yearned, that loved people, even these disobedient people Israel, and that dearly loved "the delight of his eyes". But God said, "Ezekiel, you've got to submit your emotions to my will. I want you deliberately not to show your sorrow, because I want my people to realise that an equally great tragedy is coming upon them. My house, their city, is going to be taken from them at a stroke, and it is going to be too devastating for tears. The whole country will simply be numbed by it." And this is what happened.

But between the time when Ezekiel was told about this, in chapter 24, and the time when the news came through, in chapter 33, we have a whole collection of oracles that deal with the foreign nations. They are put there as if to hold us in suspense, to help us to realise the time-lag between the moment the prediction was made, and the moment the news of its fulfilment came through. As soon as the news comes through in 33:21, then Ezekiel changes his tune. "A man who had escaped from Jerusalem came to me and said, The city has fallen. Now the hand of the Lord had been upon me the evening before the fugitive came; and He had opened my mouth by the time the man came to me in the morning; so my mouth was opened, and I was no longer dumb. I was allowed to speak now, no longer held in bondage in this ritual silence that had been imposed upon me. Now I could speak freely; and I spoke."

So this is the turning point in the book, and in Ezekiel's ministry. From being a prophet of condemnation, he became a prophet of comfort. He still had to speak pretty strict words, but now he realised that the people were broken up by the news, and he had to put the pieces together again. Because God's ultimate purpose for His people is never judgment. It is never woe; sorrow, failure. And even though you in your Christian life may sometimes go through extreme troughs of failure and sorrow and despair, it is never God's ultimate purpose. His ultimate purpose is always rich blessing, and the fulness of His Spirit, and new life and new hope. So Ezekiel turns to that.

The chapters I have chosen for today centre on the new message that Ezekiel has got; and it begins in the place where the whole book began: "The hand of the Lord was upon me . . . and set me down in the midst of the valley" (37:1). Now the word "valley" is exactly the same as the word "plain", which was used in chapter 1 of the site of the vision of God. I think it was probably the very same place. It was a place where Ezekiel used regularly to go to meet with the Lord: and happy is the man who has special prayer places; places of great sanctity for him; places where God has met with him, and where he goes back from time to time to renew his consecration to the Lord.

There may well be a place that means that to you; a place that has become a holy place for you, because you have spent time with God, and God has revealed Himself to you. Come back to it from time to time, and renew your vows and your dedication there. Ezekiel was doing that, in the quietness and the loneliness of this desert valley. And the hand of the Lord came upon him. Here is a sense of the prophet experiencing God taking over in his life.

So having seen the *setting* of this vision, let us look at the *content* of the vision. The content was that the valley suddenly was transformed, and it looked as if it were full of dry bones. And He said, "Look at them! There are very many on the valley; they are very dry. Looks like an army that's been massacred. And the bodies have been left to be picked clean by the birds of the air; now the sun is bleaching their skeletons. There they are unburied, and therefore unclean." There Ezekiel is shown the realm of death, and he could well have said, "What a magnificent army this must have been!" But God says to him, "Can these bones live? What these bones *could* be!"

You know, there are two sorts of Christian. There are the backward-lookers, and there are the forward-lookers. Sometimes people go into their half-empty churches, and they tell you: "This place was great in the days of Vicar So-and-so. Thirty years ago they used the galleries: there's dust

224

up there now." They spend their time living in the past. Christian organisations, too, can live in the past: they tell about the history of the movement, but they are not looking into the future to what it might be. Maybe God says, "It's time this closed down, and something else took over." But still they grind on, "because we've had a great past".

Don't be a backward-looker. Be a forward-looker. Look at that struggling community you belong to, and say to yourself, "What couldn't God do with these dry bones!" And God says to you about your Christian Union, about your local church, about the area where you live, about your place of work which seems so barren and so fruitless: "Can these bones live?" Test question! And what do you say? Ezekiel did not know what to say. Ezekiel was the most diplomatic prophet of them all. He did not dare say, "Well, frankly, Lord, I don't think they could", because he knew the Lord was greater than that. But he had not the faith to say, "Lord, I'm sure they can!" So he said, "Lord, Thou knowest." He was putting it back to God: "Well, Lord, you decide this one: it's beyond me." He was weighing up the difference between the logical impossibility and the divine potential; between what could humanly be expected and what could supernaturally be achieved.

The answer to "Thou knowest" was "Ezekiel, prophesy to these bones, and say, Hear the word of the Lord." "Come off it, Lord. They're dry bones! They haven't got ears to hear. What do You mean, Prophesy to these? I'll look a right Charlie standing up and preaching to that lot." Excuse the irreverence, but I think that is what Ezekiel might well have felt. "No; preach the Word of the Lord to these dry bones." And God tells us to preach to those who are dead and lost, and whose minds are closed to the things of God. He says, "Still preach to them," and we should do.

Were you brought up on the theory that you preach to the saints in the morning, and to the sinners in the evening? Well, in the morning it is just the faithful who come along, so you give them a word for Christians; and then in the evening you give them a word for non-Christians—and there it is. That's a load of nonsense, I think. Because I find that unconverted people are as often as not converted when you are preaching to Christians, as when you are preaching specially to them. Because the theory is, in our circles, so often that an evangelistic sermon is simply something that tells you about the door and the way in, and it's the ABC of the Gospel: admit, believe, commit. Yet the unbeliever needs to be told a lot more about that. If you are selling someone your house, you do not just show him the front door, and the front garden; you say, "Come inside, and have a good look round; and see what you're going to get for your money."

Of course it is not the same as that; but in the Christian life people need to be told what it is they are committing themselves to, what the inside of the Christian life is like, what the demands of God are on the Christian disciple. All too many people have turned back after making an initial profession of faith, because when they got there they said, "You never told me it was going to be like this. I thought it was come to Jesus and get; and now I find I have come to Jesus, and it is 'Hand over the lot', and I'm not sure that I'm willing for that." Take them inside and show them around: let the sinners know what the Word of the Lord is, and explain the fulness of the kingdom of God.

So, "Prophesy to these dry bones, and tell them the Word of the Lord.

And tell them that the Lord God says to these bones, 'I'm going to cause breath—my Spirit—to enter into you; and you're going to live. And I'm going to piece you together with your sinews and your flesh and your skin, and put breath in you; and you're going to live.' So I prophesied, I preached to them—and the miracle happened. The bones came together." The hip bones were connected to the thigh bones, the thigh bones connected to the knee bones . . . Hear the word of the Lord! It all came together—a magnificent miracle, all through Ezekiel preaching.

But they were still dead, and what difference is a load of corpses compared with a load of skeletons? Not very much: but at least a miracle had happened through the preaching of the Word of God. Then the Word of the Lord comes again, and says, "Ezekiel, prophesy to the breath, prophesy, son of man, and say to the breath, Thus says the Lord God: Come from the four winds, O breath, and breathe upon these slain, that they may live" (v. 9). Here the word "breath" and the word "wind" conceal the word which is the word for the Spirit of God, *ruah*. It is a Hebrew word that has an immense variety of meanings. Basically it means "air in motion," so, phew, that's *ruah*; a howling gale, that's *ruah*; the breath that I breathe, that is put into me by God as I am born, that's *ruah*; the breath I breathe out when I die, that's *ruah*; God sweeping through the personality, that's *ruah*. And I have a personality and a spirit of my own, and that is my *ruah*. So the writer plays on these words. He says, "Prophesy to the four winds—the four *ruahs*—of God, and put that *ruah* into these slain, so that they may live."

He was asking God to repeat what had happened in Genesis 2, when the Lord God took of the dust of the earth, and formed man out of the dust of the ground, and then breathed into his nostrils the breath of life. Here is creation happening all over again. Here is the Creator's handiwork: breathing into dead earth, and bringing it to life.

And Ezekiel prophesied to the winds. Do you notice the direction of the preaching this time? Before, he had been preaching to the people—dead as they were. Now he was preaching, or calling upon the Spirit of God. And if one represents preaching, the other represents praying. This is the important balance of Ezekiel 37. Why, then, in two stages? To show the difference between what men's power can do, and what God's power can do. Man's work is to preach, and through preaching great things are done. But there is never any revival just through preaching. There is never any spiritual life just through preaching. It is God's work to breathe His Holy Spirit; and the result of that work is the miracle of the new creation, the new birth, the new people of God. Does that mean that man has nothing to do with the success of this miracle? Indeed he did; but it was preaching to the wind, praying to God, that produced the final result. So if this teaches us anything, it is the limited power of preaching, and the unlimited power of God.

In Christian work we need to remember that though man's part is important, God's part is essential. Has this not a word to say to those who are relatively experienced in the task of preaching? Because I find that it is the constant temptation, when you have done it Sunday by Sunday, to rely on the fact that you have been doing it now, Sunday by Sunday, for several years. You have worked out how to prepare a sermon; you can even give lectures at a theological college on homiletics, and how it should be done by other people. But you never have miracles of new birth happening that way.

That is only when your preaching and preparation are paralleled by praying, and crying to the Spirit of God for new life to sweep through you, to sweep through your congregation, to do the real, lasting, reviving work. Do you pray as much as you prepare? Is your preaching balanced by your pleading with God in the silence of your own room? The limited power of preaching, and the unlimited power of prayer.

So much, then, for the content of this vision. Now how about the *interpretation* of it? This is not basically a prophecy about the resurrection of the dead. Verse 11 tells us that the point of this prophecy is to compare the dry bones that Ezekiel saw, with the people that Ezekiel was ministering to. "These bones are the whole house of Israel, here in the desert, here in exile. They say, Our bones are dried up, our hope is lost, we are clean cut off. But I say to you, I'm going to open your graves and raise you from your graves. And your grave is your despair, your hopelessness, your disbelief." This is a promise of—A NEW SPIRIT for the house of Israel; this is a promise for Ezekiel's parish. No wonder they had despair in their hearts, because Jerusalem had now been wiped out, the temple had been gutted by fire, the city walls had been pulled down, and the news had come through of families who had been tortured, who had been killed, and starved to death. The people were in despair about this, and God said to Ezekiel, "Now you know how they feel. They are as hopeless as this. But between you and me, Ezekiel, there is going to come a great revival, a national and spiritual awakening."

So primarily this refers to the national renewal of the people of Israel after the exile. They were buoyed up by this, and for the next fifty years, until eventually they went back to their land, they lived by this prophecy, and they said, "God is going to renew us, and He is going to take us back." And eventually the time came when they were led back to the promised land. Wonderful! Ezekiel 37 has been fulfilled. But was it? They got back home all right, but I do not see many signs of a new spirit within them. Within a few years of getting back to Jerusalem they needed to be whipped up into enthusiasm again by Haggai and Zechariah, to persuade them to build the temple—which they had started doing, but very soon packed in.

When eventually the temple was all ready, then Malachi had to come along to tell them, "What do you mean by offering this kind of worship at God's temple? It's a disgrace, the way in which you are offering animals that wouldn't be fit for a person's table; the way in which you are withholding your tithes, and involving all the people who should be receiving those tithes—the Levites and the priests—in having to go out and till their own land, and not do the service of God. You aren't fulfilling your duties, the maintenance of the ministry of God's Word in this place." New spirit? National revival? Not many signs of it.

So the hope that Ezekiel was speaking of, primarily, was dashed. Then more recently, when the Jews went back to their new state of Israel, some twenty, thirty years ago, then people began to say, "Ezekiel 37 is being fulfilled at last! The Jews are being brought back to their homeland. They're going to have a new spirit. They're going to believe in God." They are back there: but you ask any missionary in Jerusalem what the attitude of the Jewish people is to the Lord Jesus Christ—and it is the same message—oh, no. Even to their own Lord of the Old Testament; there is more materialism rife in

Israel than there is in any other part of the world, or many another part of the world: they share it as we do. The hopes have not been fulfilled.

So we look elsewhere for an interpretation of this prophecy of renewal. And we find it in—A NEW PEOPLE; and we find it both in the life of the individual, and in the life of the church. We find it in the life of the individual, in chapter 36, which fills it out and spells it out in greater detail. Chapter 36:24—and as you read this, do not just apply it to the nation, but apply it to yourself as an individual member of God's holy people. There are four great promises that God makes here, for the individual, in reviving power. First, "I will take you from the nations, and gather you from all the countries, and bring you into your own land." This is God saying, "Unbeliever, I am going to take you where you are: yes, I know you are in the far country, but that doesn't disturb me. I know you've been living in your sins and your disobedience and your rebellion now, for as long as can be remembered: but that doesn't worry me. I am going to come to you and take you just where you are."

That is the wonder, of course, of that vision that came to Ezekiel from the holy place, Jerusalem, right to the polluted, defiled, desert land of Babylon. God goes out there into enemy territory to draw His people to Himself. God always finds us in the place where we are. And if we are God's people, we've got to go out to the places where people are, to draw them in. It's no good just saying, "I'm going to preach the Word of God. Let them hear, or let them forbear. Let them come to my church; let them come to my meeting-place." We have got to go out and take them where they are. That is the way God does it. He goes out. It does not matter how heathen, how defiled the place is: He goes, and His messengers go as well; and He gathers people in.

Is the ministry of your church outreach, or is it in-drag? You know the difference. Are you really going out to people in their homes, where they associate, their places of entertainment? Going out to reach them, where they meet in their clubs and in their social activities? Go out to meet them, and go out there not just because you want to share their social activities, but because you want to win them for Christ. The effective Christian church is often the one where more members are going out during the week than are gathered together in holy huddles within the church premises. *As long as they go out in the name of Christ.* Go out the way the Lord did.

He says, "I will sprinkle clean water upon you, and you shall be clean from all your uncleannesses, and from all your idols I will cleanse you (v. 25). Because you have been out here in the desert of Babylon, I know very well you feel defiled and cut off. But I am going to make you clean." Isn't that wonderful! God is going to purify us. If there's anything the unbeliever needs, it's purification, and the sense that he has been washed and made clean. Just as you, when you are dirty, never feel right until you've had a good soak and a good bath, so it is for the person tainted with sin. He is never really assured of his salvation until he knows that God has made him clean.

The alcoholic is terrified of the taint that his former life had for him. And when he is cleansed from his alcoholism, he will send his suit to the cleaners to get the taint and the smell of alcohol out of it. He can't abide it, because it reminds him of the past. The person who is healed of mental disorder is very often constantly perturbed by the possibility that it might return. Yet when Jesus Christ takes hold of a person, He makes them clean and He makes them whole, and they can say, "God has made me whole." That is what Jesus did with the demoniac at Gadara, the man who was shouting and screaming around the tombs outside the town, who said his name was Legion, because, he said, "I'm full up with a whole regiment of demons, dozens of them inside me." He went frantically and madly shouting at Jesus Christ—and at anybody else who came near. And Jesus said, "Get out!" The demons said, "Send us into those pigs over there." And Jesus, I am sure, thought to Himself, "If that man sees his demons go into those pigs, then he'll know they've gone. All right! Demons, get out! Go into those pigs." The demons got out and went into the pigs; and *they* went mad and went rushing over a precipice, headlong into the sea. But who was the great beneficiary from that? Why, the poor man who had been mad. He had seen his madness go, and he could go back to the village singing to all the people—

> Gone, gone, gone, gone,
> Yes, my demon's gone.
> Buried in the deepest sea,
> Yes, that's deep enough for me.

He was assured, you see. And every time he could say, "But I know it's gone: it went there, there it was."

Jesus Christ has given the assurance of our cleansing by His blood. We are cleansed by His blood, and every time we are reminded of the blood of Christ, we can say, "There went my unholiness. I am clean." Every time you come to the service of Holy Communion you are reminded of the body broken and the blood shed, and the word comes, "This is my blood, which is shed for you, and for many, for the remission of sins," and you say, "Yes, yes, I'm clean. It's all gone."

He will cleanse you; He will give you a new heart (v. 26): "A new heart I will give you, and a new spirit I will put within you; and I will take out of your flesh the heart of stone and give you a heart of flesh." The word "heart" in the Bible means almost everything that a man is: it means his mind, it means his will, it means his emotions and his desires. God says, "I am going to give you a new outlook, new willpower, and purified and changed desires. I will not, however, give you a new personality. You'll still be the same person. You'll still work and function in the same way. You can't expect that kind of difference, because you're you: but I'll put a new motivating force in you."

Sometimes we are worried because, when a strange and difficult personality becomes a Christian, they don't immediately change their personality overnight. They won't: they'll still have the same problems of personality to grapple with. But they will now have a new power within them that will enable them to cope with those difficulties in a far more effective way. They will have the power of the Spirit of God.

Then He says (v. 27): "I will put my Spirit within you, and cause you to walk in my statutes and be careful to observe my ordinances." He does not say, "I will give you my Spirit so that you can walk on air." He does not say, "I shall give you my Spirit so that you, everybody, and the people of Israel, will be able to have visions of the way Ezekiel is privileged to do."

229

He does not say, "I'm going to give you my Spirit so you can all be preachers." We've got quite enough preachers; we need a few more listeners at the present time! He says, "I'll give you my Holy Spirit so that you can walk in obedience." The fulness of the Spirit is not for the spectacular; it is for the day-to-day, consistent routine of living for Jesus Christ—and, my, that's spectacular enough! And that should be the summit of our ambitions. Oh, that we may be filled with the Spirit of God to walk in His laws which He sets before us!

The result of this transformation of the individual—because this is the individual interpretation of the vision—is that people will say, "What an incredible difference! This land that was desolate has become like the garden of Eden" (v. 35). And they will say of that ineffective Christian person, "Why, he's become like a watered garden; he's become filled with the sweetness, the presence, the love, the gentleness, the softness, the beauty of Jesus Christ!" Oh, if ever anyone said that about me, I think I should die happy. Wouldn't you? They'd say, "What a transformation! Because he was cleansed, and the taint of his sins was purged and removed. He was given this new power, this new motivation within him, and the Spirit of God to transform his daily living." And people would say, "He's like the garden of Eden—really attractive and fruitful and live."

The second result will be (vv. 37–38): "This also I will let the house of Israel ask me to do for them: yes, I'll let them pray, and pray this prayer, 'O God, please increase our men like a flock; like the flock for sacrifices, like the flock at Jerusalem during her appointed feasts, when you can't walk anywhere through the streets without tripping over sheep going up to the temple, where they're going to be sacrificed.'" Sheep in Jerusalem at sacrifice time were like cars in the City of London, or Christians in Keswick! Everywhere you jostled with them. He said, "I'm going to make the people of Israel like that. I'm going to make my church like that, full of men. Their numbers have been decimated by warfare and famine and starvation and the siege; but I'm going to build up their numbers. Yes, there is going to be numerical advance in the church of Christ, when I cleanse, and when I give my new heart, and when I fill with my Spirit."

It is a sign of an effective Christian church when *men* are being influenced for Jesus Christ; men who are like flocks for sacrifice, vast in their numbers, but also going to the altar, dedicated to the Lord. Is your church full of men? It should be, if the Spirit of God is effective there; men who are dedicated, who are offering for Christian service, who are willing to go anywhere and do anything; men who will hand themselves over to God for the ministry of the church; men who will say, "Lord, here I am—an offering and a sacrifice." There will be dozens of them when God's revival comes to your heart, to our church, to us all.

There's the personal application of this. There is also the general application, which comes in the same verses, 37:24–28. Because, as we are beginning to see, this vision of the valley of dry bones is a central theme which repeats itself in different patterns throughout these chapters of hope that Ezekiel is putting before his people. In these verses we have the general application of this prophetic expectation to the people of God. Here is not the individual; here is the community, the new community under one Shepherd. "My servant David shall be king over them; and they shall all have one Shepherd."

230

Oh, but this is of the Jewish people, because the Jewish people returned from exile, and though they began with a Davidic ruler, the ruler Zerubbabel, he soon disappeared, and they didn't have anyone of David's line to guide them and to direct them. But eventually One did come—a Ruler of the house of David, great David's greater Son.

This is what Ezekiel 37 is ultimately talking about. And in Him there is going to be—A NEW COVENANT; a covenant of peace: "I will make a covenant of peace with them; it shall be an everlasting covenant with them; and I will bless them and multiply them, and will set my sanctuary in the midst of them for evermore" (v. 26). Here is the echo of Jeremiah 31:31 and following, which is His prophecy of the new covenant: "A new covenant I am going to make with my people Israel. Not like the old covenant which they rebelled against and disobeyed; but this is the new covenant: I am going to write my law upon their hearts; and I'm going to be their God, and they're going to be my people. And they shall all know me, from the least of them to the greatest. And it comes when David my servant is King among you."

Is Jesus Christ, the Son of David, King among His people? When He does come as King—as indeed He has come to His people as their King: whether they accept and acknowledge Him as King is a different question—when He does come as King He will make a covenant of peace: peace because through the blood of the cross God and sinners are reconciled; peace because when you acknowledge the Lordship of Jesus Christ over your life there is a peace within you that passes all understanding; peace because peace is the technical Hebrew term used when everything in a covenant is going right, when both sides of a covenant are keeping their obligations. Then it is said the covenant is "at peace". That covenant is a thing that you have with individuals, and so whenever I meet you in the street, then we are in covenant, and I say to you, "Peace, *shalom*." And you say, "Yes, our relationships are at peace. *Shalom*." And when you come to God you can look Him in the face, and you can say, "*Shalom*, Lord. Peace. The covenant's right. The relationship's pure." And He looks down on us, and He says, "Peace, peace, *Shalom*." Through Jesus Christ, the relationship that works peaceably.

We may have been stirred and convicted and made to feel quite uncomfortable through some of the things that Ezekiel was saying to us yesterday. But today listen to the Word of God: "I will make you clean, and my covenant with you will be peace." Isn't it wonderful?

The Living God

(4) THE WATER OF LIFE (47:1—48:35).

The last nine chapters of Ezekiel are not so forbidding as many people think. As we come to the end of the book, it is remarkable the way in which Ezekiel has balanced everything that he wanted to say. He began with a vision, and he ends with a vision. The first vision was ill-defined, dazzling, awesome; the second vision is precise, measured, the architect's dream. The first was a vision of God, indefinable, incomparable, majestic; the second vision is about man's approach to God, and is clear and revealed in minutest detail.

Both of them are shot through with symbolism, because, as we have noticed more than once, Ezekiel was a priest; and symbolism was his stock-in-trade. Had he been more of a prophet, he would have preached a sermon; but because he was a priest at heart, he described a vision—or he prescribed a ritual. But whichever way he did it, he was throwing a symbolic meaning at what he wanted to say. Therefore when we read these words we must look at them through symbolic eyes, through priestly eyes, and not through over-literalist eyes. We should no more think of a literal temple which the Lord wanted built on the top of a mountain than we should think that that vision of the chariot throne of God was an unidentified flying object, a flying saucer, the way that some people have tried—quite erroneously—to interpret it. Because both of them are symbolical.

There are clear indications that these last nine chapters are intended to be symbolic, and not literal. For a start, it begins with a city perched right on the top of a high mountain. Again, the division of the land is a straight, criss-cross pattern of lines, completely ignoring all the natural divisions and boundaries of the hills and valleys of the land of Israel. The culminating thing is this river of life, that flows from out of a mountain top, and increases in depth as it goes, without the aid of any tributaries. No: this is clearly not to be understood literally, but symbolically; and Ezekiel gave us these clues so that we should read it the way that he intended we should read it.

But if this is not intended to be a blueprint for a literal temple, either after the return, or in the Christian era, or in the last days that will come, what does it symbolise? As I read these passages (from chapters 40, 43 and 47), I think they can symbolise three different things. First, this pattern of the temple and the city, where God is going to make His dwelling, can represent the new Israel, the Christian church. The river of water flowing out of this is like the progress of the Gospel through the centuries. "Founded on the apostles and the prophets", the twelve gateways of the city. A river that increases as it goes, and incorporates many fish—the enormous extent and multiplicity of the Christian church. Perhaps understanding the trees by the banks of the river as churches that are established there, and that grow. If you look at it this way, then this is what you might call the historical interpretation of the prophecy.

Alternatively, you can look at it a different way, and you can see this not so much generally as the Christian church in the Christian era but the Christian church within eternity. Here we have the way in which this passage is used by the writer of the Book of the Revelation, to expand on what heaven is going to be like: the new Jerusalem where the temple is going to be replaced by the living God enthroned amid His people. This could be called the futurist interpretation of the prophecy.

Alternatively, you can look at this passage and say, "Here is a magnificent picture of the Christian's experience of the indwelling Christ," the believer's experience of his indwelling Lord, where at the heart of his life is the temple— the principle of worship of almighty God. And right alongside the temple is the altar of atonement, standing for the crucified Christ, from whom the rivers of living water flow, which irrigate a needy world. This could be called the personal interpretation of the vision.

So there are three possibilities opened before us: the historical, the futurist, and the personal. For my own part, I don't believe that these interpretations are mutually exclusive, because I find that in the Bible there is never *one* pattern of symbolism, just as there is no *one* fulfilment of prophecy. Prophecies seem to get fulfilled again and again and again. The pattern recurs; and each time the pattern recurs you look back and say, "Well, I never realised it was going to come out like that!" But having read that fulfilment, you say, "It's still not complete," and it seems to be carried forward to yet another day. Then the fulfilment happens again.

Many of these things that we have read about in Ezekiel referred very definitely to the return of the Jews from Babylon to their home country. But this did not exhaust the meaning of the prophecy; and so we see that many of those ideas were taken up again, and seemed to be fulfilled in the coming of Jesus Christ, and the establishment of the Christian church. But yet again, that has not exhausted it; and New Testament writers are drawing on the same symbolism and saying, "There's still more to come to fulfil—to fill out—those words which were given to us by God of old time."

So never say, "This is the fulfilment of prophecy," as if to say that by fulfilment a prophecy has been exhausted. It never has; and it never will be until the great culmination. And when the great culmination comes, we shall be able to read our Bibles from Genesis to Revelation, and say, "Ah, now I understand what it was all about." Prophecy is given for us not to speculate about the future but to praise God for, when we see it fulfilled: as Jesus said, "These things have I spoken unto you, that when they are come to pass, you might believe." So if you have worked out analytically and carefully exactly how everything in the last days is going to be fulfilled, then I'm rather sorry for you, because when it eventually comes to pass you won't be able to turn round to your next-door neighbour and say, "There you are! I told you so!" because no one will be able to say that. We may be able to speculate within limits, but Scripture is far greater than our limited human speculation, and God is going to surprise every one of us—even the greatest prophetic pundits of us all. Because the Word of God is greater.

So I say there are different interpretations, and we shall find truths in many of these; but we shall not find the whole truth—I believe—in any one of them. There is this constant overlapping in the interpretation of prophecy. So we are going to look at different aspects of this vision, and see, I hope, the richness of the symbolism as we study it more closely: the way in which the Lord said to Ezekiel, "Look at this with your eyes, and listen with your ears, and take note of what the Lord will tell you."

I want to look at three focal points. The first is the major one, as far as time is concerned; then a second one, shorter; and a third one, shortest of all.

The first focal point is—*The River of Life.* I want you to look, first, at *its source and origin* (47:1): "Behold, water was issuing from below the threshold of the temple toward the east . . . and the water was flowing down from below the south end of the threshold of the temple, south of the altar." Now it is quite true, of course, that it was from Jerusalem that the Word of the Lord went forth. "Out of Zion shall go forth the law, and the Word of

233

the Lord from Jerusalem" (Isa. 2:3). It is also true that it was from Jerusalem that the Christian message went out. It was in Jerusalem the Spirit of God was poured out upon the apostles; and the apostles then flowed out, taking the Word of God to a barren and a heathen world.

But more than that: the temple represents the temple of the living God. The altar is symbolic of the sacrifice of Christ, who receives and who consecrates our offerings, the offerings of ourselves that we bring to Him. It is from Christ, the living altar, that there go forth the Gospel blessings which are like a spring of water welling up to eternal life. Where do they actually come from? Where is the source and origin of this miraculous spiritual water that God provides for His people? Why, it is from below the threshold of the temple.

I do not think I am being fanciful in saying that Ezekiel possibly was consciously trying to say that it is from the unseen source, the hidden source, deep in the heart of God, that this spiritual power, this satisfying river, begins its flow. In the life of the Christian it is the hidden springs of God that he draws upon, and from which he drinks, that are the secret of his spiritual effectiveness: the life that is hid with Christ in God, hidden below the threshold of the temple, bubbling out from beside the altar—OUR SUPERNATURAL RESOURCES. We do well to ask ourselves, Are we drawing on these unseen springs for our spiritual sustenance, or do we rely on occasional boosts from a Convention, or from a church service, or from a meeting—or is it from under the altar, ourselves alone with the Lord who satisfies? Its source and origin.

Then let us look at *its direction and progress*. In a rather similar passage in Zechariah 14:8, the waters flow from the Mount of Olives, and they flow down in two directions—both eastward and westward. Ezekiel is concerned to describe only one flow, and that is the flow toward the east: "He said to me, This water flows toward the eastern region and goes down into the Arabah" (v. 8). The Arabah is the rift valley of the river Jordan, that finishes up with the Dead Sea, and then continues further south, down toward the Gulf of Akabah. But south of the Dead Sea it is simply a dry desert valley; never a spot of water down there, because the water has petered out. It comes happily running down to the sea of Galilee, down through the Jordan defile, but at last it gets to the Dead Sea, and there is stagnation; and it never goes any further.

To the Jew in Jerusalem, the east was always the place of death. You only need to stand on the Mount of Olives and look eastward over those barren deserts toward the Dead Sea, and you will realise that naturally and instinctively the Jew would turn his back on that, and look over westward towards the more fertile plains of the Sharon, and toward the Mediterranean Sea. That is the way he instinctively looked, and he kept his back toward the east. This magnificent vision tells of God pouring out all His water toward the region of desolation and death; because it is a principle of God's activity that He seeks out the most desolate and unpromising places, and makes a bee-line for them. For God is the pioneer evangelist in person, going straight for the areas where only miracles will do. It is a pity His church and His people don't follow suit!

Notice also the progress of this river. It ran fuller as it ran further. This is the opposite of many Christian movements, which begin with tremendous impetus and initiative, but turn into an organisation with a secretary, and travelling secretary, and all sorts of other people; and they do their publishing; and they gradually peter out, and struggle to stay alive. But God's Spirit at work is always an accumulating work; it always grows. If an organisation you are connected with is not growing, then ask yourself whether the Spirit is still wanting it to function, because where the Spirit is, there is constant deepening and increased accumulation.

On the personal level as well: if you are exercising the gifts of the Spirit, you will find they will grow in you. And if you want the gifts of the Spirit to grow, then you must use what you've got. The way to great faith is by exercising the little faith that you've got. The way to depth of knowledge is by using the limited knowledge that you've got. Spiritual giants are people who were spiritual, even when they were pygmies. And we all start as pygmies: but as long as the Spirit of God is within us and growing, then we shall grow into the spiritual giants of our dreams.

The way to avoid the benefit of the river that flows fuller as it goes is, of course, to sit on the bank and to study the river, to wonder which way it is going, to plot its progress, to measure its speed. In most churches there are people who are very happy to be bystanders. Oh, they are glad to see the Spirit of God at work. Good! They like to go and measure it, and tell their friends about it, and boast about what God's doing. But get their ankles wet? No! Go on, get in; have a paddle! And before very long you'll be having it up to the knees; and before very long you'll be swimming in it. Get involved, and get stuck in. I don't think Ezekiel would have put it quite like that, but symbolically that's what he was trying to say.

Then, the river's *life-giving power*. "When it enters the stagnant waters of the sea, the water will become fresh. And wherever the river goes, every living creature which swarms will live, and there will be very many fish; for this water goes there, that the waters of the sea may become fresh" (vv. 8–9). The Dead Sea was the place where Sodom had been, the place that to the men of the Old Testament was a symbol and a reminder of the judgment of God. Here, the place of judgment is going to become a place of life: and this is the power of the Gospel, that turns dead men into living men, death into life, and darkness into light; it makes bitter waters wholesome and fresh, in rather the same way that the salt that Elisha threw into the Jericho spring did. Everything will live where the river goes.

Where was once nothing but slime pits (Genesis 14) has now become a fisherman's delight, because the river has flowed in. It wasn't due to a new evangelistic strategy; it wasn't due to any organisation for encouraging the work of the Spirit: it was due to the river of the water of life that flowed from the cross. Here is the miracle of all miracles, life out of death; and it is God's work, and God does it still. Never say about where you live, about where your church works: "Nothing ever happens here. The people where I work are too hard. They don't respond to the Gospel." Don't you believe in miracles? Don't you believe in the water of life? Don't be deceived by that word that is all the more deceptive because it comes from the Bible, that people say, "Today is the day of small things." I don't believe it. I believe that is an excuse for saying our God is a God of small things: and He's *not*. This is the day of big things. It is the day of miracles, because the day of Jesus Christ is always in power and in miraculous effect, and in life-giving transformation. Constantly be expecting the miraculous to take place. It helps if you expect.

For five years I was vicar of two country parishes in Essex—five of the happiest years of my life, I think. Wonderful people, and a wonderful place to be living. It was the first time I had been in charge of any work, and for the first three years I was constantly feeling, What must I be doing in my parish? I must be at it. I must be doing God's work. Everything that had to be done, as so often in a country parish, appeared to fall on the vicarage doorstep. And it was all your work, and your wife's work, and your children's work, and everybody else's. But it was centred on you. And the whole pattern influenced my attitude to the work quite wrongly.

Then I was brought up with a jolt, because a "quiet day" that the evangelical clergy of the diocese had together was addressed by Canon Houghton's brother, Bishop Frank Houghton. The result of that "quiet day" was that I began to look at my parish in a totally different light. I no longer thought of it as "my parish" where I was working, but as God's parish where God was working. Instead of trying to be the spiritual director of the parish, I tried to become the spiritual detector of the parish. I went visiting, not so much to see what I could do for the Almighty, but to see what the Almighty would do; and to find out which people's hearts He was touching. I went to church to preach on a Sunday morning or evening, and I would come away and I would say, "I wonder who God is speaking to today." And very often as I stood at the church porch I could recognise, by a look in a person's eye: "God's spoken to *him*. I must call on him—not to do a bit more good, but to see if I can help; to see what God in fact has been doing, during the past week, in that man's life." It was God's work; and God is the God of the miraculous, the One who transforms people steadily and quietly. It's not dependent on the pastor or the minister: he's there to be the spiritual detector of God's activity. The power is God's: the life is His alone to give.

By the sides of the life-giving river of life, are the saints who line the banks, and who draw their resources, like trees, from the river. We are reminded of Jeremiah 17, and the tree planted by the waterside, whose leaves never wither, who never fear when heat cometh, and whatsoever they do it shall prosper. Here to me is a picture of the effective Christian. As I read this picture, especially in Ezekiel 47:12, I ask the question, Could this be said of me? Five points: First, if you are by the river of life, you *never grow old*. That's a great comfort to those who are over sixty; but it is not intended quite that way. You never wither. And yet there are plenty of Christians who do wither as they grow up, because they get further and further away from the river of life. Or else they are trying to live on an old, increasingly stagnant reservoir of spiritual blessings that they were able to store up when they were that much younger. And they are living on that, and not on the daily fresh, life-giving power of the Spirit of God. Am I growing old and withering in the Lord's service? Am I as keen for Christ now as I was ten years ago? That is the question I ask myself, in the light of Ezekiel 47:12.

Again, the effective Christian is the one who is *constantly bearing fruit*. There is a steady supply of converts through his life and witness. There is fresh fruit every month. There is never an off-season; you never grow weary in well-doing. You never take a spiritual holiday; you are never in recess.

You are on the go all the time. Effortlessly God is producing fruit in your life, the fruit of the Spirit, a different fruit every month for nine months, and then they start the nine-monthly cycle all over again: of love, joy, peace, gentleness, self-control, and all those other great fruits. There they are, coming month by month. The immense variety and the depth of the person who is constantly fruitful! Lord, am I fruitful? Do I bear fruit every month of the year like that?

Also, the effective Christian is someone who is *supplying the food for others*. "There will grow all kinds of trees for food." Their fruit will be for food—no, not for themselves; for other people to benefit from. Because there are Christians, younger Christians than yourself, who depend on you for their spiritual sustenance. Oh, I know it's not right: I know they should learn to stand on their own feet and draw their own sustenance from the Lord; but as long as there are mothers and fathers, there will be children, and they will be dependent on their parents for their spiritual nourishment. If you bring forth fruit, you will need to feed your children; and their spiritual nourishment will come through you. Lord, am I supplying the needs of others; and are people coming to me and going away hungry, or finding food through my life and witness and ministry?

The effective Christian will exercise *a healing ministry*: "Their leaves will be for healing." The Christian church seems to attract to itself sick folk. I know a vicar, who said to me, "My parish is more like a hospital ward than a mighty army! All sorts of bent and troubled and problem people seem to congregate here." He wasn't resentful about it at all: that's how it should be, because a church should be a healing community. People should be healed through coming there; and the fruitful Christian, the effective Christian, will have this healing ministry to others. And the best medicine to provide is the medicine of cheerfulness.

Also, the effective Christian *stays close to Christ*. Because "the water for them flows from the sanctuary". Do I stay close to Christ, Lord? Do I keep near day by day? So these magnificent pictures of the effective Christian, through the life-giving power of the water of life. That is the first thing we are going to focus on, the river of life.

Now let us look at the second thing—*The Sanctuary*. The one thing that strikes me in chapters 40–48, which I've only just realised, is that nowhere is this place given a name, the name Jerusalem. When Ezekiel is taken there in 40:1–2, it is simply that "He brought me in the visions of God into the land of Israel, and set me down upon a very high mountain." It could have been anywhere. Never does he mention the word Jerusalem. Oh, I know the book of Revelation takes up the symbol, and talks of—THE NEW JERUSALEM, and I am quite certain that that was what Ezekiel had in his mind as a setting for it: but he is not going to call it Jerusalem. As if to say, Jerusalem has sinned so much, that that name will not be attached to this new and glorious place that is going to be set here. It's going to be so wonderful, so different from the Jerusalem that was past.

But as we look at this vision of the sanctuary, how do we see it? Do we see it as the church militant, the new Israel; or as the church triumphant, the church in heaven? Again perhaps we see both, because there is little essential difference. Certainly Revelation 21 reinterprets this vision of the city of God, replacing the twelve patriarchs with the twelve apostles, the foundation members of this new city, each with his own gate, three on each of the four sides—one to a patriarch, one to an apostle. And as we look at this picture of the city of God, it speaks to us, I think, of the perfection of the church.

Yes, even though Jerusalem had been such a failure, yet God was still committed to His people: God did not abandon the church. He was totally committed to it. And even though the Christian church today is often so ineffective that we despair of it occasionally, I am glad to know that God Himself never despairs of the church. "Christ loved the church, and gave Himself for it, loving and cherishing it, even as His own flesh." And if Jesus Christ was as committed to this imperfect church that you and I belong to, then it is not for me to withdraw. It is not for me to desert it. It is not for me to disown it, to go for a kind of churchless Christianity. It is only the apostate church that we are entitled to abandon, and I don't see signs of real apostasy in the church of God today, even though things look pretty bad.

Jesus Christ identified Himself with His fallen creatures—people like ourselves. He identified Himself with the church that we belong to. If only we were more Christlike, and therefore more church-conscious, we should be able to contribute more to the building up of the body of Christ. Because Christ looks at the church and sees it perfect, and is determined to present it perfect before the presence and the glory of His Father one day. The perfection of the church is graphically described here, as also is the completeness of the church. And again the book of the Revelation picks up this idea. Because one day the number of the redeemed will be sealed; and Revelation 7:4 ff. describes the sealing of the members of the church: "I heard the number of the sealed, a hundred and forty-four thousand sealed, out of every tribe of the sons of Israel, twelve thousand sealed out of the tribe of Judah, twelve thousand out of the tribe of Reuben . . ." and right the way down to "twelve thousand out of the tribe of Benjamin."

Why does he say all that? Because he wants to say that there are 144,000— twelve thousand times twelve, symbolising completeness. As if to say that every member of every tribe will be there. There's not a soul missing. This is not a literal 144,000, the way the Jehovah's Witnesses understand it: what a ridiculous way of looking at things? Why, not even all the JW's would fit in that number! No, this is again the perfect symbolism of not a man being missed. God is determined that His church is going to be complete; and everyone who should be there is going to be there. God could quite easily have closed the gates of heaven long before this, and said, "We've got enough! What a great crowd; we've got enough. Let's stop now!" But He doesn't; He leaves the gates open because He is a long-suffering God. He is not willing that any should perish, but that all should come to repentance; and that every man jack of them should be there.

But one day it will be complete, and one day the gates will be shut, and the seals will be affixed: and this will be the goal of the church's life. But until then, the church is open, and I see here Ezekiel stressing the openness of the church until it comes to its state of completeness. How does he say that? By saying that round the walls of this city, on the four sides, there are twelve gateways—three on the north, three on the south, three on the east, three on the west. Isn't that a wonderful way of saying that whichever direction you come from, there'll be a gate open for you. It doesn't matter what

238

nationality you have; it doesn't matter which way you come. As long as you are coming to Christ, there is an opening in every direction. Keep the church gates wide open; keep the church doors wide open, and let them know that they can always come, because Jesus Christ opened the kingdom of heaven to all believers. The freedom of the Gospel.

Then, finally, our third and last focal point takes us to the very last verse of the book: Ezekiel 48:35. We have looked at the river of life; we have looked briefly about the sanctuary, the church of God; and now we look, finally, at—THE ABIDING PRESENCE OF THE LORD. "The circumference of the city shall be eighteen thousand cubits. And the name of the city henceforth shall be . . ." here's the name coming up at last! ". . . The Lord is there." Hebrew, *Jahweh Shammah*—not too different from the old name of *Jeru Shalaim*—Jerusalem. Yes, because the name of Jerusalem had been transformed, as well as its nature. Then it was a city of rebellion; now it is a city of glory. Then it was a city that was called, somewhat anomalously, the city of peace; now it is going to be called by the name, "The Lord is there", the Lord lives there. And these words *Jahweh Shammah* can be written as the epitaph over the whole of Ezekiel's twenty-five years of ministry, and forty-eight chapters of revelation. There was the Lord, right at the beginning on the plain, revealing Himself to the prophet. There was the Lord in the temple, even when the abominations were being committed, and the most disgraceful things being done in His presence. There was the Lord with the exiles, giving them new hope, and the new promise of life in the Spirit. There will be the Lord in the last days: He will be there with His people for ever. It is the epitaph of the whole of the book.

Also in those words, "The Lord is there", there is to my mind a word of assurance for the anxious Christian. Because these words could be written over every new situation that we move to. Are you going to a new one soon? A new job? Moving to a new home? Going to a new sphere of service? Beginning your training for the Lord's work, here or overseas? Written over the door, "The Lord is there". Or it may be some place new, but it's the old place: the place of defeat, of barrenness. And you are going back from Keswick, and you want so much to know the victory of Christ. Look, over that old place of defeat are written the words, *Jahweh Shammah*—the Lord is there. He doesn't live in this tent; He lives there. And you are going there in His name, to know His life-giving power, to know the strength and the victory of His Holy Spirit. You'll be there, and the Lord will be there too.

Also here in these two words is *the promise of eternal glory*. The Christian life is spent in the past, in the present, and in the future; and if we leave out any one of those three dimensions our Christian life will be unbalanced. We live in the past: yes, we do! We constantly look back to the deliverance that God has wrought for us. We look back to the cross: we look back to that great historic thing. We look back to our own experience in the past, to how God saved us—and never lose the wonder of your conversion; even if it was a gradual conversion still look back to the life that it was like before you knew Christ, and let the difference between past and present constantly remain in your thinking. Live in the past.

And live in the present, because you've got to live it out here and now. And unless you stress the importance of the present, alongside the past and the future, you'll be a very poor Christian indeed. But also live in the future, because the future is what God has reserved for you in heaven, and you are entitled to look occasionally into those wonderful experiences that will one day be yours. You are entitled to look at the book of Revelation, and to wonder at the marvels of the great and glorious city where there will be no need of sun nor moon, for He will be the glory there: He will be the light. And Jesus Christ, yes, the real Christ, you'll be able to see and know in a way that you have never been able to on earth. He will be there; He will be there to greet you; He will be there to welcome you; He will be there to take away all the sorrow, and all the sighing, and all the pain; He will be there to give us that eternal crown of glory that fadeth not away. Yes, the Lord will be there. Look forward to it, Christian brethren. One day you will be there, and you will find the Lord. And what a meeting, and what a welcome that will be.

So Ezekiel began with glory, and he ends with glory. Isn't it a wonderful book? Haven't we a wonderful Lord; and a wonderful Saviour?